T0248348

Praise for *Bearing Witness*

Arel's *Bearing Witness* expands how we think about religion in public, presenting museum workers as mediators of a complex public healing process. Pairing her expertise in trauma studies with ethnographic research in the field of memorials, she provides a rare and spiritually sensitive glimpse into the daily labor of bringing people into relationship with the past. In this outstanding work of public theology, Arel leads us into unbearable histories by showing how we, if guided by those who touch the past purposefully, can make meaning in the fragments.

—Shelly Rambo, Boston University School of Theology

Bearing Witness is a moving meditation on the lives and work of people who conceive of and work in museums and other commemorative sites designed to memorialize the tragic, traumatic events that many of us would like to forget. These terrible, murderous events took place in the killing fields of Cambodia, the Nazi death camps of Poland, the Twin Towers of New York, the neglected neighborhoods of Soweto. Stephanie Arel's sensitive interviews with the guardians of these sites of traumatic memory reveal the importance of their work as mediators between the victims of evil and those who, for various reasons, make pilgrimages to the sites where thousands, or millions, of them suffered and died. She also beautifully shows how these intermediaries transform the emotional toll of their work into forms of healing and cries for justice.

—Edward Berenson, New York University

Combining the keen insight of an ethnographer, the perceptive observations of a psychologist, and the penetrating inquiry of a theologian, Stephanie Arel explores the array of emotional, physical, and spiritual impacts on individuals who have elected to live a life of service by working in memorial museums. She vividly captures the complex challenges for these "guardians of memory," who must engage as professionals in their areas of expertise while continuously confronting the evidence and heartbreaking stories of trauma. With impressive scholarship, Dr. Arel posits that the act of bearing witness by memorial museum workers is more than a calling; it is evidence of a fundamental belief in the possibility of a better future. Yet, the work of those who tend to the pain of others and who daily facilitate the obligations of remembrance comes at considerable personal cost, and through her analysis, Dr. Arel offers a constructive road map for how these "wounded healers" and the institutions for which they work can negotiate challenges unique to this field.

—Alice M. Greenwald, president and CEO (retired),
National September 11 Memorial and Museum

Stephanie Arel's continuous commitment to improving the mental health of memory practitioners is incredibly important for post-conflict communities, such as Bosnia and Herzegovina. Having worked in the Balkans for over two decades, this is the first book I have had the pleasure to engage with that presents both theoretical and empirical knowledge on such important issues, which I as a memory practitioner have been dealing with in both personal and professional capacity.

—Velma Šarić, founder and president,
Post-Conflict Research Center

BEARING
WITNESS

BEARING WITNESS

The Wounds of Mass Trauma
at Memorial Museums

Stephanie N. Arel

Fortress Press
Minneapolis

For those who worked at the National September 11 Memorial & Museum
from September 2017 to September 2019

CONTENTS

Preface   ix
Acknowledgments   xxvii
Introduction:
The Wastelands of Mass Trauma   xxxi

1. Public Suffering
   Interpreting Mass Trauma through a Theological Lens   1

2. Fragments
   Living among the Dead at Memorial Museums   21

3. The Aftermath of Trauma
   Enduring Suffering   45

4. Negotiating Publics
   Visitors, Survivors, and Family Members at the Door   79

5. The Vocation of Memory
   The Memorial Museum Worker as a Wounded Healer   113

Notes   143
Bibliography   207
Index   231

PREFACE

The Research

Defining Workers

Eighty-two memorial museum workers from eleven countries testify to their responsibility in memorializing atrocity. They embark on the work with intention: to facilitate remembering; to honor people and ideas; and to care for those suffering from trauma, just as they tend to buildings, artifacts, and stories. The intention requires endurance as the worker lives the trauma commemorated. Their daily tasks demand that they endure trauma's effects to attend to what remains after grievous atrocities.[1]

Workers' testimonies reveal private hopes. They express care and commit to recovery, for individuals and communities, longing to make a positive impact on those who suffer. They envision their service as performing a public good in the act of bearing witness to historical and social atrocities. Workers serve as the fabric of the institutions they represent, taken for granted by those on the outside, and some-times by those on the inside. They form the trauma narrative in words and images, and the narrative weaves itself into their lives. In cultures where identity entails what a person does for a living, the trauma story matures into a part of self-definition.

Workers comprise all staff paid by the spaces, activists committed to commemorating mass trauma in areas and situations devoid of funding or governmental support, and volunteers who give of their time to help efforts at commemoration. The interviewees remain anonymous unless they granted permission for use of their names, or their statements derive from other public pieces.

Twenty interviews took place in group settings. The remaining testimonies represent approximately sixty-two individual voices: sometimes two together and sometimes—in Bosnia and in Cambodia—with a translator. Both survivors and family members or intimate friends of victims and/or survivors represent interviewed workers. Family members of the dead include brothers or sisters, and children or grandchildren. Community members not individually affected by the event also serve as workers at memorial museums.[2] Of the workers who have no intimate involvement with the traumatic event commemorated, 60 percent likely bring personal trauma histories into the workplace.[3]

The word "survivor" addresses large swaths of people affected at varying degrees. The South African apartheid government intended to separate races, victimizing Blacks, and everyone interviewed had some direct experience of the political system. Very few survivors work at Holocaust sites, although survivors (at diminishing rates) contribute to the causes of commemoration. For instance, Yad Vashem's annual Holocaust Martyrs' and Heroes' Remembrance Day features survivor stories: each year six survivors light six corresponding torches to represent the six million Jews murdered during the Holocaust. These survivors share their stories, which reflect the theme of the year. In Cambodia, survivors frequent the sites, selling books, talking to tourists, and sharing their stories. Their presence reflects lived memory: traces of familial, communal, or national memory interweave into everyday lived experience, even that of the worker.[4] This will change as generations come into being after the atrocity, and those who witnessed the horror dwindle.

Each worker mediates memory, standing as a conduit or connective tissue;[5] the worker links a tattered past to the present to give structure to loss. The structures that they create support those who survived. Each worker challenges violence, insisting on alternative futures, often in tension with political agendas and economic pressures.[6]

Gathering Testimonies

The immersion and subsequent interviews began in 2017 in New York City at the 9/11 Memorial & Museum, expanding first to France and Poland and then to Israel, South Africa (two trips), Bosnia, Cambodia, and Louisiana. Interviewees from Germany, Serbia, and central Africa joined at points. The recorded interviews replicated natural conversations. Unstructured interview questions circulated around key themes: the emotional impact and meaning of the work; trauma histories, either independent from or inclusive of the trauma commemorated at the specific site; and the resources needed for workers who commit to facilitating the memory and mourning of others. Modifying questions suited the interviewees' specific experiences.

Flexibility of method encouraged relaxed atmospheres. The interviews sometimes took place on long car rides, or as segmented conversations that included visitation to multiple sites. Four interviews took place over Zoom; the remainder occurred at memorial museum sites or in local cafes. Interviewees talked in some depth generally over an hour at a time. The style and means of approach shifted constantly depending on an interviewee's country of origin or cultural habits.

The most immersion in ongoing activity of those commemorating mass trauma occurred at the 9/11 Memorial & Museum. My placement there lasted two years, and followed the pattern of an average workweek including all special events, allowing for familiarity with the dimensions of the research setting, the sociocultural dynamics involved in memorialization, and how those dynamics changed at certain times of the day, week, and year.[7]

An engaged ethnographic method resulted. Studying the exposure to trauma reveals some biases and resistance to exterior critique by both institutions and academics observing from afar. The differences and particularities inherent at each site challenge interpretation while revealing the high-stakes work concerning the confrontation of trauma and the mediation of memory amidst rival parties invested in the act of commemoration. The interviews and their summation capture how local parties interpret the moral and ethical process of memorialization in their personal and communal contexts.

Describing these contexts establishes a framework for understanding how the intersection of moral processes and ethical discourse in the field of memorialization, globally understood, defines the human costs and the consequences of confronting trauma. Soliciting and engaging multiple perspectives generates an agenda for practical action. Clarifying the obstacles of confronting trauma facilitates increased understanding and handling of these by the workers.

Missing Testimonies

Societies endure mass trauma at alarming rates. An exhaustive study of these exceeds the limits of this text. Missing testimonies include those from Armenia, Latin America, Japan, India, Sri Lanka, and other parts of Southeast Asia, Europe, Africa, and Russia. Also, writing from a US context begs a deeper engagement with the legacy of slavery as a mass trauma of human design, and with the treatment of Native Americans forcibly moved to reservations, enslaved, or executed.

Studying mass trauma requires interdisciplinary research. The depth of global suffering demands understanding from myriad angles.[8] The effects of each atrocity cohered but also expanded over the study, leaving pockets of scholarship unexplored: in sociology, in museum studies, in memory studies, in theology, in history, and in psychology. Further, each country, each event, and each trauma have contours and impressions that were impossible to fully grasp or to capture.

Despite the limitations, the testimonies unveil a phenomenon: working at a memorial museum constitutes a calling, a vocation. In the grueling act of attesting to mass trauma, workers perform a good. They listen and give voice to the voiceless, acting to help others learn about and process trauma. They mediate a call to remember, to refute indifference, and a need to listen. They work toward mending souls, souls of individuals, entire communities, and their own. They tend to deep wounding in their work, a vocation that attends to traumatic memory and the depths of human suffering.

Memorial Museums and Their Situations

Institutions that commemorate the Holocaust, the Khmer Rouge regime, apartheid, the Bosnian War, September 11, and slavery introduce unique experiences of facing and responding to trauma in its aftermath. Public memorialization rebuilds after trauma and honors loss in particular, complex contexts. Each movement to commemorate transcends personal, or even group, recollection; the context of each situation demands discernment.[9] Memorial museums establish themselves in complicated social, political, and economic settings. Grasping these settings enables deeper insight into the plight, struggles, and strengths of the worker.

Memorial museums open and operate under a wide variety of circumstances. Funding originates from various sources: governments, individual and corporate donors, the international community, and/or ticket sales. Politics influence the sources and amounts of money institutions receive, as well as whether the spaces receive international recognition. Sites of death become memorial museums, in their original form or reconstructed, according to public demand, legislation, and/or expectations from the international community. Similar dynamics influence the building of memorial museums on grounds not marked by death. Each site addresses a particular catastrophe with missions and visions that identify affected communities and that function under a distinct set of political arrangements.

Contending with the Holocaust in Poland and Israel

Nazi forces systematically persecuted and finally murdered six million Jews between 1933 and 1945. Other victims included 25,000 Sinti and Roma, and about 15,000 prisoners of war from the USSR and other countries. Poland stood at the center of the killing during World War II, occupied by both Germany and Russia. The war's end failed to free the country from an oppressive regime; Stalin's provisional government instilled itself, transforming Poland into a communist country in 1945. Auschwitz metamorphosed from a killing ground into the focal point of establishing a postwar Polish identity, evidencing the complicated relationship between memory and history.[10]

An act of the Polish parliament established the Auschwitz-Birkenau State Museum on July 2, 1947, at the site of two concentration camps—Auschwitz I, which served as the main camp housing, and Auschwitz II-Birkenau, which operated as an extermination site. Together they cover close to five hundred acres at the foot of the Beskidy mountains in Oświęcim, the southern part of Poland.[11] A twenty-minute walk separates them.[12]

A first and partial exhibition opened at the camps on July 2, 1947, less than three years after the Russian liberation. The first exhibition at the site presented the history of extermination and the conditions in which the prisoners lived. A second exhibition opened in 1955, and with some minor changes, remains what visitors see today.[13] Three words capture the mission at Auschwitz: "Remembrance—Awareness—Responsibility."[14]

The southern suburb of Kraków houses another camp, ninety minutes east of Auschwitz by car. Only monuments and newly erected signs indicate what happened at different places in the camp.[15] Visitors at Kraków-Płasków use imagination to contemplate more obscure traces of the past assisted by the signs assembled by Roma Sendyka, a professor at Jagiellonian University, and her students in November 2017.[16] The camp will transform into a museum. Kraków City Council proposed a resolution that entered the Kraków Museum into force on March 1, 2021. The mission of the proposed building includes joining the past and the present inherent in KL Płaszow as a "reference point" for encouraging "open civic attitudes for the future."[17]

The Galicia Jewish Museum operates in an old furniture factory a short drive from KL Płaszkow. The museum opened in April 2004 to attest to the Jewish past in Poland, a past distinguished from the Holocaust. A collaboration between the British scholar Jonathan Webber and British photographer Chris Schwartz initiated the museum, piecing together an exhibition of the relics of Jewish life prior to World War II in Galicia.[18] "Traces of Memory" consists of one hundred and fifty of Schwartz's photographs, intended to "challenge the stereotypes and misconceptions typically associated with the Jewish past in Poland and to educate both Poles and Jews about their own histories, whilst encouraging them to think about the future."[19] The Galicia Jewish Museum maintains close cooperation with the British Embassy, the Embassy of Israel, and with the Embassy and Consulate of the United States.[20]

In 1948, the newly formed state of Israel enabled survivors of the European Nazi attempt to exterminate the Jewish community to come to Israel. The country mobilized to recognize the Shoah, inaugurating Yad Vashem. Yad Vashem fuses with Mount Herzl or the Mount of Remembrance extending from the edge of the mountainside. An act of the Knesset (the Israeli Parliament) established Yad Vashem in 1953 under the Martyrs' Heroes and Remembrance Law. The law outlines the manner and content of commemoration, including the governing bodies of the institution, its budgets, and its functions.[21] A new Holocaust History Museum replaced the original structure in 2005 and remains what visitors see today.

The mission of Yad Vashem evolves. The museum's latest objective addresses the "dwindling" generation of witnesses who lived through the Holocaust and who ensure "a certain moral strength" in Holocaust commemoration.[22] A central question emerges in the face of their increasing absence: "How will Holocaust commemoration remain relevant to members of the fourth and fifth generations, both Jewish and non-Jewish?"[23]

Commemorative practices intersect in Israel and Poland, although each country observes different annual dates of memorialization.[24] Auschwitz's meaning continues to create conflict and make an impact on Polish identity. The president of Poland signed an amendment to the Law on the Institute of National Remembrance on February 6, 2018. The amendment made the public claim of Poland's responsibility or complicity in the Nazi war crimes an offense punishable by three years in jail. Amnesty International responded two days later, asserting that "Laws prohibiting insult or disrespect of public institutions or national symbols, or laws that are intended to protect the honour of the state are not permitted under international law and standards and are contrary to the right to freedom of expression."[25] The Polish government moved to change the law: charges levied in a civil court replaced the possibility of criminal prosecution.

The effects of the law rippled through the field of commemoration, straining United States, Israeli, and Polish relations. Yad Vashem objected to a statement jointly issued by Prime Minister Benjamin Netanyahu of Israel and his Polish counterpart, Mateusz Morawiecki, asserting that the wartime Polish government-in-exile attempted to stop the murder of Polish Jews ordered by the Nazi regime. The institution argued that this statement belied documentation and research conducted over decades that painted a different picture. Strife followed in the form of conflict between researchers at Yad Vashem, its spokespeople, and the Israeli and Polish governments.[26] Several high-ranking individuals in the field lost or left their jobs, and in 2018, the average memorial museum worker in Poland hesitated to speak about commemorating the Holocaust.[27] Contention continues to reverberate around the Holocaust and Auschwitz. Spray-painted anti-Semitic inscriptions covered nine barracks of the memorial museum on the morning of October 5, 2021; phrases included biblical quotes in German and English.[28] And a Polish diplomat lost his job in 2022 after calling the regulation of Holocaust speech in Poland "stupid."[29] The political climate exacerbates stress for the worker confronting traumatic content.

Confronting Genocide in Cambodia

Bombing erupted at the Cambodian border in the final years of the Vietnam War to weaken communists in northern Vietnam and their supply routes.[30] The efforts resulted in Vietnamese communists' deeper infiltration into Cambodia and motivated ordinary Cambodians to join the revolutionary forces of the Khmer Rouge.[31] The Cambodian communist group marched into Phnom Penh on April 17, 1975.[32] They forcibly removed residents from the capital and other cities, displacing millions to the countryside to turn the country back to "Year Zero." The Khmer Rouge killed close to two million people through enforced labor, starvation, and torture, with the aim of forming an agrarian society.[33] Socioeconomic and intellectual development halted, as the regime closed schools and forbade religion.[34]

Khmer security forces took over a former high school in April 1975 and gave it the code name S-21, or Security Prison 21. S-21 served as the major killing center in Phnom Penh, imprisoning over 20,000 enemies of the state, including members of the Khmer Rouge's own ranks. The Vietnamese invaded Cambodia in 1979, halting the prison's operation,[35] and, with the establishment of a new, more moderate communist government, S-21 became recognized as a historical site. S-21 transformed into the Tuol Sleng Genocide Museum in 1980.

Ticket sales support the memorial museum, but various projects receive financing from the Ministry of Culture and Fine Arts of Cambodia, the Korea International Cooperation Agency (KOICA), UNESCO,[36] the German Federal Ministry of Economic Cooperation and Development (BMZ), the Okinawa Museum,[37] and the United States.[38] The site articulates its purpose: "To honor the victims of the crimes committed by the Khmer Rouge who were prisoners in the prison S-21."[39]

The primary burial site for Tuol Sleng lies ten miles outside of Phnom Penh. NGOs helped establish the "killing fields," or Choeung Ek, as a memorial, but not without the local community's support.[40] Over 5,000 human skulls are assembled in a glass memorial stupa erected in 1988 as a traditional Cambodian pagoda to prove the death toll there; the stupa's introductory panel reads: "The Most Tragic Thing."[41]

The Japan-based JC Royal Company bought Choeung Ek under a thirty-year contract in 2005, enduring criticism from the international community. Workers regard the commercialization of the space differently; they believe maintaining the space as a memorial allows the souls of the dead to rest. One worker contends that the dead both permitted the development of the site and allowed their graves to go on display, attesting that "Only the bones are here [now], but if the spirits were here, they would feel warm because their deaths are already valuable."[42]

Independent guides usher visitors through these sites and other parts of the Cambodian countryside, still scarred with the effects of Pol Pot's regime. The guides want tourists to know both the wounding the country endured and its rich cultural history. Those working in the countryside navigate a threat. An estimated four to six million uncleared land mines continue to kill those who come upon them.[43] Laid by multiple government forces during the genocide, land mines injure or kill about fifteen Cambodians a month, resulting in the highest ratio per capita of amputees in the world.[44]

Political dynamics also influence memorialization in Cambodia. One guide reports that the Ministry of Tourism in Cambodia sets limitations for what guides (at least those who are independent) can say about Cambodia's history. The edict exerts pressure on opposition party members and independent press outlets that object to the Royal Government of Cambodia, whose leader, Prime Minister Hun Sen, has held power for over three decades. Workers requested anonymity and expressed wariness about social media posting.

Facing Apartheid in South Africa

The all-white National Party gained power in South Africa in 1948, and its government began enforcing a policy of racial segregation described as apartheid, or "apartness." The legislation upheld racist policies against nonwhite citizens of South Africa forced to live in separate areas from whites and to use separate public facilities. National and international opposition and pressure on South Africa failed to eradicate apartheid. In 1960, Britain's prime minister,

Harold Macmillan, urged the Union Parliament to make changes in the race policy to reflect the multiracial British Commonwealth.[45] South Africa responded by withdrawing from the Commonwealth in 1961, under diplomatic and economic pressure from the other members.[46] Apartheid intensified. In 1962, the then leader of the African National Congress (ANC), Nelson Mandela, was arrested for being a threat to the apartheid government. His release occurred twenty-seven years later, in 1990. The apartheid system formally ended on April 27, 1994, with the country's first general democratic elections inaugurating Mandela as president.

Post-apartheid movements attempted to develop a new national identity while reconstructing the country's values. Memorial museum sites signified an aspect of reconstruction. The South African government conceded in 1995 to the building of a casino on a swath of land in southern Johannesburg under the condition that the owners also construct a museum.[47] The result was the installation of the Apartheid Museum in 2001. From the museum's parking lot, a red roller-coaster appears over the horizon, contrasted with seven stone pillars that reach toward the sky at the museum, each imprinted with a value from the 1994 and 1996 South African Constitutions: democracy, equality, reconciliation, diversity, responsibility, respect, and freedom. The Apartheid Museum operates independently, leased to the Public Benefit Company and reliant on ticket sales and sales from its shop and bookstore.[48] The museum aims to remind visitors "of the importance of fighting against racism, discrimination and prejudice."[49]

Nearby Soweto demonstrates the residue of apartheid influence on the country. Apartheid established the township as an inferior zone of residence created by forced removals of Blacks from within Johannesburg to its edges.[50] In the Soweto uprising in June 1976, 20,000 students objected to the introduction of Afrikaans as the medium of instruction in local schools, an event that led to the death of nearly two hundred, including Hector Pieterson. The Department of Environmental

Affairs and Tourism and the Johannesburg City Council erected both
a memorial in his honor (2001) and an adjacent museum (2002) as a
form of reparation.[51]

Nelson Mandela's first house serves as a museum in Soweto as
well. The Nelson Mandela National Museum (Mandela House)
opened as a refurbished site in 2009, funded by a campaign conducted
by the Soweto Heritage Trust. The mission focuses on a "meaningful
experience" for all visitors and the creation of an "environment of
mutual respect, dignity, and reconciliation."[52] Independent tour guides
offer tours through the neighborhoods, the memorial museums, and
the surrounding areas, sharing both points of pride and the legacy of
apartheid.

Robben Island lies eight miles off the coast of Cape Town, two
hours away from Johannesburg by plane. A leper colony, a lunatic
asylum, and a naval base preceded the island's use as a prison, established in 1961 by the apartheid government.[53] Nelson Mandela spent
eighteen of his twenty-seven imprisoned years on the island. The
Robben Island Museum (RIM), which opened as a museum in 1997,
functions as a public entity with a mission to educate others about its
multilayered history, to facilitate sustainable tourism, and to engage in
good practices for managing the island as a World Heritage site.[54]

In 1995, the South African government instilled a court-like
body to help the country heal by collecting information about human
rights violations during apartheid. The Truth and Reconciliation
Commission inspired the establishment of Freedom Park in Pretoria,
just north of Johannesburg. Freedom Park opened in December 2009
as a result of the National Heritage Resources Act and in consultation with various political formations, faith-based groups, traditional
healers, artists, and historians. A monument and memorial recognize
those who sacrificed their lives for a free and democratic South Africa,
and understood as a pilgrimage site, it dispels "myths and prejudices
that have concealed and distorted the image and achievements of
South Africans."[55]

The legacy of apartheid continues to haunt South Africa, as is evident in the wealth gap, one of the highest in the world, and which remains mostly unchanged since apartheid's end. White South Africans make an average of three times as much Black South Africans.[56] The process of reconciliation continues, as does the discovery of the dead and disappeared.

Surviving Ethnic Cleansing in Bosnia and Herzegovina

The early twentieth century challenged the former Yugoslavia in its efforts to recognize a unified identity. World War II and the rise of communism complicated political solidarity and cooperation across the Balkan states. Interregional and interethnic tension mounted throughout the 1970s and 1980s, emphasized by economic and political crises that led to Yugoslavia's dissolution. Conflict escalated among the new states, manifesting military violence that exploded in Bosnia Herzegovina.[57]

Shots echoed from the roof of the Holiday Inn in Sarajevo on April 6, 1992, as Bosnian Serbian military forces fired into a demonstration for peace.[58] The shooting cascaded and marks the seizure of Sarajevo; later in the month, Banja Luka fell to the Serbians, and the "slaughter" had begun.[59] The United Nations refused to intervene in the ensuing war, bringing intermittent aid to the area (interrupted by Serbian fire and attacks) and later extending protection to what were called "safe areas." Protection of the safe area of Srebrenica failed on July 11, 1995,[60] when Serbs killed more than 8,000 Muslim men in an act of ethnic cleansing. The attacks inspired a NATO bombing campaign on February 29, 1996, forcing the siege of Sarajevo to be lifted. The Dayton Peace Agreement followed, putting a formal end to the war. Efforts to memorialize the "slaughter" ensued, initiated by individuals and small social groups dedicated the recovery of Bosnia.

The Historical Museum of Bosnia and Herzegovina opened before the Bosnian War in 1945.[61] The most challenging period followed the siege, and the museum transformed: now it houses fragmented artifacts and residues of the Bosnian War. The museum struggles for basic survival, abandoned by the government, which places collections and infrastructure in jeopardy.[62] A worker remarks: "We don't have a heating system at the moment; it's not working. It was destroyed during the war and after the war, we do not have the money to repair the building." She says this wearing a down coat inside the space while giving a tour. The museum strives to "open up a dialogue . . . We actually firmly believe that this is the place where people can come and speak about their histories," turning the museum from "nobody's museum into everybody's museum," open to all.[63] The History Museum of Bosnia and Herzegovina lacks legal recognition and state funding, sharing this status with six other cultural institutions of national importance—including the National Museum, the National Gallery, and the National Library of Bosnia and Herzegovina.

Tarik Samarah opened Gallery 11/07/95 in 2012, as the first memorial gallery in Bosnia and Herzegovina. Images, maps, audio, and video materials display the genocide that took place in the Potočari area of Srebrenica in 1995. A museum-gallery hybrid presents a series of black-and-white photographs documenting the genocide, facilitating the memorial museum's aim to be a decisive voice against all forms of violence, "not only of the war in Bosnia and Herzegovina, but also of the suffering of innocent people and the indifference of others."[64]

An interactive web survey resulted in the establishment of the War Childhood Museum, a five-minute walk from Gallery 11/07/95, when, in 2010, Jasminko Halilović posted a simple question: "What was the war childhood for you?" More than 1,000 people responded. A book and a museum followed, the latter opening in 2017. The memorial museum documents and digitizes materials related to growing up in the Bosnian War, presenting the archived materials for the purpose of education.[65] The international community recognizes the museum and donates support to the nonprofit and nongovernmentally supported entity.

Jasmin Mešković wanted to bring the reality of the Bosnian War into visitors' (especially other Bosnians') awareness without an arbiter when he organized the Crimes Against Humanity and Genocide Museum in Sarajevo with Suada Nožić and two others. They constructed the space without exhibition designers and refused aid from any source. Jasmin asserted, "it was made just with our funds, our knowledge; it was self-made." The space opened in 2016, with a main intent of providing education. Suada affirms this: "When you visit, maybe you will forget some sentence in the story, but you will never forget the total story of the war." The museum survives on income from ticket and bookstore sales, receiving no state funding.

The Srebrenica–Potočari Memorial and Cemetery for the Victims of the 1995 Genocide honors the 8,372 victims executed by the Bosnian Serb Army in eastern Bosnia and Herzegovina. Honoring victims remains central to the organization established in September 2003. Burials continue at the site on the Day of Remembrance for the victims of the July 11 Srebrenica massacre, as bodies continue to be identified and nearly 1,000 remain missing.[66] The memorial-cemetery complex receives funds from different foreign embassies, including assistance from the Imperial War Museum in London.[67]

The memorial museum field struggles with memory politics and the representation of history in Bosnia. Serbian politician Ana Brnabic[68] opened a 2018 conference by denying that the genocide in Srebrenica happened. The premier of Serbia, Aleksandar Vučić, provides a contrast to Brnabic's stance by acknowledging the genocide.[69] Memorialization proceeds, but not without contention. Prijedor, a Serb-majority town in northwestern Bosnia, also experienced ethnic cleansing and has met resistance in establishing a memorial site.[70] Police restricted the May 31st commemoration of the 3,176 victims from the town, placing a ban on the peaceful white armbands march through Prijedor in 2022. The bands reference the forced wearing of white armbands or the displays of white claws or flags on homes of non-Serbians to distinguish them from the Serbian population. Family members and survivors ignore the regulations, for instance, by laying flowers and reading the names of 102 children killed in the city center, while wearing the white armbands.[71]

Witnessing Terror in the United States

Ramzi Yousef drove a van into the parking garage of the World Trade Center in New York City on the morning of February 26, 1993. At 12:18 p.m., 1,200 pounds of explosives erupted, killing six people and injuring close to a thousand. The Diplomatic Security Service regarded this event as a sign that "terrorism was evolving from a regional phenomenon outside of the United States to a transnational phenomenon," laying responsibility on Middle Eastern radicals.[72]

Eight years later, on September 11, 2001, nineteen militants hijacked four airplanes and enacted suicide attacks against four targets in the United States. The men, associated with the Islamic extremist group al-Qaeda, flew two planes into the twin towers of the World Trade Center in New York City; a third plane flew into the Pentagon in Arlington, Virginia, outside of Washington, DC, and a fourth plane, purportedly aiming to hit the US Capitol crashed in a field in Shanksville, Pennsylvania.

Recovery at Ground Zero took nearly a year; recovery workers removed the last piece of debris on May 31, 2002. Original plans outlined the building of an International Freedom Center. A worker recounts the story: "a museum about 9/11 was not part of the original mix . . . But the plug got pulled on the International Freedom Center very dramatically in the fall of 2005. And with the cancellation of that project by Governor Pataki, guess what suddenly was going to come into the mix? The World Trade Center Memorial Museum."

Construction of a memorial plaza began in 2006. Dedication of the space took place on the tenth anniversary of the attacks, September 11, 2011. The National September 11 Memorial & Museum opened three years later, on May 21, 2014. The main exhibition site lies seven stories deep, at the bedrock foundations of the World Trade Center.

The memorial museum honors the 2,983 people who were killed in the 1993 and 2001 terrorist attacks. As a "place made sacred through loss," the plaza provides a public space for grieving all that was lost on September 11.[73] Developers, government agencies (not federal), and private sources, including Michael Bloomberg, funded the new museum.[74] Visitors frequent the memorial plaza at no cost, but operation expenses demand the sale of tickets for the museum itself.

Recognizing Historical Iniquity in the United States

The early establishment of the United States featured the massacre, torture, and oppression of Native Americans[75] and Africans.[76] The first enslaved Africans arrived in Virginia in 1619.[77] White colonialists forced Black Africans into labor and indentured servitude after kidnapping them in Africa, shipping them across the Atlantic, and selling them into bondage.[78] Some Caribbeans and Native Americans shared a similar fate. Slavery fell out of favor in the early nineteenth century, outlawed in the industrializing North; the South continued to depend on slave labor to maintain plantations. The Civil War erupted over the differences in 1861. The North won, and four years later, the passage of the Thirteenth Amendment formally ended slavery in the United States.[79] The South resisted the change in status of Blacks residing in America, not the least because slavery as an institution supported the Southern economy.

A Louisiana plantation substantiates this claim. The Whitney Plantation enslaved just over one hundred people at its height in the mid-1800s, becoming a large sugarcane and rice plantation.[80] Independent purchasers bought and sold the plantation several times after the abolition of slavery and before Louisiana lawyer John Cummings procured the property in 1998. Cummings self-funded the restoration of the plantation over the course of fifteen years, and with the help of historian, Dr. Ibrahima Seck, turned the site into the United States' first museum commemorating the horrors of slavery. The museum opened its doors in 2014 with the goal of educating "the public about the history of slavery and its legacies."[81] Cummings donated the museum in 2019 as a nonprofit organization that operates on ticket sales and independent donations.

Other sites memorialize slavery. The National Museum of African American History and Culture opened to the public in 2016, showcasing the history of both slavery and African American life in the US. The museum houses a Contemplative Court for visitors to recover from what the museum's director of education calls, "a very emotional place."[82] Bryan Stevenson founded the Equal Justice Initiative in 1989. The organization inaugurated the Legacy Museum: From Enslavement to Mass Incarceration in Montgomery, Alabama, in 2018 as a complement to the National Memorial for Peace and Justice: together the spaces compose a memorial museum complex. Some local Southern communities seek to recognize slavery and its legacy in the form of lynching. High school students in North Carolina have committed to developing a local memorial to victims of lynching in the state; their director asserts inspiration from Bryan Stevenson's project.[83]

Worldwide commemorative practice advances, provoked by malefaction. Each site responds to complicated histories, cultural attitudes, politics, and religion. Memorial museums participate in restoring order to communities suffering from mass trauma, addressing their situations[84] by recovering and reassigning meaning. Workers confront the unthinkability of human-to-human violence, interpreting sites of death and then rebuilding from fragments. One method involves sanctifying such places. Establishing sanctity leads to immortalization by memory, giving memorial museums religious qualities and functions.[85] The door to theological interpretation opens.

ACKNOWLEDGMENTS

In February of 2016, inspired by a job posting about fellowships at the 9/11 Memorial & Museum, I went to visit. I spent over three hours immersed in the content of trauma. On the train ride back to Connecticut, I called a friend who had just visited from DC and who brought her grandchildren to the space to find the picture of their aunt on the memorial wall; she was a flight attendant on American Airlines Flight 11. The photo and the space captivated the children. Inspired by the depth of emotion I experienced at the memorial museum, and the response of the family of the victim, I wrote a proposal. Two months later, I would begin my work there.

I would like to thank the Andrew W. Mellon Foundation, who funded the fellowship and my time at the National September 11 Memorial & Museum. Thank you to June Bowling, who read and helped me revise the original proposal for the position. I sought out Marty Borell, whose work at the Florida Holocaust Museum in Florida impressed me. He was instrumental in helping me examine best practices for creating a project that would give back to those suffering the aftermath of 9/11. I also had the privilege to work closely with Edward Berenson as I was jointly appointed at New York University. His direction compelled the research, and his reflections on the topic enriched the process.

The book is dedicated to the workers at the 9/11 Memorial & Museum from 2017 to 2019, who all helped me understand the depth of their work, the dynamics behind getting up every day to attend to trauma, and the feelings involved in navigating 9/11 chronically. I want to recognize Liz Mazucci, who introduced me to 9/11 and the museum world, and Noah Rauch, who trusted my suggestions, proposals for further research, and my knowledge of trauma. He was instrumental in my acquiring the position, and actively supported the amount of research I was able to collect for the book. Without his encouragement and his unfailing "yes," this book would not have been written. Thank you also to Alexandra Drakakis and Jennifer Moses: our conversations about the text and its topics enabled me to think more profoundly and more expansively. Also, Armin Alilović treated me with grace, extending a welcome in Bosnia and Herzegovina, acting as my guide and translator.

I am indebted to each and every person who sat with me, shared their vulnerability, and revealed intimate thoughts about their vocations. This appreciation extends to the named and unnamed memorial museum workers in the book. I came away with a profound respect for the important work they do, and the personal toll exacted.

Closer to home, I am grateful to Rebecca Daugherty, who has remained a stable companion and editor throughout the writing. Together we have spent endless hours on endless edits. Thank you also to Rabbi, Emeritus Professor Joseph Edelheit, who helped me shape my scholarly and theological voice. Xochitl Alvizo and Kathryn House, as usual, have been by my side with insightful theological discussions, assurance, and love. Amanda Popoli has been throughout a friend, coach, and advisor—who I will never surpass—in the nicest way of course. Many students from Fordham University have contributed to the research and expansion of ideas in the book. My thanks to them all. One deserves special recognition. I met Aphrodite Stamboulos when she was a freshman. She asked to help, and her help has been immeasurable. Her skill set far exceeded my expectations, and for her time I am appreciative.

In the book's production, I had the good fortune to work with an editor of eloquent prose and competence, Carey Newman, whom I met years ago, and from the first meeting knew I wanted to work with him. He watched over the progress of the book from day one, brought it into focus, and guided my hand at better writing.

I am also indebted to my husband, Andrew Arel, who through all the travels, the moments of complete exhaustion, endless work hours writing, and car rides to airports, never asked "why?" but "how?" His reliable presence and sense of humor always put things in perspective and alleviated my stress. He took for granted that the book would be finished and finished well; this posture alone gave me confidence to continue.

Finally, I thank those who have had their hearts in their hands at the site of mass atrocity and allowed me to be a part of their grieving.

On one anniversary of September 11, I stood in front of a name on the parapet with a member of the victim's family. He asked me to say a prayer. This Prayer of Saint Francis came to mind in that moment. I leave you with what I said that day.

Lord, make me an instrument of your peace:
where there is hatred, let me sow love;
where there is injury, pardon;
where there is doubt, faith;
where there is despair, hope;
where there is darkness, light;
where there is sadness, joy.

O divine Master, grant that I may not so much seek
to be consoled as to console,
to be understood as to understand,
to be loved as to love.
For it is in giving that we receive,
it is in pardoning that we are pardoned,
and it is in dying that we are born to eternal life.
Amen.

INTRODUCTION

The Wastelands of Mass Trauma

Human-to-human mass violence intends to destroy the other. Perpetrators rape, beat, shoot, and burn bodies, disposing of human remains. Populations diminish. Communities suffer. Those who remain face overwhelming loss. Trauma culminates in fragmentation. Confusion abounds. Survivors search for answers, wondering why they are alive.[1] Approaching each new day challenges endurance. The self fragments, walling off the inner life devastated by evil to protect the "good" and live in the present.[2] Social groups rupture. Members die, disperse, and disappear. Familiar bonds disintegrate. Political, economic, and religious systems falter or fail.

Traumatic conflict erupts in every corner of the globe. No culture is immune. Group-on-group violence haunts every past. The Holocaust, the Cambodian Genocide, apartheid, the Bosnian War, terror on 9/11, and the inhumanity of chattel slavery challenge the capacity to go on—to be or live—in the face of large-scale destruction. Questions emerge around how to feel and process personal pain in the face of public loss.[3] A struggle ensues. Living becomes a burden, a chore. Joy belongs to an unrecoverable past. Recovery looms, intense and insurmountable.

Anger and determination motivate efforts at reconstruction. Grief, felt and unfelt, finds an outlet. Reparation thwarts the perpetrator's aim to ensure bewilderment and fragmentation after mass trauma. Individuals reconnect and rebuild. They reconstruct infrastructure, cultural symbols, and livelihoods. Trauma survivors and loved ones of the dead promise to remember. Surviving communities insist on restitution, aspiring to hold perpetrators accountable. A new form of rehabilitation emerges in the twentieth century, inspired by a call to testify and remember: the building of memorial museums. The concretization of memory and mourning fills a need for recovering communities and answers the desire to "never forget" a past atrocity.

Memorialization recognizes mass trauma on behalf of a victimized group, assembling the fragmented remains toward a goal of prevention. Past, present, and future converge. Institutions draw on core aspects of the self and society to uplift history and cultural life before the trauma, providing present-day places for communities to reunite, testify to the egregious past, mourn, and honor loss. Commemorative institutions aspire further, to effect a future good. The aspiration occurs in the form of education, prevention, and mindfulness. Memorial museum workers play a vital role in this process. Workers attend to trauma in the service of carrying memory forward, honoring victims, attending to survivors, and connecting visitors to memories to encourage personal transformation, and to prevent atrocities in the name of "never again."

Confronting trauma exacts a psychological and spiritual impact on those bearing the burden of the work. Workers endure mental fatigue in an encounter with horror that calls into question the good-will of others. But surviving propels memorialization. Continuing the work requires fortitude. The encounter leads to a struggle between the will to deny horrific events and the will to proclaim them aloud—the logic of trauma.[4] The debate operates at various levels—in the psyche of the individual, in families, in communities, and in nations. Tension persists as workers wrestle with the admission of horror and its minimization from critics they encounter. Individuals remove the experience from consciousness or try to ignore trauma's affects in fear that integrating pain and horror will itself be too painful; communities celebrate a hero but refuse victims the right to justice; and nations donate money for reparation but minimize the extent of the trauma or deny atrocities altogether. Trauma's debate between denial and proclamation ensues with workers at the center—remembering past horror to facilitate grieving in hope of preventing a reoccurrence.

The memorial museum attests to traumatic histories, exhibiting relics from past events with the intention of remembering, as well as educating about, a particular atrocity. The memorial museum thus adopts both memorial and historical functions in its operation. The spaces possess political relevance while providing room for public mourning, affecting connections between the past and the present, the living to the dead. Facilitating mourning expands into a promotion of recovery. Thus, memorial museums transcend the portrayal of the past as an object of study in order to provide space for public grieving and to create new alliances in trauma's aftermath. The goals assume an intimate quality reliant upon a human desire for justice.

Memorial museums therefore rely on both history *and* memory.[5] The sites embody traumatic memory and tell stories of public suffering from mass atrocity. Impartial facts and personal testimonies intertwine. Memorial museums combine both data and affect to extend emotional, cognitive, and sensory lessons that involve mending wounds. Visitor responses express the effects at the Whitney Plantation Museum in Louisiana:

People started interacting with our memorials . . . They're leaving things that are personal to them. They're leaving flowers; they're leaving cowrie shells; they're leaving toys in the children's memorial. There's just so many things that they leave there, and I think that's really beautiful. I think a normal museum would not encourage people to be leaving [artifacts], but we're a memorial, and you do leave things at a memorial. That tells me that people are being touched by it, and they're using it the way that you would use a memorial. I want our space to be useful for people in their own healing process.[6]

The invocation of healing extends the role of the memorial museum beyond a historical representation of facts into the realm of affect.

History serves as one of many tools attending to radical suffering for and with survivors against the forces of denial and time.

Perpetrators depend on denial and time to complete the destruction of people, cultures, and institutions. Memorial museums oppose annihilation by compiling the fragments of impacted communities, preserving history and testimonies. Questions surface, asking who wants to remember what and why.[7] Commemoration answers on behalf of the voiceless victims whose tragic pasts come to the fore in their honor. The memorial museum worker stands on one side of the trauma debate, abandoning a claim of neutrality and proclaiming horror aloud. The declarations echo amidst macroscopic political and economic forces, institutional leadership, and global critique. The forces change over time. But the trauma narrative remains unchanged, embedding itself into the everyday.

Memorialized trauma occurred in the past. But traumatic pasts haunt the present, breaking into consciousness as threats happening here and now. The body fails to differentiate a memory from a current event. For those dealing with trauma secondhand, observing and preserving horror enacts a consistent stress. The work demands engagement in the translation of firsthand testimony of atrocities into symbols for the cultivation of others. Memorial museums thus present fragments in the form of "collected memories"[8] to reanimate individuals and communities. Workers communicate what was lost or shattered in configurations of language and design to create a new interpretation of coherence in the traumatized community.[9] Personal testimonies transform into representations, translated into observable images,[10] exhibits, and audio material for public contemplation.

The visiting public appears. Tourists observe the memorial museum as guests not intimately connected to the commemorated tragedy. They come to the site with interest, seeking education about history or stimulation. Critics also comprise aspects of this public, contesting the trauma narrative or its efficacy at generating meaning.

They may affirm biases, develop conspiracy theories, or deny the trauma narrative. Common critiques resonate around the commercialization of the sites indicated by ticket sales, costs of entrance and tours, and gift shops.

Survivors, family and friends of the victims, and community members merge with the visiting public, but approach the memorial museum with different agendas. This public grieves. They arrive to find loved ones, connect with others who share their pain, or satisfy curiosity about content at the site. This grieving public composes a smaller number than the general visitor, but plays a central role in the service of memorialization. Some volunteer or become stakeholders involved in institutional operation. Some avoid the memorial museum altogether: the space evokes too much pain, and forgetting provides a respite from the pain.

Memorial museum workers attend to both publics. Skill sets encompass the ability to engender warm welcomes to visitors, to pay attention to the various needs of people on the site, and to provide safety. But the demands extend further. The worker guides visitors through affective exhibits and listens to testimonies. The content challenges moral neutrality, provoking a range of responses: tears and rage represent two of these. The burden of response lies on the worker who tells the story of suffering while mediating others' pain. Without this worker, the memorial museum fails to exist.

Awakening the Indifferent and Bearing Witness

The obligation to know about traumatic events in excruciating detail and to transmit this knowledge to publics subsumes work at a memorial museum. Emotional, physical, and spiritual costs accumulate. Stories of horror provoke stress. But the horror converges with messages of resilience and hope; the worker mediates both. The balance demands fortitude in the face of service to a public in need. The responsibility to care for both people and memories underscores the act of bearing witness to traumatic testimony.

Witnesses encounter trauma. They approach horror from various perspectives at differing times and verify suffering.[11] The moral witness, or survivor, endures suffering firsthand.[12] This witness endured horror and can attest to its veracity. An eyewitness, or lay witness, observes the traumatic incident but does not directly undergo it. Receiving the trauma story secondhand entails bearing the burden of the moral witness, who in the retelling of trauma may suffer again: past and present collide. The memory worker, in listening to this collision, observes its effects and inherits the trauma story. The worker thus enacts the role of an observing witness. Observation begins the initiation into a trauma story, that the worker must witness further in the collection, reconstruction, and retelling of the crime or atrocity. This witness bears the trauma story, carrying it into the future for the consideration of others.

Witnessing ensues during violent or traumatic events, but also transpires in trauma's aftermath. Memorialization constitutes this witnessing of the remnants of trauma, of its wounds, and of its scars. Moral witnesses, lay witnesses, and observing witnesses engage in the process of memorial museum construction and maintenance. Some assume the role of the worker. All workers, as witnesses, attend to the wounds that remain, mediating the traumatic event—telling about it.

The trauma story inscribes itself onto workers who sustain traumatic memory in sounds, visual images, and written testimonies. Consistent exposure to trauma tests the capacity to be calm and assured by human nature. The daily encounter with human depravity challenges trust in human goodness. Workers resist engulfment by disturbing content. The required emotional attention compounds the high-level cognitive demands of the business of memorialization. The psychological hurdle requires envisioning more than a few fragments of the traumatic event at once, to see the whole story, including the possibility of survival. The next task entails compiling the whole into a meaningful narrative for the benefit of others.[13] Reconstructing the trauma story demands compelling and rational language to convey a past atrocity.[14]

Entering the affective, disruptive, and difficult content of trauma forces an exposure to dangers.[15] The worker risks credibility, personal sanity, professional scrutiny, and public criticism. Traumas of human design capture workers who bear witness in the conflict between victim and perpetrator. The memorial museum worker advocates for victims and survivors inside of a complex trauma narrative. Maintaining moral neutrality is impossible.[16]

Engaging Theology

Bearing witness opens the doorway to religion, faith, and God. The actual lives of the workers, the perspective they offer related to guarding memory, and the challenges that they encounter in the work invite practical and theological interpretation.[17] Thinking about workers as bearers of testimony or as bearing witness invokes a religious aura. The juridical act of testifying meets the religious one, discovering from the profundity of suffering deeper meaning or testifying to God's presence in the face of absolute horror.[18] Traumatic memory invites the witness into incomprehensibility and invisibility to which nothing can fully testify. Theology enters. Theology operates in a situation, with particular contexts and definable authorities.[19]

A theology that engages with public memory and suffering has itself to be public.[20] The language, gestures, and symbols arising from the memorial museum field demand public conversation. But in this publicness lies the necessity that theology be open to radical pluralism. Globally diverse theologies result, supplanting a singular theology. These theologies attend to fragments in the wake of trauma of human design. They endure ambiguity even as they attempt understanding. Encountering traumatic memory demands the capacity to weather uncertainty. Fixed ideas about the individual and the collective collapse in the face of atrocity. A theology that recognizes multiplicity and ambivalence extends itself to touch deep human pain.

The fragmented memories of suffering—of both individuals and entire peoples—require an adaptable theology, one that listens to intense pain. The fragments function to challenge and further fragment any totally coherent narrative or indisputable answer. Theologies stable in their particularities but open to being disrupted, and therefore capable of withstanding a shattering of systemic totality, refute stagnancy and reflect an openness—generated in public—to growth.[21] The public act of remembering together engages a continual dynamic process, of co-construction and expansion; theology joins this process, inherent in recovery after trauma, when it remains vulnerable, loyal to its core message, and responsive.

Trauma of human design ruptures belief in the goodness of the other and of God. Destroyed hope leaves survivors confused, asking questions of "Why?," "How?," and "Why not me?"[22] Familiar categories of experience, history, and theology disintegrate. Traumatic events do not make sense, shattering the self, attachment to others, and the connection to communities. Human-to-human trauma intends this, separating people from each other and disconnecting people from themselves. Fragments remain, evidencing radical suffering laid bare in the memorial museum.

Realities at the limit of human experience cause theologies to struggle. What does it mean to endure radical suffering? How do communities remember a past that a traumatic event eradicated? Where do joy, love, hope, and wonder appear amidst actual and carnal destruction? Commemorating atrocity and attending to extreme fragmentation engender public conversation, debate, even additional conflict. Local contexts meet global negotiations; the suffering individual faces the demands and judgments of an entire world. Attentive theologies embark on the task of interpretation, maintaining the centrality of suffering and fragmentation. Theologians participate in an ongoing global, public conversation to learn how to ask a worthwhile, nuanced question, and how to interpret the situation.

Interpretation actualizes at physical public places that invite grief. These places—memorial museums—contain and display remnants of the past. They operate within a framework of violence and loss, while naming the space sacred. Physical buildings meld with lost lives. Death inscribes itself on walls and walkways, haunting the spaces. The structures embody the physical remains of those who died at sites of death or resurrect new meaning at nonspecific sites. A symbiotic relationship between present physicality and the immaterial past of memory transform private wounding into public pain.[23] The buildings address and recognize loss in the provision of space for grieving. Theologies of the sacred evolve in the interpretation of acts of mourning, discontent with God, and the exercise of belief despite evil.[24] The sacred manifests, not only in the holy, good, and miraculous but also in the remnants of atrocity. Trauma incurs a crisis manifested in the belief that damage lies beyond redemption,[25] challenging the good in God, in humankind, in resurrection. The sacred indicates the tarnished, marked by egregious acts of human violence and the act of mourning or working through trauma.

Serving Public Suffering

Workers bear testimony and bear witness. Their lives, perspectives, and challenges underscore the significance of remembering.[26] Workers translate memory and perform the religious acts of offering and communion. Testifying to trauma meets the religious habit of discovering deeper meaning or realizing God's presence in the face of absolute horror. Thus, the memorial museum worker invites others into a world where the visible meets the invisible, where evidence of the human capacity for evil wrestles with the belief in human goodness.

The worker listens. Workers devote themselves to hearing the memories of others. The memories emanate from personal testimonies, objects, and artifacts, making demands on the listener who attends to past fragments to translate these into a meaningful whole.[27] Dangerous memories reveal painful stories and rupture accepted, essentialized assumptions about the self and the group. The worker stands in solidarity with survivors and traumatic testimony to prevent public recollection from disintegrating into hatred. This being in relation steadies the strength required for resisting the fragmentation enacted by the perpetrator.[28] Workers model broad-mindedness and resilience at the expense of instability as disruptions reveal new and precarious insights for present reality or personal identity. Their strength emanates as they uncover and attend to mass graves, encounter ambiguous loss, engage death for the benefit of others, and balance institutional demands with public, emotional needs.

Workers represent the ethical response to public suffering. Duties that far exceed the limits of their training transform workers into caregivers, public servants, and practical theologians. They attend simultaneously to individuals and entire communities, simulating both the pastoral and the ecclesial. As caregivers in a pastoral framework, they bring distinct perspectives and expertise to account for human suffering: they focus on pastoring within their memorial museum contexts.[29] They shepherd communities of survival, navigating pain and guiding the possibility of new growth.

Secondary traumatic stress transpires in the confrontation with traumatic content and the traumatized individual. Demands of care exceed professional training in history, oral history, collection, exhibition design, and performance as tour guiding. The museum professional transforms into a caregiver supporting survivors. Parents, wives, husbands, children, and other family members and friends assume the role as workers joining the rehabilitating community. All have a lifelong commitment to carry memory forward. Honoring these caregivers and emphasizing that they too make sacrifices, they too experience wounding by the trauma they commemorate, contains the cost of caring and encourages the gratification they derive from memorialization. The memorial museum worker encapsulates the wounded healer, retrieving religious symbols of the West and East in the form of archetypes that return to consciousness to heal fragmentation.[30] The embodied healer as memorial museum worker suffers, lives through wounding, and transforms wounding into helping others.

Public service also requires support. Workers walk into the field of memory studies with a specific set of skills removed from navigating trauma and attending to those suffering trauma in the aftermath. The work exacts a toll. The logic of trauma circulates internal to the institutions. Memorial museums immerse themselves in the logic, where workers cannot distance themselves from the trauma. Time helps but fails to eradicate the issues that traumatic content presents or to interfere with the spiritual and psychological crises that emerge: How does one maintain belief in the goodness of the world in the face of trauma? How does one—without understanding the impact of trauma—maintain a sense of calm in the face of traumatic triggers? Institutions have a responsibility to speak to such wounding. Communities have a responsibility to recognize that memorial museum work constitutes a vocation and a service.

Service lies at the center of the memorial museum worker's personal mission. The worker engages in a vocation, not simply a job. Their voices and behavior echo bell hooks, "I know only that I am called to love. That to love is to serve."[31] Theologies sustain this discourse around service and the meaning of service as love. The memorial museum worker serves the public through love, what the public needs to engender healing.

Workers dedicate their careers and lives—their service—to public memorialization, to rebuilding after trauma. They honor loss in particular, complex situations. The work of honor and remembrance includes daily immersion in violent historical trauma cumulatively resulting in millions of deaths. War, ethnic and religious cleansing, totalitarian brutality, and economic objectification become the objects of everyday operations. The workers create a new discourse with which to teach, bear witness, grieve, and offer support. Workers as guides, as public servants, model a confrontation with difficult memories. But they need support. Ministering, caring, and serving rewards but also enacts psychological, physical, and spiritual costs. These costs, numerable, meet the negotiation with painful memories and accompany desire to give voice to the voiceless.

PUBLIC SUFFERING

Interpreting Mass Trauma through a Theological Lens

TWO POOLS FILL the empty spaces once occupied by the North and South Towers of the World Trade Center in New York City. Bronze parapets edge each pool, inscribed with the names of 2,983 people murdered in the 2001 and 1993 terrorist attacks. Intending to reflect the absence of the Twin Towers and the human lives destroyed as they fell, the designers, Michael Arad and Peter Walker, wrote of their creation: "Standing there at the water's edge, looking at a pool of water that is flowing away into an abyss, a visitor to the site can sense that what is beyond this curtain of water and ribbon of names is inaccessible."[1] Inaccessibility indicates a certain depth of pain and grief, Pope Francis remarked during an interfaith prayer service at Ground Zero in 2015; mourning reveals itself through the flowing water as human tears.[2]

The plaza honors victims of 9/11, marking a grieving place for the dead. The serenity on the plaza contrasts with the surrounding urban environment. New Yorkers hurry through the plaza every morning, traffic passes, and sounds of the city fill the air. But workers linger. Some stop by a name before work to pray. Others shine the parapets. White roses rest to honor a birthday at victims' names, placed there by a worker. Family members visit, leaving small mementos, at the cemetery where their loved one rests. At this place "made sacred through loss,"[3] a web of relationships forms between those who endured loss and those who commemorate it.

The National September 11 Memorial & Museum, and others of its kind, emerge from destruction, rubble, and mass death. They represent a twentieth-century response to incomprehensible violence and efforts at recovery after trauma. The nature of their emergence, from atrocities of human design, steeps the institutions in the trauma story. Operations revolve around responding to trauma, and service includes attending to affected groups; all arrive with expectations and needs. Survivors and family members seek places to mourn that recognize loss—of the past and of the victims. Communities press for recognition of pain and the resurrection of what once signified control, order, and peace. Democratic institutions create policies and laws to erect memorial structures that honor loss. Survivors build museums in the absence of governmental support. Each memorial museum emerges within a complex "situation."[4]

A situation represents an event, events, or a system in contemporary society. For the memorial museum, the situation involves the complex, particular circumstances in which war, genocide, terror attacks, and ideologies suffocate populations. The horrible reality of mass atrocity demands an encounter and interpretation directed toward its transformation. The encounter thus ensues, as a practical, not theoretical, response to present-day violence, to trauma, and to human suffering. The memorial museum embodies this response, modeled through the workers.

Responding to human suffering necessitates exposure to the other—survivor, perpetrator, visitor, and critic. Vulnerability affects all involved. Amnesia and anxiety circulate, but so do memory and trust. Understanding the competing tensions requires consideration of macrostructures—social groups and politics—as well as microstructures—the human psyche.[5] The two poles reflect variations inherent in the situation and apparent at the memorial museum, in its structure and in its service manifested as the shared experiences of the workers.

Memorial museums thus develop from a complex matrix. Psychological, spiritual, and physical needs intersect with politics, economics, and religion. The evolution requires mediation. The worker comes trained for a specific job and, sometimes, from a personal experience of the atrocity. Despite a lack of psychological and pastoral training, this worker enters into the other's pain and attends to wounding that confounds a personal sense of well-being.[6] Attending to the other motivates the work and gives birth to a public language with which to speak about human suffering. The language assumes spiritual and theological undertones. Reflections by Catholic theologian David Tracy reveal the undertones, as he speaks of theology that attends to human suffering:

> *We must learn to wait, to tell the story, to give voice to those who have no voice, to face the non-identity of our actuality to reason, to spirit, to reality, to despise as obscene any easy grasp for meaning in such meaninglessness. We must not allow these paradigmatic events to fixate our attention but to free our spirits for hope and action. We must discern the affirmations still left to us in the songs and stories of the enslaved black, the humanity in the death camps, the massive, unspeakable suffering, the struggle for minimal survival of the countless voiceless, wretched ones of the earth everywhere. We pray now because they saw fit and see fit to pray. We accept the uncanny gift of hope in survival itself they give us because we know that we clutch that hope only for the sake of the hopeless. We will tell their story because it must not be forgotten. We seek the releasement of their stories' dangerous and uncanny memories upon our all-too-canny illusions of rationality and humanity.*

These words reflect themselves in the memorial museum worker's actions. In speaking to the public, the workers give voice to the voiceless. They discern situations, amplifying every step into the trauma story, measuring their action through public responses. While management and institutional guidelines—if they exist—offer structure, the significance of the work and feedback originate from the various publics the workers serve. The response of the other—survivor, loved one, visitor—offers the measure of performance. Yet this work fails to elicit solid measurable outcomes. For instance, the motive behind prevention, or its intention to stop further atrocity, while noble, does not itself stop atrocity. The battle between good and evil, joy and terror, continues.[7] Thus, the worker wrestles with ambiguity to face atrocity, rejecting an easy explanation for the work, for the horror, for the future.[8] In the wrestling,[9] care for the other takes precedence. Care for the other draws the worker into the realm of the affective and traumatic, and away from the logical and rational. And each day, workers arrive to do jobs at the threshold of absence, of the unexplainable, accepting "the uncanny gift of hope in survival itself," on behalf of the hopeless.

Assessing the Situation

Within the situation, disparate social, economic, and political forces elicit fundamental questions to be answered or explored from radically pluralistic perspectives.[10] These perspectives engage systematic oppression, torture, killing, and destruction of the masses from particular points of reference to unearth meaning. Discerning meaning in the face of mass violence challenges anyone who dares to confront it.[11] The wrestling begins. Additional questions form about reality, about God, about the value of remembering. Each memorial museum tasks itself to provide answers in the expressions of cultures and traditions, once objects of destruction.

Thus, destruction inspires rebuilding. Rebuilding refutes the perpetrator's intent to fragment. Reclaimed and restructured spaces emerge as sacred places. The sacred grows from both the distressing and the beautiful. Traditions rendered "porous" by violence give birth to the memorial museum that recognizes the remains.[12] Architecture and infrastructure align to honor past memory while presenting a new representation of what once was. Auschwitz exhibits thousands of shoes and tons of human hair. The stupa at Choeung Ek displays the bones of the dead in lieu of cremation as tradition intends. And painted images surround bullet holes left by the "slaughter" in Bosnia because sparse funding prevents further rehabilitation. The trauma, integrated but evident, remains disconcerting but unfolds in its new formulation to invite hope in survival.

Looking through the theological lens brings the numinous—the religious, the spiritual—into focus in the memorial museum space.[13] The numinous emerges in all aspects of memorialization: in the building and in the personal artifact or photo. The smallest photo speaks of a life arrested by trauma. The space, and the workers behind it, give voice to the voiceless. Their stories abound in "dangerous and uncanny memories" disrupting "illusions of rationality and humanity."[14] The worker mediates the memories facing atrocity and rebuilding in the form of hope. Telling stories that must not be forgotten reveals an internal tenacity and an impulse to serve, giving intimate attention to the suffering of others. A method transpires from the workers' approach, a practical method informed by traumatic wounding.[15]

Speaking in Public

Communities rail with grief after mass atrocities, and workers respond. Their approach is fluid: "Our role is never to say, 'This is how you do it.' It's just to say, you are going to go through a process, and it's going to be painful." These words inform a curator's attitude at the onset of collecting after the 9/11 terrorist attack in the United States. At this point in her work, no memorial museum existed nor was apparent in public imagination. A group from the New York Historical Society convened to respond.

One of the first things this assembled group asked for was time off to pray. I had never thought of my colleagues as being religious necessarily, and they may not have been religious,

> *but they wanted time off to pray. They wanted time off to*
> *donate blood. They wanted time off to get dog biscuits and*
> *warm socks down to the rescue and recovery workers.*

They wanted time off to attend to public suffering, in public, as members of a public institution. The urgency of trauma, the pain of the aftermath, relies on such publicness. Public rhetoric and public figures engage in the response. All are implicated.

> *One of the people that came to pay his respects was Bill*
> *Clinton. Now Hillary of course was the junior Senator of*
> *New York at the time, I remember. I don't think I was there*
> *when he came, but he wrote—we had just a guest book—and*
> *he wrote the most beautiful thing. Apparently, according to*
> *some of the guards who wanted to give him his privacy, the*
> *tears were rolling down.*

Grief engulfs in the aftermath.

The perpetrator sought to instill widespread terror and anguish into the public. Refuting the perpetrator must, then, happen in public. On the public platform, in the face of public suffering, the theologian meets the memorial museum worker.[16] The parallel underscores the method and the demands of responding to atrocity, drawing workers into larger historical patterns in which they play a part. Alongside the theologian, memorial museum workers inject themselves into constellations of power and hate that breed atrocity.

An example elaborates the risks and demands of speaking in public. As Hitler gained dominance, a document circulated—the Barmen Declaration in 1934—largely based on Karl Barth's writing opposing the *Deutsche Christen*, or German Christian movement, of Nazi Germany. The declaration asserted that supporting Hitler opposed both the Christian Church and the Christian message. Thus, the confessional refused Hitler's governmental efforts to align the Nazi Party with Christianity.[17] The refusal cost Barth his career in Germany and many of the signatories their lives. The Holocaust proceeded. But Barth and his allies protested, dedicating practical efforts to resistance against perpetrators. Despite the ambiguity of the situation and even of the results of his action, Barth took an unambiguous stand against the wrong.

Public theological engagement in the situation combats ambiguity, reflecting moral positions and political stances.[18] These stances undergird memorialization, highlighting the public nature of the work. The practical action reflects moral positions and political stances, embedded into memorialization and underscoring the public nature of the job, including its risks and demands. Each situation draws those who speak about suffering into the public domain. The call to action challenges any desire to remain indifferent to suffering.

The memorial museum worker embodies involvement with suffering. The involvement includes creating a public platform for political resistance to forgetting, to atrocity, to continued persecution. They both join and host political and religious leaders who come to the memorial museum space to participate in ways that bear upon a religious community, but also relate to larger society. The most senior Islamic leadership delegates in the history of Auschwitz visited there in 2020 to proclaim messages of peace. The Archbishop of Canterbury, Justin Welby, traveled to Yad Vashem in 2017 to make reparations, acknowledging the history of anti-Semitism in the Church and affirming a commitment to continue efforts to stop anti-Semitism.[19] Buddhist monks chanted prayers at a ceremony inaugurating a memorial at the Tuol Sleng Genocide Museum in 2015, and each year the museum marks the Khmer New Year on April 8 with a religious ritual blessing workers and presenting offerings to victims.[20]

Memorial museums thus represent a plurality of voices, those of faith traditions and those who claim none, remembering and mourning on a public platform, providing a method for theological reflection. The memorial museum worker endures public suffering on behalf of the suffering group.[21] Mourning transpires together in the place of words that escape grasp in the face of the unexplainable.

Wrestling with Ambiguity

Sites of memory encounter the "unsayable."[22] Symbols, artifacts, exhibits, and architecture replace words, endeavoring to articulate the vestiges of trauma. Yet these memories, narratives, and emotions remain ambiguous. But ambiguous is "too mild a word to describe the strange mixture of great good and frightening evil" that the situation reveals.[23] The struggle between good and evil evident in trauma of human design manifests at the memorial museum. Memorial museum workers attempt to make meaning from the struggle. Their efforts at interpretation bring stories and relics to the fore, for remembrance and reclamation.

Such action involves a locally attuned, globally aware, and pluralistic approach, an inclusive discourse that reaches beyond particularities. Reflective questions emerge as traditional language falls apart in the face of atrocity. The curator at the 9/11 Memorial & Museum articulates the trajectory of the challenge after the terrorist attacks. She describes the process of collecting and the questions the collector asked before 9/11, which included precise rules, ways to cite objects, checklists, and resources, but "9/11 changed everything because all of that went out the window. We—the profession and fellow curators—had no sense of what had happened."

Confusion ensues. Old ways of doing things disintegrate or seem invalid. The situation challenges workers to think outside the bounds of the possible. Tracy invites the theologian into the realm of this thinking: "theology should play a role in the public realm because theology helps us all to ask the kinds of questions which all reflective human beings ask."[24] A lesson in listening develops, recounted by the curator at the 9/11 Memorial & Museum:

> *I see this history as a gigantic jigsaw puzzle. In the beginning, I had no idea where the pieces were supposed to go. I didn't really know the World Trade Center that well beyond as a tourist. We occasionally visited it, but I didn't know. What I*

didn't know was so profound. I didn't know about the Port
Authority. I just didn't know so much. Over the years, I feel
like the more I listen, the more I read, the more I hear, I
learn from people that come in and share their stories, the
more I am able to patiently—and patience isn't necessarily
my strongest virtue—put pieces back into the puzzle. My
goal is to get that whole puzzle somehow back together,
which is an impossible goal. There is this fascination, I guess,
where does this puzzle piece go? How does this connect? This
huge sense of satisfaction when I find a piece of the puzzle I
hadn't had before, it was like, yes, I was always looking for
that green shaded piece, and suddenly it pops in. There's this
enormous sense of patience being rewarded when listening
carefully.

The memorial museum and its workers listen, accepting the inability to provide answers, as they simultaneously give speech to pain, narrating and curating it. Developing such speech challenges in the face of trauma, characterized as "unsayable" or impossible to know.[25] The memorial museum becomes a place where the challenge to speaking and the impossibility of knowing exist alongside the traditional ways of speaking and knowing.[26] Providing quick answers collapses mourning and traumatic processing.

The worker models the capacity to tolerate the insecurity of having no precise answer and lives in a vulnerable place, speaking to and engaging publicly in the ongoing dilemma of human suffering. But the memorial museum worker knows that the encounter with loss includes being undone, unmade, and disrupted.[27] Like the theologian, the memorial museum worker runs this risk of exposure to and disruption by the other. Any attempt at encountering the other or immersing oneself in the fragmentation of the human community must involve an acceptance of disruption.[28] In the willingness to be disrupted, the capability to defy indifference materializes.[29]

Memorial museum work entails a process, putting the puzzle pieces together, a process reflected in memory. The worker aims to convey histories, personal and societal, that are always affected by other situations: politics, the economy, and cultural mores. So, the theologian listens for an opening, a "*kairos*," a hope, a liberatory notion, and "a power not one's own.[30] The liberatory sentiment surfaces in Archbishop Emeritus Desmond Tutu's words. Tutu acknowledges the despair that ambiguity perpetuates, an acknowledgment memorial museum workers enact daily: "we all experience sadness, we all come at times to despair, and we all lose hope that the suffering in our lives and in the world will ever end."[31] But, he contends, "There is no such thing as a totally hopeless case."[32]

Acknowledgment alone cannot simply be incorporated into this hope; action is necessary. Memorialization calls workers to consider what they have seen and heard, to consider the best action, and to speak. A biblical imperative emerges, contextualized by Daisy Machado in her work with Elena, an undocumented woman and survivor of rape and mutilation: "consider what you have seen, take counsel on what action to take, and speak."[33] Workers make a choice to enter the trauma, take counsel, and speak it aloud. Visitors also have a choice. The visiting public returns to the world with a call to behave differently, having been changed by the content of trauma. The worker initiates this sending, the ministerial moment of the theological journey. The memorial museum embodies the trajectory. Dr. Ibrahim Seck brings the point to bear at the Whitney Plantation:

> *Black people, white people, young children say, "Thank you so much. Why did nobody teach me about this?" We always tell them, "What is important now is to get involved. This is just a spark you got today. Now you are a missionary . . . It is not only to tell you the story. What is useful is just to tell you the story. What is important is what comes after."*
> *Leading someone to action involves a lot of emotion, a lot*

of education, and a generous understanding. Once you get through it too now, whatever the color of your skin, you are ready to be a missionary and do something about the legacies of slavery.

Conflict and ambiguity may be the situation, but possibility surfaces in conversation, behavior, and action. That possibility centers itself on the other.[34]

Centering the Other

While ambiguity entails asking impossible questions and listening for answers that may never completely come to fruition, listening itself implies an interaction with the other. In the aftermath of mass trauma, the memorial museum worker listens to the various voices that speak to the situations of suffering. Listening entails hearing not only words but nuances, the ways in which words are used, the symbols and metaphors involved, the gestures that accompany words, the tones of words, and body language.[35] Observing behavior and interactions, subtle cues of enjoyment or fear in the presence of others, makes demands of the worker, which the worker invites but which also have a psychological and spiritual impact.

The impact surfaces in the engagement with suffering where reparation of atrocity takes place—at the cemetery, at the reconstructed set of symbols that becomes a memorial museum. Mourning transpires here.[36] Memorial museum workers welcome the grief of the other, performing a sense of shared hospitality.[37] This engagement is intimate, ecclesiastical although it takes place outside the protection of the church, synagogue, mosque, or temple, and outside any narrative that promises a solution.[38] No solution arises. Possibility lies in presence: being available to the other. Thus, the memorial museum embodies *metanoia*: living in the present world, alongside life's duties, problems, failures, and successes to take more seriously the pain of others.[39] A posture evolves. Kind and compassionate gestures—unfolded arms, eye contact, open chests, welcoming expressions—facilitate trust in a person, in a relationship.[40] The body speaks of being with the other, in solidarity.

Characteristics of good listening include concentration, attunement, the freedom from anxiety, and suspension of judgment to lead to perceptivity and compassion.[41] The hermeneutics of listening introduces the complexity of a situation. Media rhetoric and critical voices cloud interpretation. In the din of appraisal, memorial museum workers continually refocus on the other, the victim, the survivor, the loved one, and the visitors. Everyone comes to the memorial museum with a story. And the worker hears.

Listening happens from all sides. The grounds speak, as do those who mourn; both signify something other than themselves. Workers expose themselves to the other—in a confrontation with meaninglessness, absurdity, the threat of "nonbeing," and extreme fragmentation—of the self, the community, and the nation. Setting aside preconditions, assumptions, agendas, and biases leaves an aperture made unstable by vulnerability and ambiguity but through which relationships and pathways emerge. Listening to expose a pathway resembles the dedicatory acknowledgment Phillis Sheppard makes to those whose vocation calls on them on "frightening days":

> As a womanist and practical theologian, my vocation
> demands that I listen not just to the horror stories that I hear
> from my students, colleagues, or the texts we read (or from
> within), but it also demands I listen for the ways that the
> past and present converge to expose a way forward. This push
> toward the way forward is an ethical demand to act on the
> teaching that all humanity is created good and welcome.

Workers face this ethical demand. The pressure to maintain goodness in the face of atrocity requires that they have resources, resources that help them continue to draw meaning and purpose for the work. Because the work changes them.

"You bring a lot of yourself to the interviews. Doing the interviews does change you, and it's the opposite of compassion fatigue. The more interviews you do, you become a better listener, and you do become more compassionate on the whole," one worker reports.[42] However, a risk of the availability to listen to traumatic testimony and to be vulnerable to change is fatigue. Thus, the listener also needs care or an environment where the heaviness of trauma's receipt can be processed, reflected upon, and integrated.

The heaviness registers at another level with the centrality of the victim in memorialization. Names, images, and personal possessions of the lost imprint themselves in every aspect of the work. At Auschwitz, researchers toil to make the depth of Holocaust history known in order to make every victim known. In Cambodia, those who died violent deaths speak to the workers. In Louisiana, enslaved ancestors' energy inspires the tour guides. At the heart of memory lies the stories of the voiceless, whose voices provide a sound footing. The memorial museum builds upon on this foundation. Bringing the stories to bear reveals a critical task of the memorial museum worker: integrating trauma into the present.

Integration requires effort. Effort includes continual attention to the way that pain mobilizes to claim the worker—physically, emotionally, and spiritually. A guide prays that God will inspire and lead his tours as he begins his work each morning at the Apartheid Museum. His colleagues concur: we are "stewards of history" and "guardians of memory."[43] As guardians, they care for the dead and witness the mourning of the living. The Srebrenica Memorial Center displays "guardians of memory" on its website in echo, seeing the work as providing a deep practical need for the survivors of the genocide. And an engineer at the 9/11 Memorial & Museum asserts, "I wanted to be a part of a project that I knew was important, significant, and meant something. I wanted to be a part of something that had meaning. There are a million high-rises. You can build those any day. I told myself, 'You can do a museum, and it will make a difference.'"

Affecting the Cognitive

Workers commit to making a difference. Effecting change requires a full-bodied response to trauma. Affectivity and cognitive processes collide in the encounter with human suffering. The mediation of memory begs for a conduit embodied by the worker. Henri Nouwen guides the method, articulating a paradox in Christian leadership: "the way out is the way in . . . only by entering into communion with human suffering can relief be found."[44] Workers enter into communion with suffering as "guardians of memory," attending to human pain and nurturing serious goals at various times in various contexts. The communion requires absolute presence—emotional and intellectual, affective and cognitive. Such presence necessitates that workers be present to personal pain as well. This takes courage. But the only way out of pain is through. Traumatic suffering requires remembrance and mourning. The curator's words reverberate, directed at the other who approaches: "you are going to go through a process, and it is going to be painful, but it will be the best therapeutic process you ever have gone through, if you are open to the pain and you know what to do about the pain."

In this effort to mediate pain, the worker protects memory, displaying artifacts and composing narratives that restructure the trauma story. The telling and restructuring enables a negotiation with traumatic histories, in images and symbols, that releases repression, facilitates mourning, and encourages the "working through" of trauma.[45] This "working through" trauma manifests even in the memorial museum structure. Visitors follow a trajectory of trauma, its effects, and its responses, always on a pathway toward a transformation that falls within the realm of the sacred. The arduous journey of contending with trauma's effects comes to the fore, emphasizing a reflective process that invites a connection to meaning, not a projection of rigid frameworks or theological concepts.

Pain destabilizes totality and rigidity. The destabilization happens at all levels of the work. After 9/11 for instance, there "was the peeling away of all the artifices in our occupational life that keep us in separate worlds, those with academic degrees and those without, those with blue-collar jobs, those with white-collar jobs. Those who are recognized as thought leaders as such and those that are followers." The curator assesses the situation: "All of this meant nothing. It meant nothing in part because of the stories that were beginning to emerge of what had happened that day and the rescue response and what people were beginning to reconstruct about the events." The cognitive stable elements slipped from grasp. The slipping allowed something else to enter—the deeply affective as an equalizer. Pain continues to be present as sadness, confusion, anger, and rage, but also joy and hope. The affective infuses itself into all perceptions of memorialization, combining fear with dread and awe, physically representing something that can never be explained by facts and logic.[46] And thus, the memorial museum brings all who enter to the threshold of the uncanny.

Approaching the Uncanny

In 2002, Suzanne Morgan founded Sacred Space International. Morgan, an architect with a specialization in liturgical design, established the organization in response to the events of September 11, 2001. The attacks on the World Trade Center provoked religious friction, to which Morgan responded. Her educational strategy used religious architecture to promote interfaith dialogue. In 2010, the organization partnered with PBS to produce the documentary series *God in America*. A publication emerged from the partnership: *Visiting Sacred Spaces: A "How to" Guide.*[47] The comprehensive guide informs readers about how to prepare for visits to "sacred space," how to maximize the visit, and then how to decompress afterward. The list includes "Memorial

Sites" among those sacred and set aside for the "public good." Memo-rials join houses of worship, Indigenous grounds, and historical sites as solemn, spiritual locations requiring visitor decorum.

The how-to guide also suggests visitors take time for "quiet contemplation."[48] Contemplation engenders discussion: the authors encourage conversation about religion, articulating that religion underlies the formation of many sacred spaces.[49] The sacred, defined as something set apart from the secular, surfaces in its memorial form as the marker of an event or person, a burial ground, a cemetery, a site of conscience and memory.[50] Within this framework, both specific and nonspecific sites assume a hallowed status. Memorial museums assume the condition of being sacred, a consequence of both self-naming and external classification.

Media outlets and publications characterize Auschwitz as "holy soil"[51] or as "hallowed ground"[52] constituting a place of pilgrimage where visitors embark on journey to undiscovered parts of them-selves. President Obama remarked at Yad Vashem, "Nothing equals the wrenching power of this sacred place . . . If you come here a thou-sand times, each time our hearts will break."[53] The Tuol Sleng Geno-cide Museum envisions itself as a commemorative and religious site that encourages visitors to be "messengers of peace."[54] The Apartheid Museum preserves "sacred memory,"[55] physically distinguishing itself from the secular landscape of the nearby amusement park. And in Pretoria, Freedom Park asks that visitors remove their shoes when walking through the sacred ground of the *Isivivane*, or mound of stones representing the nine provinces of South Africa. The Srebrenica Memo-rial characterizes itself as "a sacred and holy place," and all that survi-vors have left of their loved ones.[56] The 9/11 Memorial & Museum self-identifies as "this place made sacred through loss."[57] Dr. Ibrahima Seck describes the Whitney Plantation Museum as sacred:

It is sacred ground because it's a place where people suffered so much. Slavery was a very horrible and violent institution.

*People were put to work just like animals, working from
sun-up to sun-down, at the pace of the whip . . . People died
on those places making sugar. This place was also full of
blood. This is sacred, and this is a place where people suffered
too much. That is what makes it sacred: it's about human
beings.*

Building memorial museums on the grounds of the original
trauma shapes them into sacred space in the sociological sense of being
"set apart"[58] and in the theological sense where some essence underlies
the experience not limited to the encounter of a finite object. The sacred
hovers between a positive, creative power and negative, threatening one,
informed by the memory of trauma. Mediating space introduces the
uncanny, the numinous, and uncompromising ambiguity—no final
answers arrive, and the reality of remembering overwhelms.

Memorial museums exhibit content that escapes human grasp:
unspeakable loss and experiences that have no logical explanations.
The display of both tragic loss and the mysterious nature of human
resilience evokes both dread and awe. The sacred accumulates.[59]
The space—the artifacts, testimonies, and the lives that the space
implicates—transcend reality while remaining a part of that reality.
The transcending constitutes the sacred. Naming something sacred
induces the uncanny, the mysterious, and the immortal through affectivity and materiality in the memorial museum.[60] The affective atmosphere juxtaposes apparent opposites presence/absence, past/present,
visible/invisible, and earthly/transcendent to underscore ambiguity,
but grants access to the numinous through the symbols of what was
lost.[61] Finite stories, objects, and space possess an essence of the infinite.
At the threshold of the numinous, memories communicate trauma,
producing a force capable of transforming a person's life.[62]

Memorializing loss through the consecration of space, the
care of artifacts, and the attention to stories immortalizes an event.
Recollection of the traumatic event becomes larger than humanity.[63]

Approaching the traumatic introduces the *tremendum*,[64] that which lies beyond language, and which disabuses the notion that the sacred aligns solely with the good and healing. Human suffering acquaints humanity with mourning as sacred.

Mourning interrupts time. The act of mourning at memorial museums emerges as rituals, which, like sacred space, distract from the profane of the everyday. Any worker hearing the sound of bagpipes emanating from the memorial plaza at the 9/11 Memorial & Museum understands. The sound recognizes death and transforms time, bending it toward the sacred. To envision the memorial museum as sacred is to make it sacred through such ritual actions.[65] Rituals proliferate. Restitution ceremonies commemorate the return of Nazi stolen paintings and other artifacts to rightful owners at the Museum of Jewish Heritage in New York, while Yad Vashem observes Yom HaShoah, annually commemorating the nearly six million Jews who died during the Holocaust.

The rituals iterate themselves, traversing time and geography. Cambodia observes a National Day of Hatred, also called a National Day of Remembrance, on May 20 when memorial museums commemorate the genocide enacted by the Khmer Rouge through the reenactment of death scenes, and every year during Pchum Ben, a day for caring for the dead, the "hungry ghosts" representing those who died a violent death walk freely to have the opportunity to receive gifts from their relatives. Monks and museum workers make offerings themselves at the stupa at Tuol Sleng Genocide Museum. December 16 marks the Day of Reconciliation in South Africa, a title changed from the Day of the Vow under apartheid. The day recognizes the struggle of apartheid, beckoning to all South Africans to "renew their commitment to the ideals of human dignity and equality" in honor of the holiday.[66] In 1994, Nelson Mandela declared June 16 Youth Day to mark the 1976 protest of oppression in education by thousands of Black pupils from Soweto. Human rights activists from Bosnia and Herzegovina initiated White Armband Day, May 31, as a response to authorities denying the building of memorials or public commemorations after 2012.[67] The 9/11 Memorial & Museum spends a large part of workers' effort for the year planning the observance of September 11. Every year the Whitney Plantation Museum organizes two ceremonies, one in February during Black History Month and one for Juneteenth. A priestess from New Orleans and the drummers of Congo Square in New Orleans attend to bless the grounds.

Ceremonies and ritual enactments align with religion, indirectly or directly, but all are reminiscent of its practice, its publicness, and its attachment to a serious goal.[68] Rituals address the catastrophe while bolstering the ability to cope with its effects. Through the repeated mourning ritual, "a sacred collectivity" confronts anxieties about death, supported by common action.[69] The action—wrestling with catastrophes, commemorating them, and drawing purpose from the work—inscribes the sacred into the experience of mourning, an inscription beneath language, at the heart of human suffering and emotion.

Memorial museums envelop religious and spiritual language of pain, anger, betrayal, dignity, hope, and transcendence, addressing the human spirit, pressing a return to the deep language of the soul and a move away from systemization.[70] Stories, objects, and places play important roles in restoring a sense of coherence, purpose, and connection, and assume psychological and spiritual meaning. Thus, the profane remnants of atrocity lie before the uncanny awaiting reinterpretation. The parapets at the 9/11 Memorial & Museum thus surround thousands of human tears. The pope observes, "This flowing water reminds us of yesterday's tears, but also of all the tears still being shed today."[71]

Pope Francis attends to the tears and sees at the parapets a sign for possibility. "Here, amid pain and grief, we also have a palpable sense of the heroic goodness which people are capable of, those hidden reserves of strength from which we can draw. In the depths of pain and suffering, you also witnessed the heights of generosity and service. Hands reached out; lives were given."[72] Theologians recognize and assuage the suffering from public atrocities. The memorial museum worker joins the conversation, proffering a living theology in "generosity and service." The workers respond to disparate situations with similar methods: reaching out their hands and granting life, as they address the unspeakable. Their efforts at assessing the situation and listening to traumatic testimony center their work on the other. Places and efforts at death transform into places of life. The transformation demands a confrontation with trauma, with the uncanny, and with meaning.

FRAGMENTS

Living among the Dead at Memorial Museums

ATROCITIES BEGIN WITH the diminishment of a people. Hate speech circulates in rhetoric and images, subtly or obviously placed. Messages humiliate and threaten entire cultures aiming at annihilation. Nazi propaganda likens Jews to vermin, snakes, and oppressors in cartoon illustrations.[1] A sign in South Africa reads, "Caution Beware of the Natives," distinguishing white, European areas from those of Black, colored, and Asian people during apartheid.[2] Conservative churches herald Afrikaners as the new "chosen people" to whom South Africa is bequeathed.[3] Songs unify the first recruits of Pol Pot in Cambodia, signifying how the "old people" join the Khmer Rouge's political campaign of reeducation and help "clean out the enemy within."[4] Novels and films portray the Ku Klux Klan as "redeemers of the south," relying on religious sanctions to justify lynching as an act of "justice."[5]

Social policies and oppressive systems sanctify the elimination of unwanted ethnic or religious groups by displacement, mass murder, rape, or threats of such acts. Rhetorical diminishment promotes violent action. Convicted war criminal and prior leader of the Respublika Srpska in Bosnia and Herzegovina Radovan Karadžić, dubbed the "Butcher of Bosnia,"[6] aims hate at the Bosnian Muslim population: "Muslims do not think that our political solution is good. Well, then we will have to crash them."[7] Osama bin Laden deprecated Americans as he threatened them prior to the terrorist attacks on the World Trade Center: "We believe that the biggest thieves in the world and the terrorists are the Americans. The only way for us to fend off these assaults is to use similar means . . . We as Muslims believe our fate is set . . . The war has just started. The Americans should wait for the answer."[8] The answer arrived in the form of airplanes striking the World Trade Center towers in New York City and the Pentagon in Washington DC on September 11, 2001.

Eliminating cultural and religious symbols accompanies the annihilation of a people. Social life fragments or nearly disappears. Nazi forces and civilians smashed windows of stores and synagogues on Kristallnacht. Then the regime hunted, imprisoned, and killed nearly six million Jews. Apartheid ideology dichotomized the races. Separating Blacks and whites in civil society transformed into a project of social engineering: two thousand police forcibly removed the Black South African residents from Bohemian Sophiatown on the morning of February 9, 1955, and bulldozed the town.[9] Slave owners in America Christianized Africans as a form of social control, enforcing a Christian order of duty: slave to master and master to slave.[10] But slaves' being baptized posed a problem; theoretically, "only 'heathens' could be enslaved."[11] The solution emerged in colonial legislation ensuring that baptism did not neutralize ownership nor necessitate a slave's freedom.[12] Pol Pot demanded the destruction of Buddhist temples, or *Wat*, dissolving centers of religious, educational, and social life in Cambodia. Demolished Muslim mosques became the debris that blanketed bodies in the mass graves of some Bosnian towns during the war.[13] And the September 11 terrorists targeted the World Trade Center, a symbol of economic power and global commerce. Each assault aimed to crush and erase a people, their cultural heritage and the symbol systems that went along with them.

Fragments remain. A guide at the Kraków-Płaszów concentration camp calls a ravaged landscape "rubble." He points to the remnants of a Jewish cemetery.[14] Grass grows wild amidst the broken stones of a former funeral parlor and graveyard. In 1943, the Nazis bombed the cemetery; only fragments remain. His job requires more than a simple tour of the camp. He reconstructs a Jewish cemetery destroyed by Nazis, then recreated as a prison camp in the visitor's imagination: "What I am asking you to do here is to imagine things that aren't here, right?" He details a full image of an atrocious past, testifying to the annihilation of the Jews, amidst the present scene of recent reconstruction.

Memorial museums reclaim symbols, providing public space for mourning and recovery, acting as a corrective to destruction. Reconstructing rubble counters the annihilation of religions, cultures, landscapes, infrastructures, and people. The current absence of a formal museum site at Kraków-Płaszów requires ingenuity from the guide. He cultivates the plight of his grandfather in the mind of visitors at a former gravesite that doubles as a depository of violence and mass deaths during the Holocaust. His efforts attempt to "diminish the distance" between the atrocity and the present landscape.[15] Sites of death absorb chronological time, pulsating with the past. The memorial museum shares the resonance of death constructed either apart from or situated at the death site itself.

Painful pasts mold memorial museums. The structures protect victims from oblivion in return. A struggle transpires. The evocation of agony begs mourning. Workers stand at the center of the struggle to facilitate the grieving process—for individuals and communities. They maintain the grounds of the dead to honor them, bridging gaps of time, making death transparent. At non-site-specific locations, workers endure the certitude of death made ambiguous or dispersed. In both cases, workers preserve destruction, modeling ways to reconstruct lost social and cultural symbols; they display respect and reverence, asking of visitors the same.

Identifying the Cemetery

The wounds of history lie open at memorial museums. The wet earth reveals clothing and bones still emerging through the dirt after heavy rains at Choeung Ek. Over six thousand tombstones extend across the grounds of the Srebrenica Memorial Center, and the National September 11 Memorial & Museum occupies the location of the former World Trade Center complex and where the twin towers stood signifying the place of death for nearly three thousand people. Each site invites silence and, for family and loved ones, provides access to the life that existed before the mass trauma.[16]

Memorial museums address death at or near its vicinity. Identifying victims unfolds as a challenge; time renders bodies found or missing. Former lives fall into anonymity unless testimonies or memories of victims surmount the efforts of perpetrators to suppress them. Memorial museums represent a force against forgetting the lost: both of those discovered and those disappeared. The institutions serve as the cemetery, offering a burial place—even in the form of an exhibited name—for the fragments in the form of memories or bodies. Memorial museum sites carry a common burden of death in the face of the inability to bury victims. The sadness is permanent.[17]

Auschwitz-Birkenau's roster numbered 67,000 weeks before liberation. The Russians entered in 1945 and emancipated 7,000.[18] The other 60,000 people died in death marches within a matter of days. Prisoners, mostly Jews, walked tens to hundreds of miles through the Polish countryside.[19] Few survived. Their bodies litter the Polish landscape at Auschwitz, extending deep into the forest. The dead join legacies of extermination at the camps; Nazi forces murdered one million Jews, 70,000 Poles, 25,000 Sinti and Roma, and about 15,000 prisoners of war from the USSR and other countries.[20] Auschwitz and its periphery transform into an impossible cemetery.

Various organizations bring visibility to mass deaths. Both independent nonprofit and governmentally funded projects allocate resources to verify acts of violence made evident by mass graves.[21] Disinterring the dead substantiates narratives and evidence of murder, assembling data to identify victims and making the return of remains to survivors a possibility. Difficulties abound. Infrastructure and government policies inhibit disinterment. Deliberate damage to bodies complicates identification or hides abuse. Unexploded ammunition and chemical weapon contamination threaten safety in and around post-conflict grave sites. Despite the challenges, exposing mass graves disallows a rewriting of history by perpetrators and can enable the emotional processing of traumatic events.[22]

Interaction with grave sites varies. Memorial museum guides in Poland visit mass graves as a preparation experience before becoming officially employed. The exercise shocks, serving as a foundation for understanding the experience of the visitor who may come to a site and be unaware of the atrocity that happened there. A worker from the Galicia Museum shares her experience and its cost: "We went to Zbylitowska Góra. It's outside of Tarnow, and at the site [the Buczyna Forest] where eight hundred children were murdered from the orphanage by grenades, that site scared me to death. I had nightmares about it." Seeing mass graves evokes distress, and memory of distress imprints itself on the life of the worker.

The Killing Fields signify landscapes of death in Cambodia. The Documentation Center of Cambodia (DC-Cam) dedicates resources to identify the burial grounds used by the Khmer Rouge.[23] The organization registered 19,733 mass graves, 196 former Democratic Kampuchea prisons, and 81 genocide memorials over a ten-year period. Choeung Ek represents one of the killing fields, and the major killing center for prisoners of S-21. To date, 9,000 bodies have been excavated from the site.[24]

A worker from Tuol Sleng, the former S-21 prison, remembers her first encounter at the site: "My sister was a Killing Fields guide. Her first job was a tour guide at Choeung Ek. She brought me there in 1999. It was the first time I saw the scar right in front of my eyes. I could not sleep for one month, I think. The image of the scar kept reoccurring to me because back then is not like right now." The "then" the worker refers to indicates a time when visitors walked directly on the ground where shifting soil and weather would reveal bones and clothing. Time transformed the site. Now wooden platforms provide a walkway over the soil and any physical remnants that continue to appear.[25]

The worker characterized Choeung Ek as a "scar" on Cambodia and as "scary." She explained the source of the fear: those who endure violent deaths have souls that "are still going on and on around there." According to the Buddhist belief in *preta*, or hungry ghosts, the murdered wander the grave site, continuing to speak to the living. "It's horrifying," she says. The horror fails to prevent her working in the field, "on scarred land." In fact, she connects meaning to the horror: "I learned during this project why we [Cambodians] keep the scar, for Cambodians to see death by other Cambodians." The cemetery transmutes into an educational center that communicates an egregious history.[26]

Mass graves attempt to bury history. Uncovered bodies speak hidden truths. South Africa's dead blanket the landscape. The apartheid regime incited inter-civilian violence and politicized death to make naming and categorization of mass graves difficult.[27] Murders transpired during covert operations and as a part of "defense" during protests. Innocent victims died at uprisings or disappeared altogether, and those imprisoned succumbed to torture.[28] A guide drives through Soweto, where he has lived most of his life, recounting his observations of apartheid's impact. He stops the car on the road, pointing to where he watched the shooting to death of a young Black boy. He details another event: the Soweto Uprising June of 1976. Black children marched through the streets denouncing the introduction of Afrikaans in schools; many gave their lives in protest. The nearby Hector Pieterson Museum recognizes the youth that died.

The number of daily deaths during apartheid vary dependent on region and period. A report by the South African Institute of Race Relations (SAIRR) in 1990 recorded ten people per day dying of political violence.[29] South African educator John Aitchison draws attention to the victims:

Behind these statistics lie people, people who live and die,
who have holes made in them by 137 knife thrusts, who are

burnt to death, who are blasted by shotgun blasts, who go to lawyers and appear in court as witnesses and are then gunned down by the people they testified against . . . people who are interviewed by journalists, then detained and interrogated by policemen.[30]

Aitchison's assertion directs attention to the embedded, complicated nature of apartheid. Safety did not exist. Political and social circumstances intended to protect brutalized and murdered human bodies, Black bodies, robbing the dignity and the self of Black people.[31] Perpetrators hid bodies in places only known to themselves; other bodies languished in the South African landscape, their deaths justified as the elimination of an ominous threat. Thus, building a site-specific memorial museum poses a challenge because no single site exists. Death's residue accumulates everywhere.

Of bodies recovered from mass graves since the Bosnian War, over six thousand are buried at the Srebrenica Memorial Center. Exhumations continue to reveal remains in Prijedor, a city in Respublika Srpska, the Serbian Republic of Bosnia and Herzegovina. A forensic team worked for two years investigating the Tomasica grave site there. As one of Bosnia's largest mass graves, the site covers over five thousand square meters and descends ten meters. Identified victims include 275 full skeletons from Bišćani, Rizvanovići, Sredice, and Čarakovo. Sudba Bubi Musić, a survivor of the genocide in Bosnia and an activist dedicated to memorialization of the massacres in Bosnia, communicates the nature of the work and the loss involved in proper burial after the discovery of mass death.

Sudba explains the emotional costs of doing such work: "Every single day, there is a new confrontation with a new horrific story. It was hard to hear them and to organize commemoration, to organize funerals. That surrounded me for plenty years, my God. It was too much." A total of 7,573 people remain missing across the country.[32] The ambiguity provokes an intense desire both to discover bodies of friends and family and to be heard. Sudba tries to serve the longing:

"People just need a little bit of attention. They're traumatized, and nobody understands them." He envisions his role as "ready to accept them, warm with love."

The disappearance of bodies and graves also haunts the North American landscape, where slave bodies rest surreptitiously buried in the brush and forests at the periphery of plantations.[33] In Florida, shopping malls and apartment complexes obscure Black cemeteries from the civil rights era.[34] The Legacy Museum in Alabama sits on the site of a former cotton warehouse where the enslaved labored. Memorial museums emerge slowly, recognizing slavery and its legacies, including the lack of victims' bodies. At the Legacy Museum, jars of soil replace tombstones to indicate the death site of victims of lynching, thereby naming and honoring the dead.[35]

Roughly 40 percent of 9/11 victims remain unidentified.[36] Their bodies materialize from the rubble of the destroyed World Trade Center towers in small fragments. Evolving DNA-testing methods help identify the fragments, many smaller than a fingernail, but some will go nameless. An underground repository preserves the remains at the National September 11 Memorial & Museum situated at "ground zero," in the original footprint of the World Trade Center and the debris after its destruction. A massive wall separates these from the public. A Virgil quote hangs from the divider, etched out of World Trade Center steel: "No day shall erase you from the memory of time."

Memorialization defies the obliteration and brutalization of bodies to provide burial processes—even if symbolic. The sites cradle the remains of the dead, serving as actual and figurative cemeteries. Reconstituted cemeteries replace mass graves and bodies rendered to oblivion. Funerary landscapes or collective representations result, manifesting as sacred replicas of the living community.[37] The new physical locations in the form of the memorial museums provide places for mourning and for the living to connect with the dead.

The memorial museum thus bridges present life and egregious pasts. Workers mediate communication between the dead and the living. They assume the role of conduits between worlds, differentiating the past and present, witnessing death and human suffering as ways of bringing meaning to life. Meaning derives from understanding what to do with grief and loss, and the worker becomes a guide.[38] The public grieves. Families find photos and names of the dead buried, cremated, or disappeared. Survivors process profound experiences as witnesses of both death and horror. Visitors cry before, during, and after tours, accessing buried pain. Lack of such access inhibits a fully human life.[39]

Looming Losses

Mass trauma unsettles, robbing communities of the ability to grieve the dead and engage in traditional funerary rites. Without burial processes honoring the transition of life to death, the reality of death fails to integrate social and psychic structures of the survivors. The wait for physical remains commences. Loss compounds: the absence of a body leads to the absence of a place for grieving. Families have no place to pay homage. Confusion ensues, perpetuated by a lack of facts around individual death. Survivors and loved ones experience a sense of helplessness, asking unanswered questions. Where is my loved one? Are they dead or were they spared? What happened to the body? When and how will my loved one be discovered? A plea resounds for knowledge and for the erasure of ambiguity. Pain arrests the living in vagaries and doubt. The natural grieving process halts.

Ambiguous loss results.[40] The term describes loss that fails to be marked, identified, or located in the form of a body. Bodies verify death and facilitate the normal life process of grief. Being asked to grieve in the absence of a body, in the absence of the certainty of death, creates gaps in the perception of reality. With a body, loved ones conceptualize someone missing or absent as still living. The absence of official or communal verifications of loss undermines certainty in life.[41] Physical absence thus distorts psychological presence.[42] A combination of the known and the unknown collide, producing a disordered relationship between the living and the missing, riddled with questions and uncertainty.

Atrocities intersect with the concept of ambiguous loss.[43] Nazis abducted and then murdered the victims of the Holocaust; families neither saw loved ones again nor had verification of their deaths through physical remains. Political violence claimed victims during apartheid: bodies disappeared from surreptitious assaults. Children filled mass graves in Cambodia during the time of the Khmer Rouge regime, their clothing and bones surfacing from the soil slowly over time. Serbians collected men from their homes and massacred them at undisclosed sites during the Bosnian War. Enslaved people's bodies rest deep beneath the earth at the outskirts of former plantations. And close to 1,200 families will likely never have verification their loved one died on 9/11.

Unrecovered bodies magnify the inexplicability of trauma. Death's obscurity obstructs mourning. The ambiguity interferes with coping and grieving, leading to depression and withdrawal, potentially eroding human relationships.[44] Unresolved grief challenges answers to unsettling questions: Where and how did my love one die? Where are the body's remains? Where and how can I grieve?

Sudba survived the Bosnian War. He contributes to commemorative work and negotiates ambiguous loss as a result of ethnic cleansing: "Thousands of beautiful empty houses" fill his neighborhood. But no bodies live in them. However, the psychological presence of the owners haunts Sudba. "You have to see it to realize how empty those places are and how huge a tragedy it is to this country. It is devastating." The deserted homes transform to "nothing more than monuments. Empty beautiful houses, which are keeping memory of some family alive . . . This emptiness and loneliness, monuments of loneliness and emptiness, surround me."

Sudba responds. He seeks work in the field of commemoration. He participates in the healing process of the Islamic community in Prijedor, conducting the opening ceremonies of rebuilt mosques, and organizing funerals for discovered victims' remains. He expresses the

intensity of the work both as a need for the care of the community and
as an act that takes a toll on his well-being:

> *In 2007, we had 305 identified persons. Can you imagine
> how much of job the person who is responsible for all of this
> has? After every single funeral, I went to the emergency to
> take some help for me. It was so hard, preparing bodies or
> bones. I was there for all this time, and I recognized some of
> my school friends or important persons from Prijedor, then I
> am taking care of putting him in a white blanket. To prepare
> them, in the Islamic way, to prepare, to show my respect.*

Prijedor mirrors Srebrenica on a smaller scale, and Sudba's efforts
anticipate the role of the commemorative institution and its workers
to provide a physical space for bodies or names and grieving.

Mass trauma and death prevent proper burials or delay them
considerably. The absence of normal funeral rites immobilizes grief.[45]
Memorial museums counter the immobilization. Memorial museums
and their workers mediate the funerary process at the funerary landscape. Memorials, tributes, and exhibitions recognize the lives and
deaths of victims. The pathway forms to make ambiguous loss "real
loss."[46]

The worker assumes the role of the mortician or the undertaker.
Sudba models the service. He addresses and dresses the dead, having
faith that what he contributes to the community helps the community
heal.[47] He perseveres in the face of ambiguous loss, caring for bodies,
honoring the dead, providing a critical function that helps loved
ones grieve and carry on with life. The process counters the relational
disorder that ambiguous loss engenders.[48]

Sudba understands this. And before creating his first NGO and
engaging in more formalized processes of commemoration, he began
taking care of a cemetery:

> *I created my job. I took a map; I made the map. I numbered*
> *the map and wrote in the names. Then, later, we started*
> *to erect some small gravestones, and it started to be a*
> *personification of tragedy and postwar tragedy. From year*
> *to year, people realized that I could help much more. I was*
> *the president of the local Islamic community, just to help the*
> *reconstruction of so many devastated mosques and burying so*
> *many people we lost.*

He shares a sentiment that creating and restoring grave sites honors the dead, cares for the living, and facilitates historical knowledge for others.

Teresa Klimowicz shepherds grave restoration in Poland. She uncovers the obscured loss of Jewish people in her childhood town of Lublin. Her project, "Well of Memory," asserts as its aim community connection to the cemetery alongside an obligation to take care of it. Her work intends to create a space for loved ones to find family members. She thus calls the cemeteries "artifacts of history . . . important as historical sources about genealogies":

> *If you clean the bushes from the cemetery, then you can*
> *read the gravestones, and you find the names. So, we do*
> *registries of those names and then, the Jewish community,*
> *people who are looking for their roots, can use the names as a*
> *database and see whether the name of their relative is at that*
> *cemetery and whether the gravestone was preserved. Because*
> *in many cases, because of the war and the Holocaust, there*
> *are no registries of the people buried at that cemetery. These*
> *documents were not preserved . . . The only way to find out*
> *who was buried there is to read it from the gravestone.*

Teresa's work of finding and recording names begins to counteract ambiguous loss. Absent bodies assume some presence in grave restoration. The living have a place to find loved ones and to grieve.

Sudba and Teresa work to heal disparate communities. Their work models ways in which individuals combat ambiguous loss after mass atrocity. Each care for bodies and restore places for mourning. Memorial museum workers emulate the paradigm, tending to bodies through retention of personal testimonies and artifacts. Constructed buildings become memorial museums, standing in for the physical remains of those who died, the new cemetery. A symbiotic relationship forms between the past and the present, a restored relationship that speaks to ambiguous loss.

Displaying the Dead

Memorialization follows the trajectory of Sudba's rebuilding and Teresa's grave recovery. Preserving memories about mass death provides an example of burial without bodies and responds to challenges about integrating ambiguous loss into present life. Remembering joins mourning in a complicated path, not linear, and not always evident. Memory refuses to stand still, as does the grief that accompanies tragic death.[49] Addressing evolving memory and grief, memorialization testifies to egregious death and represents it. In the process, spaces emerge for mourning and connection.

Honoring Memory

Teresa articulates the critical nature of the discovered tombstone in grave restoration. The tombstone names the dead, historically identifying individual biographies often detailed with names of the survivors or epitaphs enabling a tracing of the past.[50] Socially, the tombstone functions as a lasting memory and tribute to the deceased, completing the entire ritual process surrounding death—visitations, funerals, wakes—serving as the final stop for the bereaved to express and grieve the death of loved ones. Culturally, the tombstone signals sacred ground, set apart from the secular world, and determinative of the comportment and language of those who visit.[51] Mass death robs victims of the opportunity to be remembered, breaching historical

legacies, interrupting life with unexpected grief, and defying ceremo-
nial, religious, or sacred means of honoring death.

Memorial museums attend to deprivation of the historical,
social, and cultural aspects of ambiguous loss made palpable by mass
atrocity. Specific sites emerge as cemeteries. Family members and loved
ones gain a precise location to remember, pay respects, and mourn;
those who grieve leave mementos and entrust peace offerings. Within
the physical building, walls of names and photos of the dead replicate
the tombstone's purpose: to identify where the dead rest—actually or
in memory.

The portrait identifies victims of mass atrocity. These portraits,
along with photo evidence of torture and other crimes, attempt to
reverse destruction.[52] The photos connect generations to each other,
offering the living links to the past that facilitate a working through of
grief and trauma.[53] The images erase ambiguity and verify life, however
painful, providing a visual vehicle for loss. They "capture that which
no longer exists, to suggest both the desire or the necessity and, at the
same time, the difficulty, or the impossibility, of mourning in the face
of massive public trauma."[54]

Memorial museums portray these images of the dead. Designated
rooms and halls represent the victims in life. Pages of Testimony and
portraits of Holocaust victims adorn the Hall of Names at Yad Vashem.
An adjacent computer center allows the public to seek information on
the fates of the victims and/or information about their lives. A Memorial Exhibit at the 9/11 Memorial & Museum features the same interactive viewing experience. Different rooms exhibit different types of
victims' photos at Tuol Sleng: mugshots from various angles testify
to capture and death by the Khmer Rouge, while other rooms expose
images of tortured bodies. Each image testifies to a life and death to
answer questions created by the body's absence. Bodies, tortured and
killed, become present, and photos of the dead, alive, connect viewers
to victims' history. The totality of egregious death emerges, facilitating
public mourning.[55]

The lost meet the living. Visitors frequent the Memorial Exhibition at the 9/11 Memorial & Museum to find images of loved ones. Family members enter to see a life commemorated and substantiated. Audible messages from loved ones and colleagues play as the victims' images project onto a screen in the interior exhibition space. A worker at Gallery 11/07/95 in Bosnia observes that people visit there as well to find a name, a photo, or any evidence of a loved one's past. A ritual reenactment of remembrance emerges, ratifying past existence and attesting to grievous human loss.

The lists of names provide outlets for both grief and identification. At the memorial site of 9/11, the parapets engraved with nearly three thousand names encompass two flowing pools of water. A worker describes accompanying a family member of the dead to her father's name:

The one time that I really realized how important this place is, I was managing a nighttime project, and I was leaving work. It was midnight or 10 or 11, I don't remember. I was leaving, and this girl was walking by with flowers in her hands. She was crying. She was with some guy, and she was saying how she just wanted to go see her dad. Of course, at that time the plaza was completely closed. You're not supposed to go in. I look at her, and I look at the cops, and I was just like, "I'm going to escort her in." I told security, "She's with me." I'm not supposed to do this. I could have gotten in trouble, but something told me, "Just do it." She never came here because her family refused to come. They didn't want to be part of the spectacle, so that was part of her experience. I spent some time with her there. I let her do her thing. She wanted a picture with her father's name, so I took a picture of her with it.

The father's name on the parapet evokes the daughter's past loss, prompting human interaction in the present. Victim, family member, and worker intertwine. Meaning emerges. A personal connection ensues, inspired by the name as a tombstone.[56] What follows accounts for another dimension of the process of memorializing victims at sites of mass trauma. The worker wants to understand and know more. She devotes time to knowing the victim and his daughter. "She was going to New School, like I was going to Parsons; she was on the Dean's list you know; she was basically doing well." She sees parallels between herself and the daughter, empathetic links not unusual for those immersed in labor around distressing topics. Her lack of action inspires guilt. "I haven't done it yet, and I feel guilty about this, but one of the things I want to do is take a really nice photo of her dad's name and then print it or something. Then send it to her and say how proud her dad would be now because, and then mention all these things, so she's almost like, 'How does she know this?' I feel like her dad wanted me to channel how proud he is of her."

Knowledge of the deceased transforms, imbued with personal meaning, important for the life of the living.[57] The daughter mourns near the evidence of her father's death. Witnessing this moment changes the worker. The past confronts the present, affecting the lives of all of those who the memorial museum greets, including the workers. The workers mediate the connection between the living and the dead, confronting the demands of public grief that leave an imprint on them.

Testifying to Death

Photos also evidence egregious death. These images confront the viewer with horror. The visitor encounters such images once. The worker encounters them daily. When meeting depictions of past horror transpires at site-specific museums, the emotional impact of content increases. A worker expresses the dilemma at Tuol Sleng. He walks to his office through the exhibit of black-and-white photographic mugshots of those captured by the Khmer Rouge, and then through a room of the images of tortured bodies. This, he recounts, "is the most difficult thing" that he does every day.

Tuol Sleng depicts scenes of torture through which he traverses daily. The memorial museum also displays photos of the dead, obscuring faces as much as possible. The Crimes against Humanity and Genocide Museum in Sarajevo spares little detail in demonstrations of torment and suffering. Other sites establish differing rules about displaying death in photographs.[58] An entire ethics exists around the display of death. An Apartheid Museum worker asserts: "Our policy is not to display dead bodies." At Auschwitz, the remains of the dead— piles of shoes, luggage, and glasses—serve in the stead of photos to ratify systematized torture and death.

Images that convey death appear sparingly and with warnings at the 9/11 Memorial & Museum. The Historical Exhibit alcoves signal forthcoming disturbing material: visitors choose to witness videos of people falling from the towers or to listen to audio recordings as passengers on highjacked United Airlines Flight 93 say goodbye to their loved ones. A worker there recounts planning the historical exhibition:

Piece by piece was carefully considered. There was, for instance, a big debate about whether to show people falling from the buildings, and in the end, they decided to show that but in an alcove. Video footage shows some of the fall, but you don't see what happens to the victims.

She continues, "There are not any images of deceased people anywhere throughout the exhibition with the exception of maybe Father Mychal Judge, who was being carried after. It's not a graphic image. We don't do that."

Survivors of 9/11 recognize the photo of firefighters carrying Father Judge's lifeless body from the rubble of the World Trade Center. The well-known Franciscan friar and American priest officiated as chaplain to the New York City Fire Department for nine years. The image of his dead body in a chair being carried out of Ground Zero holds meaning for those who knew him and those who knew the people he served.

Photos, thus, provoke personal memory and emotions—both good and bad. A guide reflects on the encounter with traumatic images, noting another important aspect of the job: some memorial museums separate the museum from the office space; others do not. A highway separates the 9/11 Memorial & Museum from much of the office space. Guides enveloped by the traumatic content without pause report the difference, noting that workers in the office space can *choose* whether to be exposed to museum content. "They have a choice. The guides do not . . . When I come up here, I feel more relaxed. It's a great escape." She and others placed in the museum remark on the absence of leadership in the museum space: "I think most people don't want to go into the museum and be reminded of death."

The concern abounds across the globe. Workers at Auschwitz discuss the potential building of space in the large parking lot away from the camp; currently, jobs ensue in the barracks where the residue of death remains. The Tuol Sleng offices have the same tension—the prison functions dually as an office and memorial museum, where the work space inhabits a site of torture and a place of death.

Reclaiming Symbols

Memorializing death expands. Preservation of destruction conjoins efforts at reconstruction. Preserving destruction verifies the atrocity, while reconstruction insists on a community's capacity to rebuild. Rebuilding interweaves personal testimony with historical details. Death becomes contextualized horror in a larger narrative—one that attempts to make sense of events impossible to comprehend. The narratives foster recovery: forming an entire story, which includes the interweaving of fragments of traumatic memory to make the narrative whole, leads to meaning for individuals and the community.[59] The memorial museum models the narrative construction and reconstruction.

Buildings themselves contain entire symbol systems that tell a story. The Apartheid Museum erects six pillars corresponding with the constitution, Choeung Ek assembles a stupa declarative of Buddhist practices around death, and the 9/11 Memorial & Museum imprints exhibits in the footprints of the World Trade Center towers. Memorial museum construction thus responds to attempts at annihilation of a society. Without inherent cultural symbols, a society ceases to exist. Restoring the symbols through memorialization, even as fragments, links the present to the past as the expressions of a society's history. The expressions refute denial, repression, symbolically framing and creating stories and characters significant to larger audiences.[60] The working through of trauma progresses from there. A constant tension pulsates, implicated in the process of trauma recovery.[61] Telling the trauma story is hard; reconstructing meaning after trauma even more so. Memorial museums create new meaning through elevating cultural symbols; however, the spaces also preserve destruction, to tell the stories of trauma. Recounting trauma serves communities, but real people accomplish the work.

Through the workers' efforts, memorial museums employ symbolic reconstruction to communicate a progressive graduation from loss to its overcoming. In Kraków, old ghetto walls merge with a playground. A guide reflects on the collision of the present with a past the Soviets intended to erase when they built playgrounds in Jewish spaces. The walls evidence the Holocaust, while the playground indicates a lighter present. Together they create a pathway to a better future: "When I see kids playing there," he remarks, "it feels less like an ominous place and more like a space where history is being folding into the present."

The memorial museum absorbs past memory to inform the present. The Whitney Plantation immerses the public in a tragic past to teach narratives of resilience. Memorials to slavery, original slave quarters, and narratives about the African economic and cultural contributions to American society intertwine. Education prevails as Black and African American visitors hear about the complex history of their ancestors. The Tuol Sleng Genocide Museum assimilates its past status as both a school and a former prison. The prison and execution site of the Khmer Rouge educates Cambodians about their history, countering the aim of Pol Pot's destructive regime and rebuilding the society.

Workers at Tuol Sleng feel the collision of the past trauma with the intent to reconstruct meaning. "When you are working in the office now, and you look at the floor, there are the blood stains; there are the former cells that used to detain victims, and I feel very sad. But it must be preserved actually—the buildings, the walls, the stairs, the graffiti—everything that has been written on the walls." Tuol Sleng explored cleaning the floor, but expert conservationists advised against it: cleaning would erase the stains and endanger preservation of the graffiti. For Cambodians and those who participate in educating about the Pol Pot regime, erasing the blood means failing to preserve proof of the Khmer Rouge's horrific actions. The blood indicates death but also hastens education. The graffiti reaches out to the living: one engraving implores "Bear witness," in English.

Pol Pot forbade the practice of Buddhist traditions and, utilizing mass graves, paralyzed traditional burial processes. Choeung Ek and Tuol Sleng retain the bones of the dead in response. Singularly, the act violates the Buddhist custom of cremation, which releases the dead to find peace and liberation. Both sites understood that cremation would eradicate the evidence of the Khmer Rouge. A pragmatic solution evolved in the establishment of Buddhist altars. A Buddhist stupa stands at the center of Choeung Ek, and Tuol Sleng buries the skulls under a statue of the Buddha.[62]

Assembling Fragments

Memorial museums recover fragments that remain after mass trauma. Their efforts enable connections between the present and the past. Memorialization resurrects narratives and symbols, which serve as the threads that tie communities together after trauma, and which maintain the integrity of testimonies. Workers piece the fragments together in their respective locations. The steps solidify memory in a narrative sequence manifested first in the act of groundbreaking. Elie Wiesel offers insight into the process of reconstruction initiated at groundbreaking, which lends a "physical dimension to [the] relentless quest for remembrance."[63]

Cambodians likewise recoup bones from the Killing Fields and present them unified. Workers at the War Childhood Museum collect thousands of children's stories about war and exhibit them side by side. Audio testimonies echo through the entrance hall of the 9/11 Memorial & Museum as witnesses from around the globe recount their experiences watching planes fly into the World Trade Center. A worker there interprets the function of the job to be not only "mediators" but also "connective tissue between grieving communities and what they lost." The worker thus intercedes. Reconstructed cultural symbols connect past and present narratives, but the living reconnect to the lost through the efforts of the workers.

Connective tissue supports, protects, and helps repair other tissue. Memorial museum workers support and protect past memory to repair communities. Their work with symbols congeals to compose entire narratives, collecting fragmented memory into new, cohesive alliances. For instance, a guide directs visitors to the imaging of blood in the "Traces of Memory" exhibit at the Galicia Jewish Museum:

> *The main idea is to show the blood is something unique. Blood*
> *is something unusual, something extraordinary, but at the*
> *same time, it has something to do with ordinary. We all have*
> *blood, and this is a thing which can unite us; of course, there*
> *are different blood types, but in general, this liquid is the same.*
> *So, we are going through the history also, and we're showing*
> *the idea that the meaning of blood in Judaism and the Jewish*
> *culture [is to create] a connection with non-Jewish world.*

The guide teaches her visitors that blood signifies life, emerging as a symbol for death in Galicia only secondarily.[64] As a bodily fluid, she asserts, blood connects all people, transcending its biological role to connect not only the Jewish culture with the past but also to connect the Jewish people to the rest of the world.

Life blood pulsates in a people. Blood seeps into soil. Recovering bloodlines entails healing land. Terran Young-Outsey, co-chair of the Wise County/City of Norton Community Remembrance Coalition, spoke at the lynching site of David Hurst, at Kent Junction, Virginia, on July 7, 2021: "At the site of where someone died, there is power in that soil. So, I think recognizing, remembering, if it doesn't heal outwardly, it heals the land."[65]

Teresa Klimowicz heals the land by restoring overgrown and hidden graveyards. Sudba Musić buries identified bodies, restores the mosques, and brings vibrancy back to a community gutted by perpetrators of the Bosnian war:

> *We did a great job. Up to today,[66] we have buried more than*
> *2,500 people. All the mosques are renovated; we are pioneers;*
> *we have visited all those places of death for the first time in*
> *the Republic of Srpska in the post conflict period in Bosnia.*
> *When we visited, for example, in 2003, we were under so*
> *much pressure. It was unimaginable for the rest of Bosnia.*
> *A group of people doing something like this. It took so much*
> *courage; just one moment in life really, but it took so much*
> *courage. We were the first of everything in Prijedor. The first*
> *opened mosque in the Republic of Srpska is in Prijedor; the*
> *first commemoration is in Prijedor; the first returnees are*
> *in Prijedor. Prijedor is our community. We took back our*
> *property. We are heroes of war.*

Mending land recovers fragments, providing real and symbolic grounds for healing. Sudba and his team enact this healing. Similar acts reintegrate a past repressed in South Africa. A guide describes Freedom Park in Pretoria as a place of pilgrimage. The memorial museum features the names of the dead from the South African Wars, World War I, World

War II, and apartheid, including a narrative journey informed by traditional African culture and Indigenous Knowledge Systems (IKS).[67] The guide details the walk of the visitor through the reclaimed space:

> *There's a whole garden and smoke, and you can go in. You go through the Garden of Remembrance, and there's a whole wall with the victims' names. It's a whole healing place. It's done in a very traditional African way. It involves smoke, and you sit in an outside circular space. There's a whole ritual to help South Africans heal.*

Traditional African elements create an exhibit as a healing process. A contemplative pathway spirals up the hill on the grounds of the memorial museum, called the *Vhuwaelo,* connecting all parts of the space.

The Great African Steps at the Constitutional Court in South Africa facilitates a similar mending of the land in Johannesburg, according to the guide. The steps lead from Constitution Square to the ramparts of the Old Fort and Number Four Prison. "The reason why the steps are great," the guide recounts, "is they're dividing the evil of the past at number four, from the hope of the future, which is the court. They're also great because they show oneness of society; these steps architecturally flow outside and flow inside the court. They show what is outside is the same as what is inside." The steps, like blood, flow naturally, both inside and outside.

Buildings grow toward the sky to enact another assembly of past symbols for recovery. Pillars reach up at the Apartheid Museum, and at the 9/11 Memorial & Museum memorial pools animate a New York City block. A callery pear tree grows different from the other oak trees on the memorial plaza. The tree emerges from a damaged tree discovered at Ground Zero in October of 2001, which was replanted at the original site of trauma. An oral historian remarks on witnessing a European couple's engagement under this "survivor tree." She recalls someone asking the couple, "Why here?"

They replied, "We remember that day very well and we feel
like the space now is a place of hope and a place to come
and grow and be strong." Their reasoning behind it was so
beautiful. They came because they felt hope, because we've
rebuilt something; we've done something instead of keeping it
a hole or building stores on top of the space. That gives people
hope that we can actually move on, and courage, and strength,
and all these wonderful things that we've built something
where you can go mourn. Now, look at us. We did it. We
built the space in memory of all these people. People can come
and sit and enjoy and be there. Be in the space of such a
tragic event but be happy.

The story reclaims not only land but also hope in the face of tragedy, facilitated by the worker, the primary connective tissue.

The worker at the memorial understands the sadness undulating in the grounds there but has an equally powerful vision of the space: "I've come to think of it more as not a sad place but a beautiful space that has been created by all these people, so that other people can come together . . . a beautiful space and not such a heart-wrenching place." The past atrocity and the present expressions of meaning and joy emerge in her story, laden with new meaning.

The memorial museum enables new meaning, attending to mass death and mourning to honor moving memory. The memorial museum worker mediates the restructuring of loss, rebuilding the intentional dismemberment of social groups, people, and their symbols. The memorial museum worker interferes, refuting perpetration, reclaiming blood, land, and soil. The worker confronts trauma on the behalf of others, enduring horror so that others transform painful pasts into meaningful narratives. Each space revives meaning and, in that renewal, achieves a new purpose. Remembering and mourning the trauma manifests as that purpose.

⚜ 3 ⚜

THE AFTERMATH OF TRAUMA

Enduring Suffering

A CAMBODIAN CHILD watches his best friend fall to the ground as she runs playing through the field; she dies from a gunshot wound inflicted by a Khmer Rouge soldier. A South African boy passes the bodies of burning children on his neighborhood street in Soweto during apartheid. A Bosnian girl hides in the woods pretending to be a boy to avoid being raped during the Bosnian War. An American man turns to see people falling from the burning buildings of the World Trade Center; he runs from collapsing skyscrapers on September 11, 2001. Each personal past tells a story about someone who works at memorialization of mass trauma.

Survivors endure traumatic content that they know firsthand. Others join them in the work of bearing witness to trauma's aftermath. An archivist tends to the shoe of a child killed at Auschwitz. A family member bequeathed the shoe to Yad Vashem after the death of the child's father, a survivor of Auschwitz. A project manager directs a digitization program in Cambodia, which includes sifting through photos too gruesome for public viewing. He reconstructs the story of every victim killed at the S-21 prison during the Khmer Rouge. Teresa uncovers the stories of Jews in her town, rebuilding destroyed cemeteries and creating a guidebook about the history of the dead. Guides all over the world repeatedly translate atrocities to visitors.

Exposure to traumatic content provokes physical, spiritual, and emotional stress. Trauma conflates present happenings with past events; the two collide to create a perception that the trauma happens now. Physiologically, the body responds by entering a state of hyperarousal—characteristic of the traditional fight-or-flight mechanism—or hypoarousal—characterized by freezing or withdrawal. Each memorial worker encounters trauma daily. Experience and education enable workers to develop a degree of tolerance to this type of pressure, but facing trauma daily and for long periods of time has residual effects. Performing in contexts characterized by high organizational demand (e.g., responding to high-skill activities, dealing with survivors and family members, negotiating with politicians or celebrities) and lack of resources (e.g., lack of institutional or social support) compounds the effects of witnessing trauma.

Memorialization places workers at critical junctures. Workers inhabit the logic of trauma, defined as the conflict between the will to deny horror and the will to proclaim it aloud.[1] The conflict operates on multiple levels, which the workers must negotiate. They deal with the internal proclivity to talk about what they experience daily, as well as the urge to minimize it. They face public criticism and denial of the importance of memory work from outsiders and academics, while standing before survivors, affirming pain and suffering. The work combats denial and distortion of the facts surrounding large-scale traumas, defying silence that exacerbates and embeds trauma's effects.

Each worker stands suspended between the duty of memory and the will to forget, preserving destruction, and tending the wounds that remain, to testify and remember as a source of future possibility.[2] Exploring and understanding the nature of trauma and its impact on this work reveals costs. The costs accumulate, causing psychological, spiritual, and physiological changes. The changes leave a residue that alters workers' daily lives, disrupting both the nervous system and self-perception. A guide from the Galicia Jewish Museum summarizes a necessary process for reducing trauma's impact at the close of the workday: "It's like ringing out a sponge at the end of a day. You need to let go of some of the stuff you learned and remember you're still a person."

Her words and efforts reflect Elie Wiesel's daunting question: "How could we go on with our daily lives, if we remained constantly aware of the dangers and ghosts surrounding us?" Memorial museum work immerses people in the dangers and ghosts. Together they mediate history, tell the trauma story, and remember tragedy, because in this work, "forgetting is not an option."[3]

Poland and the Holocaust

From wooded hills of the former Kraków-Płaszów concentration camp, a guide announces, "I'm here to share stories that visitors don't necessarily know. I share survivor testimony, and I share photos." His goal "to preserve and share memory" motivates his desire to "clarify the history" of the Holocaust. "This works best when I can tell a story." He chooses one about his grandfather. In his tours, his grandfather's struggles during the Holocaust transpire in a publicly given and publicly received testimony: "I feel a little weird about that sometimes. I feel like I am using my grandfather's experience. I don't think he envisioned that, twenty-five years after giving his testimony, I would be walking around and quoting what for him are the most harrowing experiences of his life, the most morally compromising and guilty experiences of his life too, and sharing them to tour groups."

The Nazis imprisoned his grandfather in one of the hospitals at Kraków-Płaszów, a precarious placement during the Holocaust. His grandfather attended the sick and weak, only to watch them be systematically murdered after they healed.

Healers became coerced murderers. "The nurses and doctors were also forced to kill people, to inject gasoline into people's hearts. In my grandfather's testimony, he talks about it: it is done quickly and quietly, and it's not part of an execution because the death takes place in the hospital, but I don't know." He shares the guilt that his grandfather experienced due to the brutality of being forced to restore health to someone to kill them; merciless memories that unravel core beliefs in the human capacity to do good. As he describes who is killed, his voice trails off. A warm wind whips around the camp to fill the silence. The guide points to the three hospital locations on the grounds. He looks up, reflecting,

> *It just feels like it digs into me, and I am like, "Is this going to be the rest of my life, just guiding in a death camp?" I think it's a strange thing because it's not like the heavy emotional weight that a lot of people who are in Poland for two days feel, but it's there and it's weirder, and it's dug into your life.*

The guide immerses himself in Holocaust history, a history that is personal. He offers a public testimony, his grandfather's, while giving his own. He navigates the density of memory, a memory that binds him and the present to his grandfather. He hopes the attachment offers visitors "an emotional experience" they will, in turn, remember.

He shares painful stories to keep his grandfather's memory alive. He perceives a dilemma in his service as an observing witness, testifying in the survivor's stead without the survivor's knowledge, in front of a visiting audience. He fears that listening visitors introduce the possibility of memory's exploitation. The desire to educate the audience transcends fear and guilt. Knowing painful memories, he believes, serves as a source of resistance against evil.[4]

The Kraków-Płaszów camp guide shares a personal, traumatic history that touches him, deeply. The trauma story depletes him at the end of the day. Testifying to trauma engenders physical and emotional exhaustion. He conveys the struggle: "I don't want to lead another tour later today. I do feel like, 'Ugh, I don't really want to.' It's not just about having to do the work of doing it; I don't really want to tell these emotional stories again today."

Interpretive guides share stories of large-scale trauma day after day. Tours follow scripts that repeat survivor accounts of horrific details and histories of death. Telling and retelling provokes contradictory responses. The guide withdraws from the content or becomes desensitized. Or the story arrests and inundates the guide. Each response requires effort from the nervous system.[5] Using extreme emotional effort to contain or control trauma alongside performing a job well instigates fatigue. A guide from the Galicia Jewish Museum reflects the intersection of emotions and execution: "I get tired giving tours . . . I'm giving Maria[6] this tour, and I'm talking about Belzec, and she starts crying, and I'm tearing up, and I tell her, 'Look, I can't give this tour every day.' But I've done three of them in one day." Simultaneously negotiating affect and the cognitive skills demanded by work, such as giving a tour, depletes. Repeatedly telling a trauma story, as on a tour, compounds that depletion, and entails risks. The risks include the underperformance of ordinary demands and an inability to function at the highest levels.[7] In more severe cases, fatigue alongside underperformance morphs into negative transformations in the self.[8]

Yad Vashem recognizes the difficulty of ushering visitors through Holocaust narratives daily, even multiple times a day. An executive staff member comments after giving a private tour himself, "You can't go through that museum multiple times a day or you will go crazy." Sites create different policies related to tours given daily. Staff numbers influence the policy. Smaller memorial museums sacrifice selectivity: whoever works gives requested tours. Independent tour guides have flexibility, whereas institutionally bound guides have a schedule on which paychecks rely. Flexible contractors generally host tours at Yad Vashem.

Giving a tour constitutes testifying to trauma. Testifying depletes psychological, physical, and spiritual resources. The diagnostic language varies, but the underlying thesis remains the same: sustained exposure to trauma, traumatic content, and people presenting traumatic wounding has an impact. Several terms describe the impact of confronting trauma: burnout, compassion fatigue, empathy fatigue, secondary traumatic stress, vicarious trauma, and ethical fatigue. Each details the effects of "people work,"[9] including exhaustion, feelings of inadequacy about job performance, and a progressive loss of perceptions of competence or accomplishment. If not addressed, these impressions develop into depression and anxiety, somatic complaints, desensitization, reduced feelings of empathy and compassion toward others, and, in more extreme circumstances, disassociation.[10]

Research on the effects of "people work" focuses on social workers, therapists, nurses, and veterinarians, all of whom negotiate traumatic content presented by individuals seeking care. Other fields have similar encounters, such as those in criminal law, emergency services, humanitarian aid, the police force, and memorial museum workers. Each labors amidst perpetual traumatic stimuli. Memorial museums submerse workers in the story of past trauma and the mediation of memory. A guide from Kraków reflects on the stress of the job:

> *I am a guide from Kraków. I've been to Auschwitz five times, over the course of being here for three years. The negative impact emotionally is that guides go to these sites continually confronted with the disbelief that something like this could never happen. There's no word in English or Polish or any language that can really describe how I feel in these sites. That's the hard part about giving tours and being here; I am constantly surrounded by the absence of Jewish presence here in Kazimierz and around Galicia. And sometimes I just walk around as if I am in a daze.*

Confronting the unspeakable, the unimaginable, day after day, contributes to intense disorientation. The disorientation challenges guides to find positive attributes to horrible stories. Auschwitz-Birkenau, Kraków-Płaszów, and Yad Vashem plunge guides into a traumatic past that embeds itself into their daily lives. The work contradicts the therapeutic job of overcoming trauma: to make the trauma a memory where one's whole being understands that the event happened a long time ago[11] and has some intrinsic meaning.

Memorial museum workers straddle a line: they work in a present that continually evokes the traumatic past. Traumatic stress triggers emotional and physiological reactions as if events occur in real time. An independent guide who transports visitors from Kraków to Oświęcim has a strategy for handling the impact of chronic traumatic memory: "I don't sit inside, so I don't, or I try not to think about what kind of place this is, like what happened here." His colleague echoes the sentiment that going inside the gates provokes a negative psychological state, "because you are thinking all the time about what happened at Auschwitz." Thus, avoiding the space enables some dissociation from the horror. A rationalization ensues: "I tell myself, 'It's just a job.' I, of course, respect what happened. I know what happened, but I try not to think about it." Going inside requires preparation; he frames the venture as a task. "It's like, 'OK. I am going in there. I'm checking my people.' I do it quickly." Then he leaves the camp to "refuel." Refueling takes place in a seating area that backs up to tall trees that provide respite from the cold, hard reality of death and destruction on the inside of the "Arbeit Macht Frei" sign.

The guide experiences the vestiges of trauma, not as a survivor but as someone confronted with traumatic content. The confrontation entangles workers in trauma's logic between the will to deny and the will to proclaim the violence aloud. The workers subsequently internalize the logic. The internalization motivates the work. Teresa articulates how, for her, the dilemma provokes action. "A whole history of my town was silenced, and I am trying to work against that silence."[12] She speaks to the situation in Lublin, Poland, a town with significant loss during the Holocaust.

Efforts to proclaim traumatic history while enduring traumatic stimuli illuminate an aspect of memorialization. For Teresa, commemoration gives voice to the voiceless and proclaims the trauma story of the silenced. Another guide in Poland interprets telling Holocaust victims' stories as giving voice to those who suffered, specifically women. The telling expands. While she recounts women's stories of sexual victimization during the Holocaust, she voices a childhood pain and that of her mother's as a victim of domestic violence. Proclamation conjoins the trauma narratives, and the guide's words about the Holocaust give voice to both her personal pain and universal human suffering.

Present suffering intertwines with past trauma narratives. Both inspire a need at the end of the day for this guide to seek the presence of others not connected to the story, or to sink into the couch to watch YouTube. Efforts at escape constitute efforts to avoid physiological changes generated by the trauma story, which alter how the body signals external threat to the brain, increasing stress hormones. More extreme stimuli interfere with the brain's ability to filter information to distinguish what is relevant from what is irrelevant.[13] Surging stimuli induce the failure of the stress systems, and this can have long-term effects.

Memorialization differs from other professions that do "people work": staff do not necessarily work with survivors, nor are they asked to respond with therapeutic or medical care to people at the site, nor do they generally deal with emergencies. But they confront trauma. The confrontation materializes as witnessing those who weep while collecting oral histories or when guiding a tour, when traversing the funerary landscape settings of their institutions, or while digitizing and documenting photos of torture and death. This type of "people work" distinguishes itself from that of the social worker and the criminal court attorney. The therapist enjoys the fruit of watching someone work through, and potentially recover from, trauma. The lawyer seeks justice, taking a perpetrator to court. Each receives feedback and, often, resolution. For the memorial museum worker, trauma repeats itself as a memory, as a narrative frozen in time. Not one guide at Auschwitz can change the horror that happened there. Reparative action on behalf of victims is elusive, and destruction remains to be preserved and observed.[14] However, hope emerges, suspended between honoring memory and understanding that telling the trauma story promotes a future good.

Cambodia

Barbara Thimm recognizes that those navigating mass trauma at sites of commemoration endure something particular.[15] As the Civil Peace Service advisor (GIZ) at the Tuol Sleng Genocide Museum in Cambodia, she expresses what she sees as a shared experience among people in the field: "I don't know exactly what the psychological costs are. I can only say in general, many people—I assure you, all of us—working at memorial sites have friends and family members, and people in our surroundings saying, 'How can you work there?' Everybody has this experience. There's nobody working at a memorial site who never has been asked this question."

Thimm's career began at the former Buchenwald concentration camp in Germany. She envisioned this work as temporary: "When I first started to work in Buchenwald I thought, 'Okay, you might be able to do this a few years but that's it. You can't do this for a lifetime.'" Her observations included the realization that the capacity to endure trauma chronically differs from individual to individual: some work in the field of memorialization for an extended amount of time and find ways to handle the content, while others last only briefly. Whatever the duration of time, working with traumatic content affects people. The impact of confronting trauma leads to the necessity, in Thimm's opinion, for self-reflection, even therapy, to address being "triggered by certain stories in different ways."

Thimm anticipated leaving the field of memorialization for good, but after a brief hiatus, she had the opportunity to work at the Tuol Sleng Genocide Museum in Cambodia. Her contributions to Tuol Sleng have helped shape its educational role as a memorial museum site. In addition to a large display of prisoner photos located at the entrance, the site exhibits photos of the dead. Some images depict what happened in the exact room where the photo presently hangs. The dead are unidentifiable, and their faces are covered to maintain the dignity of the victims, but Thimm and her colleagues believe the significance of the photos derives from their role as evidence of the crimes that happened at S-21.[16] The photos constitute one aspect of combatting the denial of torture and executions that happened at the prison, playing a part in the larger project of the memorial museum to inform Cambodian citizens about the Pol Pot regime and its willingness to slaughter and exterminate. The central goal of education functions as one means of reversing the Khmer Rouge's effort to eliminate anyone considered an "enemy" of the revolution.

Furthermore, disbelief by locals that Cambodians killed Cambodians creates a false narrative to which workers continually respond, teaching the country's youth, collecting oral histories from survivors in the countryside, and displaying photos of the thousands that were killed at S-21. Workers believe that education and commemoration enriches the country; making the genocide known promotes development and resistance to legacies of an oppressive regime.

Workers thus interpret their roles as performing a greater good for the country. When one young Cambodian woman came to volunteer at Tuol Sleng, she felt torn about the work but motivated by the idea that the museum aims to "encourage visitors to be messengers of peace."[17] Working around horror with a hope to secure a future good in visitor behavior creates a tension in workers' lives. Being torn in the act of commemoration reverberates among colleagues, but hope, through education, appeases discomfort.

> *When I was in Grade 11, I went to Tuol Sleng. I could not sleep for three or four months. I always had nightmares, and I went to sleep with my mom. I was afraid because when I closed my eyes, I saw the coconut tree beside the museum and the scene of each room, something like that. I told myself that I will never go to Tuol Sleng again. Now, I work for the museum.*

> *When I visited the museum later, when I was in year 4 at university, I felt different. I admire my current director at the museum. This director transformed the museum from*

a horrific site to something you want to learn more about.
Not only about killing, about what we can do, how we can
contribute more to our history. That's about teaching in the
right way, teaching history in the right way.

This worker possesses a complex understanding of the dynamics of education and the audience of the museum. Good pedagogical practice requires a cohesive narrative and psychological mastery of the trauma story through language, thus evading the wordlessness, and sleeplessness, trauma invokes.[18]

This worker also possesses an understanding of the impact of dealing with traumatic narratives. After collecting stories about the genocide from fellow Cambodians, she finds engaging in personal self-care critical. She learned about the need for self-care through experience after enduring both psychological and physical illness during her time in the field.

Workers remain committed and reflective on their experiences around the trauma narrative at Tuol Sleng. An archivist describes her work preserving clothing collected from the killing fields: "From the beginning of doing this job, I felt very upset for the victims because we could see these artifacts, these clothes, had been torn apart—and then fixed by others and worn again after the first set of victims had died. We could see that there had been a lot of suffering." Even so, working with the tattered remains of the Pol Pot devastation, she says, "did not get any harder. It has gotten easier because I have the experience of archeology, and I am fully trained on textiles and preservation." Just as her colleague believes that good pedagogy answers the suffering experienced from the reality that "Cambodians killed Cambodians," this young Cambodian archivist believes skill building helps her manage the traumatic content.

She talks about her experience in Poland, where she was trained in methods of preservation:

There are similarities between Poland and Cambodia
because both experienced genocides, and more people died in

*Poland during the Holocaust than in Cambodia. But there
are differences in the clothing in Poland and the clothing in
Cambodia. Because in Cambodia we neglected this kind of
artifact before. We left it with no care, and a lot of dust and
dirt have collected because of no preservation; for some time,
it remained unused and unpreserved. The condition of the
clothing is more [ravaged] than in Poland.*

The opportunity to learn from skilled preservationists increases her
capacity to confront the traumatic content and manage its emotional
effects. Her exhaustion decreases with the comprehension of a larger
narrative, one that includes both shared trauma—between Poland and
Cambodia—and finding meaning in the work of preservation. A feeling of mastery evolves. Both testimonies underscore that education
and experience lead to fewer disrupted beliefs in the areas of safety,
control, intimacy, trust, and self-esteem when encountering trauma
secondhand.[19]

The archivist's story evokes another striking element of working
in the field of memorialization, specifically related to dealing with
personal artifacts. Handling the clothing in Poland requires encountering a distinct smell. "A strong smell. It's a blood smell." The smell
triggers pain, and highlights, for her, the reality that in Poland and
Cambodia, "the population is still suffering from genocide." Her statement reveals that objects, materials, and exhibits actualize sensory
responses in workers. Museums focus on the visual to make an impact,
but the content handled prior to the visual encounter by the visitor
encumbers all the senses.

Sensory overload distinguishes an effect of trauma. The lower
brain logs trauma as a result of overwhelming stressful sensory input;
the overload arrests higher-level cognitive function. Memorialization demands both highly cognitive activities—perception, judgment, and reasoning—alongside high engagement with sensory
content: preserving artifacts, translating testimony, collecting objects
and oral histories, creating exhibits, giving tours, and often dealing

with dignitaries.[20] Workers thus balance activities requiring higher-level thinking skills with stimulated stress systems provoked by emotional and sensory data that have the potential to impede cognitive functioning.

Sensory immersion begins when one enters the workplace at Tuol Sleng. Many office spaces are in the former prison. The graffiti and blood-stained floors offer little respite. "I cannot relax and eat my lunch inside my room, because I feel so badly about it." Another worker expresses a similar effect of sadness:

> *Tuol Sleng used to be the primary school or secondary*
> *school in that time. Now when a visitor goes inside, they see*
> *nothing. No blackboard. No whiteboard. No chair. No table.*
> *No desk. Only a bed in the middle of the room and a mat.*
> *The mats look very old. Even some blood remains on the floor.*
> *When I first saw it, it reminded me of death in the villages. It*
> *is very, very sad.*

He describes the path through the museum to his office every day. He copes. Coping includes evaluating work as critical for the health of Cambodia. The viewpoint injects meaning into the confrontation with horror and makes it manageable.

A digitization project inundates this same worker in sensory content as he sorts through every single piece of evidence of the Khmer Rouge. He catalogs documents such as biographies, confessions, execution lists, entry lists, photos, and negatives. Every piece verifies the reality of the Cambodian genocide. Validating the genocide includes sorting the mugshots: front, left, right, and behind, half, and full. "We try to rebuild the stories of each and every victim . . . their stories and how they lived in S-21." Seeing the original photos of those who have been killed, he says, has traumatized him and his colleagues the most:

> *The photos cannot be shown to the public. They were first*
> *intended to verify to superiors that a revolutionary has been*

executed. It is very difficult work . . . My staff can usually scan about five hundred photos a day, but if they are scanning these kinds of photos, the number goes down to about two hundred. And we have hundreds of thousands of these pictures.

These pictures depict Cambodians who died a violent death. The cultural belief asserts that such victims struggle to find peace after death, a problem made worse by the lack of proper Buddhist funerary rites, banned during the Khmer Rouge.[21] Denied passage to the next realm, ghosts haunt the space, indicating unresolved conflicts, bad death, and trauma in Cambodian culture.[22] Ghosts persist as addressable social entities that play a role in the lives of the living.

When she started her job, an archivist at Tuol Sleng immediately recognized a victim's ghost nearby. She said, "I was afraid of this ghost haunting me. I saw it was him; he walked behind the building during the day. I knew I had to deal with it. It was the first day that I came here, maybe 12:00 in the afternoon. I had a pen in my lap, and the ghost used it to write." He let her know that he thought she and her colleagues were "working hard." She interpreted his presence and writing as an indication of his approval of her work. This alleviated her distress and demanded more of her; satisfying ghosts requires greater attention, respect, and ritual action.[23]

Respect—for ghosts and ancestors—motivates workers' actions in Cambodia. They face blood-stained office complexes, teach their fellow Cambodians about a war-torn history, and negotiate with restless victims' souls to honor those who died and those who remember. Similar to the guides in Poland, these workers trace family histories related to the Khmer Rouge. Familial narratives related to the genocide create the grounds for a deeper connection to the content.

During the Khmer Rouge, my mom told me that there were rumors that young girl would be forced to do things, to fight, and so parents married off their children as fast as they could.

*That's how my parents met. Then for a few years, my mom
ran away from the war zone into the city. My father stayed
behind, but then they reunited again and moved to another
part of the country and left everything behind. They moved
to live in Battambang; that's how they survived. If my mom
stayed with her family in the city . . . they would become the
new people who were targeted to be killed. This is how my
mom survived, but the rest of her family didn't survive. It's
because of my mom. That's why I do this work. Because she
told me a lot, but I didn't pay much attention. I just keep
it for the record until I came to do this project, and then I
started to understand, "Oh, the way she remembers the past,
it's very important." My mom is one of my inspirations.*

The mother's history, and loss of her family, inspires this workers' job
performance. Memory and skill sets fuse. Caring for family merges
with honoring victims in the work of commemoration.

Workers express a need to do the work that they do, for personal,
political, social, and educational restitution. Their work constitutes
testimony. The testimonies have both confessional and spiritual or
private dimensions and political and judicial or public dimensions.[24]
Their public contribution, and its impact, cannot be understood apart
from the private, spiritual aspects that motivate the work.

South Africa

The Apartheid Museum seeks to create opportunities for visitors to
engage in South African history and draw on crucial lessons that understanding the dynamics of apartheid offers. Recognizing the legacy
of apartheid entails exposing an oppressive, traumatic system made
visible through exhibits. In the "Hall of Execution," 151 nooses hang
from the ceiling. Each noose represents someone executed for their
antiapartheid activism during the apartheid years. The encounter with

traumatic content deters many South Africans, especially the youth, from visiting the museum. A researcher at the Apartheid Museum confirms the reticence: "To get the locals here is difficult. There are many reasons they don't come, but one is they don't want to go into the museum. It's too painful, too traumatic to revisit."

In a conversation with a colleague about the legacy of apartheid and the difficulties of confronting memory of racialized segregation in South Africa, she adds, "We need to have conversations around these topics because if we keep closed and we don't discuss them, we won't make progress." She continues, explaining the seditious effect of apartheid that ensured division among all South Africans, and which she resists in her work:

> *Not only Black and white but also Black and Black; there's Zulu; there's Xhosa; there's so many ethnic divisions, and when people were placed, taken out of the white areas, they were placed in communities that only have Zulu. Conversations will take time because, even among Blacks, there's a division. If you have a conversation with your white comrades, then you still have to deal with the fact that, I'm Xhosa, and she's Zulu. So, when we have a conversation with a white person, it's like, it's so many levels of the whole thing. It is going to take time to be able to come through that.*

She and her colleagues labor to combat this system embedded in South Africa that continues, as trauma does, to fragment people. Perpetrating systems invest in separating people from one another to maintain control and power. The social segregation, the fragmenting of a society, operates like traumatic circumstances do on the individual self—fragmenting memory. Addressing fragmentation at any level requires confronting traumatic pasts to integrate these pasts into present reality. The confrontation requires that workers refuse to resign themselves to indifference by revealing and counteracting perpetrating systems that benefit from fragmentation.

A guide at the Apartheid Museum discusses results of fragmentation in the form of the Zulu and ANC violence he witnessed as a child. This kind of Black-on-Black violence, he recalls, represented one of the final stages of apartheid. He remembers being on his way home at seven years old and seeing a burnt body in the street; something atrocious that became "normal." "I would come across a person being shot or hacked, or a person being set alight alive. It was violence by day, so people were extremely violent. Sometimes I would find that already the person is dead; sometimes I would find that the person is in the process of dying." His childhood memories frame his work.

The stress manifests while watching movies displayed in the museum. "I get worried watching, so I pay attention to the time instead." Checking the time regulates his nervous system, and he avoids an effect of trauma: the present feeling that a past horror happens here and now. Looking at his watch draws him into the present, ensures safety, and reminds him that the videos reflect the past. The videos and guiding visitors through the apartheid story leaves him in need of care. He asserts that the work itself as emblematic of the truth helps him confront violence, but he also draws strength from outside, "I pray, do a bit of exercise now and then; things like that help me work through the pain."

Guides across South Africa mediate the history of apartheid with clear recollections of the past. At Robben Island, ex-prisoners recount personal experiences to lead tours. They follow no script as they show tourists where they were imprisoned during apartheid, recounting narratives about intimate, traumatic histories in the space where the traumatization occurred.[25] During a tour in 2018, a worker guides a small group through the prior prison, "When I came in 1977, there were no beds here in prison, so each prisoner was given two mats and three blankets." He details the changes and abuses that occurred throughout his confinement, recounting the history of his arrest: "I was one of the students that organized and led the school boycotts that happened in 1976 in Port Elizabeth. That's why I was arrested and convicted. I was nineteen."

A door slams during the tour; everyone in the group jumps, including the guide. A tourist asks the guide, "When they slammed the door, was that intentional?" "I'm not sure," he answers as he looks around to uncover the source of the noise. The tourist observes his reticence: "You didn't expect it though, did you?" He shakes his head no, managing a chuckle. "Maybe they were demonstrating how they used to close the doors." His affect is light; his shoulders are heavy. The tourist continues to ask him how he worked in such a place. "It's just not easy," he responds. He has been doing this work since 2010 and manages the stressors well, with some humor. However, his body reacted when the door slammed shut. His startled response exemplifies how past trauma infiltrates the present, a small example of what is at stake for survivors doing the work of commemoration.

This guide remembers an endured trauma in the process of giving a tour. As a survivor, he encounters triggers related to past trauma exposure. Triggers often never completely dissipate and can lead to a reexperiencing of trauma. This reexperiencing injects the past into the present. Unless the trauma has been integrated, the survivor senses that the trauma happens in real time, resulting in a stimulated sympathetic nervous system. Provoked stress takes time to abate and, in some cases, may cause long-term damage, including chronic anxiety, rage, depression, and feelings of helplessness.[26]

Biological and neurological stasis alters based on a variety of factors, including but not limited to personal history (such as a worker's status as a survivor or not), individual genetic makeup, prior trauma, and ability to manage cognitive processes. Therefore, one person's experience of trauma differs from another's; people possess different abilities to manage extrinsic events based on inherited traits and past experiences, and therefore they emerge from a traumatic event—or from confronting it—with different effects. The effects depend on the age at which the trauma occurred, the length of time that the traumatic event lasted, and the degree of social or familial support an individual receives during and after a trauma.[27] Integrating trauma fails when the traumatic experience remains central to a person's identity or when a person continues to organize their life as if the trauma is ongoing. In this case, the trauma stays interior to and definitive of the self, thus defining every exterior event. Long-term effects ensue.

At a memorial museum, trauma itself defines the exterior event. Survivors at work confront their personal traumas on the job. In South Africa, the horror and continued wrestling with apartheid challenges workers. "I must say that it is a problem in our work," a researcher at the museum reflects on navigating content related to trauma during apartheid. She comments on the human responses to triggers—defined in trauma theory by constriction and intrusion:[28] "For all of us who are researching and writing and documenting violent periods of our history, you get inured to images that you've seen often. Every now and then, you come across one that you haven't seen before that is absolutely shocking and horrifying, and it's traumatic. Then it haunts you." Traumatic content, articulated here in the form of haunting images or recollections, surprises, taxing stress systems, provoking a physiological response.

Facing trauma daily at work creates a professional life that fails to offer a breather from difficulties outside of the work environment. Historical, political, and personal realities seep into the office space. Those working at the Apartheid Museum understand the struggle this intersection of the personal and political poses: "Everything is racialized, everything. We've got to get through the space; we will, but it's difficult and contested, and it's depressing." The museum assumes responsibility for fostering conversation, working toward repair directed internally among workers and externally toward the community. Engaging with politics, and beliefs of the youths in South Africa, a leader at the museum articulates one popular assertion among the youth: that life was better under apartheid than it is now.

The museum has to take that on because it's ahistorical,
but you can understand why it has currency in certain

quarters. The other belief is that Nelson Mandela was a
sellout, and that he was too reconciliatory, he didn't put
his foot down hard enough. He gave away too much too
easily. These young South Africans who are expressing those
views, they are a very marginalized community and a very
militant community. The majority of South Africans now
are young, and unemployed. It's dangerous politics that we're
entering into now, and it's like the older generation, we are
the ones who are saying that that's ahistorical if you go back
and look carefully at that period, particularly the period
of the transition from 1990 to 1994. Mandela and others
played an absolutely critical role in averting the blood bath
that everybody predicted would take place. We're having
to deal with that a lot in our public programs and the
dynamics around that. But we also have to give space to the
conversation; you can't just close it down.

The museum provides for such conversation in a variety of platforms: among workers in workshops and with the public, inviting guest speakers, activists, and academics to speak at public events.

Pumla Gobodo-Madikizela represents one such speaker.[29] She brings insight to museum guests as a professor of historical trauma and a participant in the Truth and Reconciliation Commission. Gobodo-Madikizela stresses the importance of bringing people together from "different sides of history" to build solidarity and to combat the fragmentation of trauma—at individual and social levels. She emphasizes the important psychological conception of repair after trauma, in the context of South Africa, but also in general:

I can live with my trauma; I can live side-by-side [with] my
trauma, and I can tell a different narrative; now that I have
encountered you as the perpetrator with your sense of remorse
and your sense of recognition that what you have done has

hurt and destroyed my family, I am able to take this step, the
first step, to hold your hand into the future. It's really about
that possibility, that the language is about the possibility. The
rest of the work, as I say in my new work, is about repair.[30]

Repair surfaces as a new way of thinking about how to achieve
solidarity in South Africa. Such repair involves issues of judgment to
ameliorate the social isolation that trauma precipitates. Repair work
in trauma theory aligns closely with the concept of integration, not
only of memories but also of a life history or a part of the self that
one would like to forget. Trauma inspires the desire to reject part of
life or self, the part that feels difficult to love because that part links to
the trauma, to what is considered bad, or abject.[31] The abject though
reemerges as hate toward the self or other. Resisting hate requires repair
encapsulated in the idea of integration to "love" whatever is difficult
to love.[32]

Bosnia

Many of those employed in the memorialization of the Bosnian War
(1992–95) witnessed the siege and genocide as children. They live in
communities still marked by war and participate in memorializing
events that continue to reverberate in their communities. "Everyone in
Sarajevo is walking around traumatized," a peace worker from Serbia
observes. This reality echoes in the words of a memorial museum
worker from Gallery 11/07/95 in Sarajevo: "Generations and generations of people have been affected by this war. You have children that
were born during the war; you have women who were raped during
the war, who had children. So, in another fifty years, it is still going to
be something, you know? Like the Holocaust, generations were influ-
enced by it."

She reflects on the generational and historical impact of genocide,
and in the next breath, recalls an evolution of personal awareness. At

first when she told visitors about the war and the war experience, she "was telling the story as if happened to somebody else, somewhere else in some other time, and not to me." But over time, she realized that during the tours, she shared her personal life, her personal trauma. "I started to realize more and more that I was so unconscious about some of the things that happened to me."

Working in the space thus facilitates a stage of trauma recovery—remembering.[33] The stage includes telling the trauma story, piecing details together, contextualizing the memory, and eventually making meaning of the horror. The process entails an interpretation of conveying and telling trauma as useful or, as the worker asserts, "good in its purpose." In the end, she concludes that "the reason why this place exists is really important, because in Bosnia Herzegovina, people complain, 'We don't want to talk about the war.' But you have to deal with your stuff; you just cannot push it under the rug, because it's going to explode one way or another. In some way, in your life, or in the society."

In the nearby National History Museum of Bosnia, another worker shares the sentiment about facing the trauma. She does so in a bullet-hole pocked-marked building that preserves damage done during the war. Stars created by artists now frame the bullet holes in order to, in her words, "reheal the museum." She reflects on naming the trauma that happened during the siege, with a shattered stained-glass window behind her: "It's emotional. Sometimes, I go from panel to panel, and I explain the context of everyday life during the siege. Sometimes, I have groups that stay here with me for hours, and we talk constantly about it." The conversations involve personal details in a professional context. The intertwining of the personal and political mirrors that which occurs at the Apartheid Museum. For this guide, the intersection provides reciprocity: "Sometimes, I have this moment with a visitor, a blink of an eye can be very moving. We discover that all of us are in a way eyewitnesses, all of us are connected to the siege." The connection supports the worker who, in Bosnia, faces the dialectic of trauma in political efforts to deny the war and ethnic cleansing.[34]

Those who commit to memorialization in Bosnia testify to a trauma political leaders want to deny. Bosnian Serb nationalist leader Milorad Dodik called the Srebrenica massacre a "myth" and a "deception."[35] In July 2021, the United Nations responded, making genocide denial illegal in Bosnia.[36] Workers combat such denial, telling a story about torture and death in a postwar environment without post-conflict or interethnic reconciliation.[37] The lack of reconciliation meets the release of war criminals;[38] one worker recalls coming face to face with a perpetrator convicted of war crimes in her apartment building. The response to working in this tension happens at a variety of levels. At the individual level, a person hovers between constriction—numbing and withdrawal—and intrusion, which includes flashbacks and sensory impressions from trauma. At the communal or political level, the tension lies between those who wish to deny or nullify trauma versus those who attest to its validity. People's lives and memories hang in the balance.

Velma Šarić, a Bosnian journalist and the founder and president of the Post-Conflict Research Center in Sarajevo, has spoken about this balance in documentaries and lectures. Her global efforts include supporting memorial museum workers, as well as contributing to a commemorative art exhibition made of one hundred thousand ceramic bones to commemorate the Srebrenica genocide.[39] Honoring victims has taken a toll.

> *As additional burden on my own childhood teenage memories, which I'm carrying, and I never had my own layer of processing these things because I consider my work a responsibility to share these stories and tell these stories. When I'm translating what Kristen filmed, I try to repeat every single word a witness would say . . . the biggest issue came from the woman victims of sexual violence, maybe because I'm*

a woman, and maybe because I was deeply affected by doing
these documentaries and doing all these other projects around
and trying to raise awareness about stigma and silence
through a couple of different projects . . .

I would have horrible nightmares when I heard voices say to
me, you have to do something about these victims. You need
to do something about these women, and I would jump from
my bed screaming, "But yes, yes! I will! I promise I will!"

Intrusion emerges as nightmares, not an uncommon occurrence for those working in the field: workers from every situation reported nightmares and sleep disturbances.

Nightmares, insomnia, and flashbacks reflect an overactive nervous system signaling danger in haunting images. The original trauma engenders images at the point of trauma, and the images fail to process.[40] At a later date, the brain rekindles the images, and they break through into consciousness as abnormal forms of memory with vividness and emotional strength.[41] The heart rate elevates and respiration increases; Velma wakes, responding to those to whom she feels responsible in real time.

Intrusive symptoms perpetuate a feeling of being "crazy" as they break into present time to disrupt and destabilize reality. Reality as horror itself transforms to become absurd and incomprehensible. Sudba describes what he went through when imprisoned by the Serbians, saying over and over during his testimony, "Can you even imagine it?" He repeats this phrase multiple times as he describes his efforts at reconstructing mosques and burying human remains from the genocide in Bosnia. He reflects a tendency for the trauma survivor to describe, in repetitive detail, what happened, attempting to make sense of the experience.[42]

Another survivor of torture and detention during the Bosnian War, Jasmin Mešković, decided to build the Crimes Against Humanity and Genocide Museum in Sarajevo with a group of other survivors. Jasmin and his colleagues utilize the memorial museum platform to tell personal stories, and to testify on behalf others. The testimonies serve to counter disavowal of the war, and thus provide no respite from the past: "We lived through the war in our own unique ways; again, we live it every day that we go to the museum. And if you visit the museum, you enter the psychology of a person who survived."

Entering others' stories fosters a perspective on history and on his personal trauma, even if he struggles to manage the effects: "When you listen to other people's stories, then you realize there's even worse. There's worse than worse. At the end of the day, there's always pills. You take one and then you're feeling better." He laughs at the severity of his statement, but shrugs his shoulders, "It's just how it is. You just take a pill and everything's ok. It holds you for like a few hours, and then reality kicks in again."

The Whitney Plantation

In the summer heat of Louisiana, Ali, a guide from the Whitney Plantation, wipes the sweat from his brow. He talks about having worked on the property since 2015. He was not originally drawn to the work, and in fact, at a friend's prodding, responded roughly, "I don't want to work at a plantation. No place for Black people on the plantation in 2015 or whatever." Over time she persuaded him, with a promise that this place "was something different." She offered to pay for him to take the tour, promising that if he hated it, he could leave, and she would never bother him again. He acquiesced.

I came, and I took the tour, and I've been here ever since.
Like I said, I didn't want to work on the plantation because I
thought it was the usual plantation tour where they just bring
you to the house and talk about all the wealth that this white
family had off the backs of my ancestors. Coming to Whitney,

*I found out that it was something completely different. It was
speaking about my ancestors and telling their stories, which
have been swept under the rug for so long, discounted, lied
about, just patently false information put out there.*

Ali places himself, as an extension of the Whitney Plantation, in the logic
of trauma. He combats the denials and false information by claiming
the truth of slavery aloud. His voice counters a silence that has enveloped generations in trauma.[43] Proclaiming the truth aloud emerges as
an obligation. "Once I came and took the tour, then I just knew it was
a duty of mine to step in and do the work. Coming from the neighborhood I grew up in and the life I had as a young man. This is a place
where I felt like I could pay some penance and put out some good
in place of all the other things that I had put out in my life before."
The interplay of denial and truth, silence and proclamation, leads to a
personal reconciliation. For Ali, remembering and honoring suffering
of the ancestors contributes to his integrity and recenters his life.[44]

The historical, familial, and personal converge at the Whitney.
Ali speaks to the difficulty of navigating and mediating the trauma
of enslavement because he feels connected to not only every ancestor
the memorial museum represents but also to every other African
American:

*It's hard to talk about the trauma that your ancestors
endured. I don't feel I'm not related to any of these people.
I feel I'm related to all of them. When I speak on their
trauma, it's a very personal thing. To put up with the climate,
temperature, rain, because we give tours in the rain, the
environment, and then to just constantly retell the trauma
that people who you consider as being a part of you had to
endure. It's hard, but it's definitely worth it.*

*When I say ancestors, I mean any African American, any
African. We know we were all taken from Africa. We were*

dropped off in different places all over the world. We don't
have accurate records on who is your actual great, great, great
grandfather or your great, great, great grandmother, or uncle,
or whatever. I always tell people we are all cousins. African
Americans, especially in America, we are all cousins. We
were bred and bought and sold like livestock and traded like
livestock. We don't know. I could be standing next to a guy
who is actually, in all reality, my first cousin, and I wouldn't
know. When I say ancestors, I speak globally, really. Globally.

Connection to the ancestors resonates at the Whitney. The ancestors
refer, Dr. Ibrahima Seck details, "to our people in the spiritual world, to
all of them who were enslaved on the site and elsewhere." Seck assumes
the ancestors underlie his energy and capacity to confront atrocity:

Personally, when I lead the tour, I feel some kind of internal
energy. I'm a very low energy person when I'm just sitting
there, but once I get on the ground, I have such a feeling.
I don't know where it comes from. Sometime my colleagues
ask me, "Where do you get your energy?" My answer to them
when they ask me that question is, "Probably it is the energy
of the ancestors." I'm not here just by chance.

Connecting to the ancestors, grieving their pain, and resurrecting their
contributions to society and their resilience creates a transgenerational
community. Recreating community heals old wounds and resists fragmentation, here generationally imposed.[45]

Ashley Rogers, executive director of the Whitney Plantation
Museum, references the necessity of addressing and dressing "wounds"
incurred by trauma.[46] "A large narrative that we hear is that slavery was
a thing that happened a long time ago, and that people should move
on, and get over it, which, as we know from even our personal lives,
that the only way you can actually heal a wound is by addressing the
wound. You're going to get gangrene if you ignore a cut." She continues

asserting that the United States "never really dealt with this history," and she envisions the memorial museum as participating in providing a space for people to process that history. The creation of such a space required confronting trauma and the legacies of slavery.

> *If I really understood completely what I was signing up for,*
> *I would have been more scared. I went through years of very*
> *hard lessons about what it means to especially be a white*
> *woman and working in this field. This is a topic that I still*
> *understand academically. I studied it in undergrad, in grad*
> *school. There's a way that I will never understand the kind of*
> *emotional experience of learning this history or teaching this*
> *history, and how it affects Black Americans.*

Ashley's words illuminate the complexities of narrating a traumatic past. She articulates additional challenges about understanding her role at the memorial museum. "I was thinking of [the work] totally on an academic level and not thinking about, How does it feel to be a fifty-five-year-old Black woman who is being taught how to talk about slavery by a thirty-two-year-old white woman from someplace else?" She reflects, moved by her personal memory, "Now I understand this dynamic and understand how that could have been very, very upsetting for people. There were things that I had to learn by doing really." Racial identity emerges and complicates the approach to the work. But Ashley learns, less through the academic act of studying and more through her body, "by doing."[47] The affective collides to inform the cognitive in the memorial museums space.

Emotions and historical facts merge for all who visit the space. In an expression of grief, guests leave behind mementos, jewelry, donations, and other tokens at one of the four memorial sites on the grounds. The workers consider these memorials critical sites for mourning the victims and the legacy of slavery. One visitor leaves a poignant note: "Now I can cry without shame."

*It's so affecting every time I think about it because, thinking
about the things I didn't know about this before I got into
it, I did not realize the depths of shame that many Black
Americans feel about slavery, which is so painful to think
about. Providing that space so that people can think about
their own ancestors, and think about how much they survived
and cry, that's okay. It's okay to feel that because so often we
hear, "That's not okay. Just move on. Just get over it."*

Ashley's words haunt: the American imagination projects an ideal
that the history of chattel slavery has ended, thus, the concept of
"getting over it."[48] Reconstruction, Jim Crow laws, segregation,
and mass incarceration reflect some of the structural ways that
white supremist systems have continued to perpetuate trauma. The
Whitney calls attention to the trauma that the perpetrator—as the
white supremist—seeks to deny and forget. As with trauma theory,
the perpetrator names and defines reality, going to great lengths to
promote secrecy, silence, and forgetting for the sake of "moving
on."[49] Working at the Whitney resists the insistence to move on by
facing suffering. Dr. Seck asserts that giving tours itself "involves a
lot of suffering":

*When you go through the tour, it lasts ninety minutes, one
hour and a half. Most of it outside, may be very cold and
rainy, may be very hot, but people, I'm telling you, although
they suffer, at the end, it's just like they want some more. I
have seen elderly people. One time I had a lady who was
about eighty-four. She went through all of it walking.*

Ali echoes Dr. Seck: "It's rough work. We joke when we say it, but it's
real. Nobody comes to Whitney just because they need a job. This is
something that you have to have a passion for. People don't get out here
and walk. Y'all see this heat and humidity. People don't get out here

and walk and give this tour in these kinds of conditions just because
they need a paycheck . . . It's a calling. It's definitely a calling."

September 11, 2001

In another corner of the country, workers testify to the events of
September 11, 2001, at the National September 11 Memorial &
Museum in New York City. A worker there distinguishes professional
tasks at a memorial museum from other places of employment. His
words encapsulate the intensity of confronting trauma on the job:

> *If you're an accountant, you could work at Disney World.*
> *You're looking at Excel spreadsheets all day about Mickey. But*
> *if you're working on the content of 9/11 every day, or you're*
> *working with victims' families every day, or you're working*
> *on social media every day where you're writing this stuff every*
> *single day, it is fucking taxing. No one talks about the fact*
> *that this is something that we all will be affected by one way*
> *or another.*

He summarizes what those represented from each context have
asserted: dealing with the content of trauma takes a toll. Going to
work introduces stress. The content's impact shifts depending on a person's trauma background, but confronting the residue trauma daily
affects everyone. Those working in the museum space assume that the
office workers, those who infrequently traverse the museum, encounter
fewer incidences of death and human suffering. A presumption follows that the office guards from immersion in painful visual and audible content, or from the cemetery of the memorial pools. However,
death emerges in most aspects of the work, not just working inside the
museum.

One worker edits audio clips together with video images for
marketing or social media. Footage includes images and audio of the

falling of the towers. After completing the project, she reports hearing a constant noise. "I have this noise of the day in my head. I constantly hear the buildings, that rumbling sound." The sounds persist and, for reasons she could not explain, grow more intrusive. "It's more prevalent now for some reason."

The acoustic remnants of 9/11—falling towers, sirens, panicked people crying and yelling, footsteps running from billowing debris of the towers—imprint themselves onto memory. The brain signals impending danger, and the stress system responds with increased arousal.[50] Heightened sound sensitivity characterizes the exposure to trauma, both its ambient and explosive properties.[51] Sound's impact on this worker parallels that of war veterans' sensitivity to loud booming noises: a car backfiring evokes the sounds of shelling or explosion during war and startles. Ensuing symptoms include a sense of being persistently on high alert, emotionally reactive, and irritable.

Sound features extensively in the Historical Exhibit (HE) as the memorial museum narrates 9/11: news reports on TV screens reel off the accounts of the day; harried newscasters interrupt regular programming to broadcast planes penetrating the World Trade Center and the towers' falling. A distinct chirping sound rings out in the distance, indicating that a first responder has suffered a serious injury and has remained motionless for thirty seconds. Disturbing photographs accompany the cacophonous noise: the towers burning, people trapped on high floors of the building hanging at the precipice of life and death, and the collapse of the World Trade Center.

Many workers either avoid or request that they spend a limited time working in the HE due to the constant stimuli: "If you're working downstairs in the HE all day, seeing those planes constantly hit, that can't not affect you, unless you are just completely blind to it." However, this worker warns against disassociating from the content, observing that, "we don't want to be completely shut down at work here. We need to be emotionally ready." This readiness creates, she asserts, "a better host or associate, or a better security guard, a better retail person, a better admissions person." This worker interprets good performance as not simply navigating and communicating traumatic content but as staying immersed or engaged in it. Such engagement results in being "emotionally ready and attuned" to the needs of others, but from the viewpoint of trauma, it equates to being consistently hyperaroused.

Arousal collides with the perpetual sadness instigated by stories about death and loss daily. Loss saturates the content of the job for one worker:

> *It's not like you read one thing and you think, "Shit, I work at the 9/11 Memorial & Museum." It's every day you read this shit; every single day, and it piles up. It's sad and over time exhausting, you know what I mean? With other jobs the work might touch on something sad for a day, but then the next day something else comes up. This place, it's sad every day.*

A colleague echoes his sentiment in an interaction with a supervisor. Together they listen to an oral history of the day of 9/11 to ensure factual continuity for an exhibit. The supervisor fast-forwards through the recording to find the point of the narrative that they need.

> *She just kept fast-forwarding and wouldn't let the recording play. It was interesting because I was trying to understand her behavior, and then I was like "Oh, you are doing this because you're uncomfortable." At one point she said, "Oh it's just so sad." I was like, "Yeah, no shit it's sad." It is sad every day for those of us who are doing this.*

Loss characterizes the memorial museum setting. The spaces become vehicles for mourning that victims can never be resurrected, many remain disappeared. Deep pain, pain that cannot be eradicated, resounds, mediated by the worker. One worker observes nearly breathlessly, "It is really heavy content. This whole idea of resilience and triumph and rebirth is only like 5 percent of the content. The content is about mass death and honoring these people, which is incredibly important, and I'm honored to do it, but it's really draining."

Facing Trauma

People translate and mediate the trauma story at memorial museums. The memorial museum worker, like others who do "people work," dives into horror. The plunge provokes neurological responses. Human remains, personal effects, images and sounds of torture, and destructed remains envelop the worker in traumatic memory. When personal, professional, and institutional resources wane or are nonexistent, the content overwhelms the system.

Fatigue and fragmentation result. Functioning day to day takes an extra effort because all parts of the self fail to function harmoniously. The brain and stress systems react as if in danger. Thoughts are rapid. Nightmares invade sleep, and confusion or bewilderment ravage the day. Trauma makes its impact in small and large ways. Higher emotional responses, or withdrawal, and tasks that seem easy—returning an email, sitting down to eat, walking through the hallway—demand effort.

The impact of trauma transcends the contextual differences at each site, as does its amelioration, staying in the present, reminding oneself of safety in the present removed from the traumatic past. The past haunts the present, a phenomenon made clear—for the trauma survivor as for the worker—by awareness garnered through training and practice. Understanding trauma's effects provides a foundation for countering the impact. Sometimes those resources lie within, but often they derive from external support, such as solidarity among colleagues and institutional acknowledgment of the psychological and spiritual costs of the work.

❧ 4 ❧

NEGOTIATING PUBLICS

Visitors, Survivors, and Family Members at the Door

A DRIVER RELUCTANTLY makes a U-turn on a two-lane road deep in the woods of Oświęcim, Poland. The tourists he escorts want to return to Auschwitz to take a selfie under the *Arbeit Macht Frei* sign at the entrance. A bookseller at Yad Vashem smiles as she helps people discover books about Jewish history; she says it's the best place to work in the museum. An oral historian describes her physically and psychologically treacherous work in the fields of Cambodia collecting stories from reticent survivors of the Pol Pot regime. She listens to hundreds of testimonies about past and present pain, navigating fear and trepidation. A guide interrupts a fight at the Apartheid Museum. He challenges the distraught visitors to voice their concerns and speak to one another, supporting them in their efforts and saying a silent prayer. A worker at the History Museum in Bosnia ruminates on connecting with local visitors who share her status as a survivor of the Bosnian War. She joins them after a tour to exchange stories of suffering and resilience. A visitor at the Whitney Plantation cries in an apology to his guide. The guest had, he said, no idea about the lives of enslaved people, and he could see parallels with his upbringing, where daily labor supplanted education. A public communications worker navigates death threats from anonymous sources at the 9/11 Memorial & Museum. The callers object to a public program featuring Haroon Moghul, author of *How to Be a Muslim: An American Story*, and president of the Islamic Center at New York University at the time of the World Trade Center attacks.

Memorial museum workers serve various publics. Each public has a wide array of needs and backgrounds. Survivors approach expressing pain and offering to contribute to the memorial museum—anonymously or not. Alongside survivors, family members share memories and personal artifacts—of their own, and of the dead. Questions emerge about when and how precious belongings will be shared, shown, and stored. Guests from foreign places visit, demanding accommodation and direction. They take tours, ask for evidence of their stay through photos and selfies, and shop for educational books and mementos. Local community members attend events with a desire to feel included and heard in the public representation of suffering. Critics respond to social media content, both defamatory and approving. Workers arbitrate, operating between the publics and the institution, protecting memory. Protecting and preserving memory challenges workers to reach beyond specific skill sets to meet the profound emotional needs and demands of others; all of whom face trauma. Traumatic situations challenge business operations with the reality of "people work."[1]

Deeper meaning emerges. Responsibility transforms exhibition designers, education specialists, tour guides, and communications liaisons into theologians, philosophers, and jurors to face bewilderment, the state of being after atrocity.[2] Workers confront the remnants of atrocity, toiling alongside those who suffer, empathizing with pain, while staying attentive to pragmatic duties. The duties include their field of training, which inextricably aligns with attending to the psychological needs of others. Guides tell the trauma story, observing visitor responsiveness, prepared to intervene, counsel, listen, or defend. Curators collect personal objects sacred to the donor, and oral historians listen to painful memories of family members and survivors. Cultivating responses demands empathy and awareness manifested in the skill sets of a therapist or caregiver.

Interpreting the nature of care in the context of trauma requires insight into the moral and political contexts of memorialization both singularly, in relationship to a particular tragedy or location, and as a general field.[3] Workers discern the situation and measure their responses, to employ aptitudes that extend well beyond formal training. An ethics of care develops. Caring establishes the basis of workers' actions and motivates a willingness to carry the density of human pain. A belief underscores their perseverance: that mediating mass trauma through memorializing it transforms pain into new meaning. The ethics of care thus reflects an assumption of interdependence among humans, based on the reality that each person—survivor, family member, worker— receives and gives to each other as a practice aimed at maintaining, sustaining, or repairing the world.[4]

Dedication to reparation after human suffering illustrates a form of chaplaincy. Chaplains accompany those who mourn and offer care in trauma's immediacy. On September 11, 2001, chaplains arrived at the site of the World Trade Center attacks to attend to the emotional and spiritual needs of rescue workers, survivors, and families of the lost. In *Trauma and Transformation at Ground Zero*, Storm Swain explores the compassionate, soul-wrenching deeds the chaplains accomplished on 9/11: blessing bodies or parts of bodies recovered at Ground Zero, praying over machinery controlled by recovery workers digging through rubble that included human remains, and standing by the sides of family members and friends asking, begging, if their loved one had been found.

Chaplains listened and offered themselves to the suffering. Innumerable risks materialized: chaplain to the fire department, Father Mychal Judge, lost his life ministering in the early response to 9/11. Chaplains' voices enumerate the risks and rewards of the work in *Trauma and Transformation at Ground Zero*. They testify to facing the unimaginable and responding to the catastrophe. The practical responses of the chaplains, recorded through their testimonies, inform a psycho-theological model of care. The model, devised by Swain, employs a complex psychological understanding of caring for others in the context of trauma, unfolding in three movements: Earth-making, Pain-bearing, and Life-giving.[5] A dynamic process emerges.[6]

This triune and dynamic framework illuminates the continual demands and activities inherent in the worker's job of tending to the aftermath of trauma. Workers embody the role of the chaplain as they attend to human suffering and preserve memory. These radically interdependent activities ask the grieving community to contribute to and exchange with the worker.[7] The exchange replicates the giving of a gift first as memory in the form of an artifact, a narrative, theologically recognized as love. In return, the worker gifts care and love to a suffering public. The gifts given, the givers, and the receivers corroborate.[8] Caregiving practices foster the possibility of mourning. Mourning informs the participatory acts of commemoration that extend memory—of loved ones, of victims— beyond human life, providing a pathway through grief that engenders hope. Each movement in Swain's triad connects a theological concept with the psychoanalytic one—Earth-making is the Holding space, Pain-bearing is the Suffering space, Life-giving is the Transforming space. Swain details how each position works together to inform and ground pastoral care, fostering an imagination for commemoration and care after mass atrocity.

Earth-making engages the concept of creating space— environmental, physical, and personal.[9] Spaces constitute the memorial museums themselves, composed of physical exhibits and collections of objects, personal artifacts, and narratives that proceed from relationships. Workers join with those who suffer in remembering, through stories and objects, while continually looking toward a purpose or meaning in the face of death.[10] Together they provide access to memory and to the past. Granting access to traumatic memory signals Pain-bearing or bearing witness.[11] Workers bear pain by carrying the weight of trauma with the grieving community, tending to artifacts as fragments that speak for deep wounds. Listening without judgment characterizes the work, as suffering voices ask for meaning. Memorial museum workers wrestle with answers and engender meaning attached to memory, in an affirmation memory. With the affirmation of memory and mourning, new possibilities emerge. Trauma transforms into reconfigured significations in the conception of Life-giving. Life-giving synthesizes with Earth-making and Pain-bearing to highlight the multidimensional process of care—physical, emotional, and spiritual—that the worker offers to the suffering community.

Providing Access to Memory

Building a memorial museum entails an in-depth course of reconstruction and construction. The former constitutes the rebuilding after damage and destruction, the latter with creating something new. Both connect to physical entities—buildings and exhibits—and abstract meaning—purpose after suffering. All forms of construction intertwine with confronting traumatic memory and loss, to make sense or meaning of these, processes that continue indefinitely. Integration with trauma and loss characterizes the memorial museum that contains and sometimes embodies the core representation of the dead.[12] The reality of memorial museums' locations as cemetery or as housing the final remnants of a family's history brings to bear the aspects of Swain's Earth-making as the holding space. To build the space that holds the dead and what remains of memory relies on human relationships, or an alliance.[13] Alliances in the form of donor and collector stand central to the existence of a memorial museum.

Collecting artifacts for a memorial museum differs from collecting artifacts for art or other museums. Trauma lies at the core of the exchange. Objects related to trauma reflect victims' lives and family members' most cherished and painful memories. "We are guardians of memory," a researcher at the Apartheid Museum affirms. The worker watches over memory captured in the distance between the past and an imagined or hoped-for future.[14] Memory thus guarded and guarding—in psychoanalytic terms held—protects the recognition of past atrocities articulated, expressed, and understood through the artifact. Dealing with artifacts requires a profound engagement with their care and preservation, with decisions about how and what to display, and compassion toward what the objects represent.

Understanding the layers of intellectual, historical, and emotional depth to objects, ephemera, and media requires weighing both their historical and emotional value. Further assessment includes discerning how an item fits into the greater collecting mission of the organization, and how its acquisition may impact the institution's resources. For instance, if something needs to be conserved to go on display, does the museum have resources for conservation? The curator asks further, "How does this evaluation affect the donor?" Collecting artifacts animates the ethics of care: of both memory and the other, as the donor.

Such care depends on reciprocation, through the exchange of a gift. The giver—the donor—and the receiver—the curator as a representative of the memorial museum—participate in a relational encounter or the alliance. The relationship frames the exchange of the gift and evidences Earth-making. Together the giver, receiver, and gift create the internal substance of the memorial museum, a physical reconstruction of the past. Past memory manifests in the form of artifacts and objects, each different in substance but corresponding, woven together by narratives. No artifact stands alone but coheres with others to convey a whole relational process, between the loved one and the lost, between the memorial museum worker and the suffering public. All are held in the space of the memorial museum.

The profundity of collecting artifacts, cherished objects connected to loved ones lost to mass trauma, points beyond the object itself. The artifact symbolizes the life of a person and the meaning of that person's experiences, interpreted by both the giver and the receiver. The gift centers their relationship, and the memorial museum depends on their exchange, a "relational and communal"[15] care of memory. Such care compels an incredible amount of trust. Trust develops as a result of the giver's interpretation that the memorial museum will guard and hold all that the object signifies. The giver depends on the receiver of the object by extension.

Two different interviews facilitate an understanding of the multifarious meanings of collecting artifacts of mass trauma. One is from the National September 11 Memorial & Museum in New York City, and the other from Yad Vashem in Jerusalem. Both interviewees gave generously of their time to explore the dimensions of collecting objects that communicate the memories of mass trauma to tell a story, to tell history, or to help people share in the memory of life and suffering. Each interview echoes the other as they articulate themes, sentiments, and realizations about the role of curator: to collect items and interpret them in a public setting, while placing them in dialogue with other objects and the museum space. The testimony of each woman reveals the deep care taken in the exchange of artifacts with the residue of human atrocity upon them.

Trauma transforms ordinary objects into extraordinary indicators of the most private intimate details of a victim's life. Yad Vashem houses over thirty-four thousand artifacts embodying history, memory, and testimonies. A worker from the site illuminates their significance. "When you think about artifacts, there's everything . . . dolls, shoes, a little piece of cloth, whatever was meaningful for the original owner." Some of the artifacts represent the last possession of the person who perished. "They could be very expensive, like all this silver. Or they could be something like a shoe or something that doesn't have any monetary value, but which has feelings behind it, a story behind it." In her estimation, this story unveils narratives that chronicle a life.

> *We see the artifacts as storytellers. Each one of them has a story. Each one is evidence from what happened, and it's tangible. If you see a photograph, a photograph is something very visual, or if you see a letter; everything visual helps you connect. But it's something with these artifacts. It's like as close as you can possibly get. This is how we treat them, and this is how we feel about them, because they tell a story of the person who owned them. Like I said, sometimes, it's the only thing left from their life, their entire life, their family, their siblings, their house, everything they had before. This is whatever is left.*

She interprets the artifact both as the storyteller of a personal memory and as the tangible, historical evidence of life, death, and suffering. The artifact "is as close as you can possibly get" to evidence, transporting and giving the viewer access to the past. The distant traumatic past touches the present through the object, authenticating a life and the narrative trajectory that accompanies that life. The object eradicates distance between the past and the present, bridging life and death. Intimacy evolves.

The object facilitates an alliance. The interaction folds the viewer into a past narrative, bringing the viewer to the threshold of understanding. The curator works at this threshold, recognizing that the object unites ideas and life stories. The process implicates her. Relationships concretize through the exchange of the object, a process initiated by the donation. A curator from the 9/11 Memorial & Museum imparts the evolution of giving beginning with the donor:

> I spend a lot of my time vetting requests from the public that come in about donating to the museum, and they range drastically. I do meet all the time with 9/11 family members, survivors, responders, Lower Manhattan residents who were displaced from their homes after the attacks. Now a lot of sick responders, artists, filmmakers, collectors, people who worked in the World Trade Center before 9/11, tourists who visited the Trade Center before 9/11. It's so broad, and it's so hard to really characterize.

A variety of people, often called stakeholders, engage her; they interpret the memorial museum as a guardian of their memories. Each stakeholder possesses a personal story that entangles life, the traumatic past, and a set of expectations (for instance related to the exhibition of the artifact) that the worker balances. First, she determines the interest in pursuing a person's object(s) for the permanent collection. Most of the time, the memorial museum accepts the offering, and if the person lives in New York or close by, this curator extends an invitation to meet in person to donate the items. Even if a donor is not local, she prefers a personal visit: "If I can sit down with somebody in person, I do it."

> *Then I listen. I take notes during the meeting, and I write up their stories for interpretation in exhibitions, for interpretation in educational curricula, and certainly for our catalog records here that have now taken on an online form, and the collection is becoming more and more accessible to wider audiences. That really is the heart of what I do here. I'm constantly in dialogue with people, no matter what their level of connection to the attacks is.*

A "steady constant dialogue" comprises the central task of the curator, a person trained to ensure the proper solicitation and interpretation of artifacts. The job includes the mediation and interpretation of objects alongside an ability to be present to and aware of human emotions. Collecting objects laden with trauma demands attention to meaningful personal narratives—oral histories, testimonies of trauma, and a community's self-documentation[16]—and the needs of the museum and its exhibitions. Thus, the curator works in between disparate fields composed of institutional demands *and* human emotions, between cognitive skills and affective attunement.[17] The association contributes to the Earth-making of the memorial museum, even as it disrupts the distanciation of the professional world from personal life and skill competency from emotional vulnerability. Within the dyad of curator and donor, vulnerability to the other and felt emotions constitute doing the job of collecting well.

The donor and the curator engage in an interdependent alliance. Exhibition space emerges from the relationship, created together as Earth-making. Something new forms from the painful world the artifact represents that adds dimension to time and the space of the museum. These collected stories survive. Yad Vashem recognizes the passing of generations and the threat to memory in the assembling of artifacts that verify the painful history of the Jewish people. Combatting the threat entails creating a large archive—the Earth-making of the memorial museums. The comportment of the curator reflects the memorial museum's mission to persist in holding memory for succeeding generations once the survivor is lost:

> *Last Monday, I was at this Holocaust survivor's house, the last one that lives probably who was in the Warsaw Ghetto Uprising organized by Mordecai Aneilewicz. She was fourteen, and she would do these errands for him. She's sitting there and telling me about the two parts of the ghetto, and how she would go from one to the other. It's like you don't believe it, you're touching history.*

The woman donated a small knife, the only thing that remained from her home engraved with her father's initials: S.M., Shlomo Malinck. Her family left the ghetto quickly, but her mother was able to hide the knife because of its size. She took the utensil with her knowing that this would be the only thing left from her family.

> *The daughter kept it, and she had a long story she told me last week. The family didn't know if they were going to survive. The father perished, but she and her mother and sister survived. She's ninety-something, and she's sitting there and telling me this; she's one of the last survivors. When you hear stories like that, of course then it touches you.*

The story engenders empathic attunement.[18] She connects with the survivor, and emotions circulate in what Swain calls a "feeling with the other."[19] This "feeling with" characterizes the collection process that occurs at people's homes or in private offices, neither of which is neutral territory. Private and public worlds collide, shifting levels of power, safety, comfort, and intimacy. The home represents the least stable circumstance, and may even present a threat, but workers endure the risk to create the essence of the memorial museum.

Collectors understand that the artifact signifies the most intimate memories of someone's life. The meaning requires attention and responsiveness, alongside an energetic pace. The 9/11 Memorial & Museum curator describes her approach to reciprocation:

> *I have grown accustomed to being ready to move quickly when somebody reaches out. For the most part, I'll always just do whatever it takes to accommodate them. I've definitely gone to a lot of people's homes, and by myself, some strange situations like that. But I feel very motivated to respond to people.*

She continues, describing the nature of the alliances she makes. Each connection requires attention to detail of facial expressions, of body language, even of words to achieve attunement:

> *I never want to say the wrong things. You know certain words are going to upset people. Like the word "closure," I'll never ever use that word. You just learn certain things on the job that make people upset. I feel more comfortable now than I did in the beginning because I've been doing this for as long as I have, but it still feels stressful because, again, it's a sensitive situation, and you don't want anybody to feel uncomfortable at all, or regretful that they decided to take the time to do this.*

Her attention evidences an ethics of care. Benevolence toward the other holds moral value, even in the face of risk or uncertainty. Value emerges in the recognition of the relationship and in the restorative activity of the exchange of the gift.[20] Each collector envisions the constant giving and receiving of the artifact as a gift as delicate, serious, sacred, and fully dynamic.[21] Intimate encounters root this dynamic as care performed in service to memorialization. Memorial museums rely on this relationship, this dual cocreating for its observable content. Personal artifacts add a dimension to relationality. Objects represent narratives shared with the public, which foster the interpenetration of an other's experience.[22] Identification with the story that the artifact conveys connects humanity across time and context.

The curator speaks to this connectivity in Yad Vashem's weaving together thirty-four thousand stories in the reinterpretation of the historical museum in 2005. The new museum emphasizes the individual person, the family, or the community that perished. Care and reciprocity between the curator and the donor assume a central role in the most recent operations. She conveys the essence of the connections through an anecdote.

A grandchild of a Holocaust survivor called Yad Vashem to say, "My grandfather just passed away today. It's urgent. Please come and take something that belonged to him." The "something" was a single shoe. The family thought that the museum should house the shoe, the evidence of their story from the Kovno Ghetto in Lithuania. "You see this shoe, it belonged to a girl called Hinda." Hinda was born in 1942 in the ghetto. She was two years old in 1944, at the time of her death.

> *Hinda's parents had to go to work every day. The elderly,*
> *the old people, would take care of the children. One day the*
> *parents returned, and the ghetto was empty. They found*
> *out that the Nazis took the old people and the children. The*
> *only thing the parents found in Hinda's bed was one of her*
> *shoes . . . Out of agony, her father carved the date of that day*
> *at the same time, 1944, March 27. For him, this was Hinda*
> *because it's the last thing that was ever left of her . . . For us,*
> *it's a very important and precious artifact because, like I said*
> *before, it's not like something very, very expensive. It's not a*

*yellow star that it's automatically understood. It's something
very simple. It's a shoe that if you would see it in the street,
you would say it's garbage, but if you know the story behind it
and what it represents, it is everything. This is what we try to
collect here.*

Hinda's parents escaped into the forest. At the end of the war, they had another daughter, the caller's mother. "This is Hinda," the curator asserts, "but if her parents didn't survive, we wouldn't even know she existed, and they kept it and of course, for them, it was the most *yaqar*, in Hebrew, or precious in English." Holocaust memorial museums exhibit thousands of shoes across the globe. In the exhibits, the shoes pile high, unidentified, and unclaimed. Each is another Hinda, precious, and facilitates the interpenetration of a past or foreign other into private internal experiences.

The collector at a memorial museum works not to identify the most beautiful, the most innovative, or the most popular pieces but to gather the most precious with discernment and care. At once the multiple skills necessary to navigate the job emerge with the challenges of interpersonal alliances around trauma. The aesthetic, cognitive curatorial practice of assembling traumatic pain in the form of objects requires attunement and a "feeling with" the donor that "touches" the worker. Together they create the space of the memorial museum, the holding space of traumatic memory.

Bearing Pain

The curator enters the private world of the donor. The private world includes memories, emotions, and pain.[23] Memorial museums operate in the domain of private and public pain. Internal experiences of horror and loss manifest to be outwardly presented to various publics. Workers mediate the transition. They bear the pain of the trauma story in its emergence from various angles, sometimes in unpredictable ways. The unpredictability reflects trauma and contextualizes the work, which always occurs in the suffering space and obliges the worker to bear pain.[24]

Family members grieve at memorial museum sites before the name of loved ones. Visitors tour the sites to learn history and hear memories. Survivors tell their stories on the memorial museum grounds, and community members approach, some hesitantly, to see the transformation of destruction. Each encounter entails confronting trauma, which provokes pain. As a result, the memorial museum worker bears witness to pain in various iterations and personifies "feeling with" by entering another's suffering. The entrance carries a risk of being deeply affected.[25] Pain begets more pain, a result of attending to a public in pain.

Caring for those who suffer exposes workers to both the negatives of fatigue and fragmentation and the positives of connection and empathy.[26] This reality manifests in the work of oral historians, those who collect the testimonies about trauma. An oral historian from the 9/11 Memorial & Museum reveals how the affective experiences inspired by both pain and connection intertwine. The worker interviews a 9/11 widow whose husband was a firefighter. They sit together in the kitchen of the widow's home. She shares the story of the last morning that she saw her husband. The couple's parting is unusual. Instead of saying goodbye in the house, the wife walks out onto the driveway and waves goodbye. He waves back. The worker reflects on the impact of this testimony:

> *I don't know; I have not had tears running down my face during most of an interview for years, but that one, I just couldn't . . . Maybe it was how he said goodbye to her that morning, how it was different than their usual goodbyes. They had a very prolonged goodbye, a more meaningful goodbye, and that was their last. It just makes me think, "How did I say goodbye when I walked out the door this morning?" That*

was good for me. That was a really good. We connected on
some level, and when she came to the museum, she said, "I
saw you crying." It's just that she got me. Her story got me,
but I felt good.

Shared suffering generates an empathetic attunement. The widow's story touched the worker providing access to personal pain.[27] The worker felt pain. In this case, pain stimulated reflection: the 9/11 Memorial & Museum worker listened to a "difficult" narrative that inspired "a good feeling about humanity on the whole." Both pain and joy emerged from recognizing a commonplace event, saying "goodbye." A worker in Bosnia echoes the experience, reflecting that the everyday stories of final partings represent some of the most sacred narratives. Everyone says, "Goodbye," daily. To have a goodbye be the last and to recount it touches the depths of human pain and vulnerability.

In another episode at the 9/11 Memorial & Museum, a firefighter's wife announces a visit to New York and her husband's desire to share his oral history. The oral historian outlines her method, which includes arranging the meeting with the survivor himself. The wife insists otherwise:

I agreed because I didn't want to fight with her. So, they get
here; they come to the office, and she says she would like to
stay in the interview. I said, "Well, we don't usually do that.
It's better rapport." She was doing all the talking, and she
said, "No, I'm staying." I looked at him, and he said, "She
can stay." Well, he cried during the entire interview. I could
barely ask a question. Usually, when somebody is crying
during an interview, they either look around and reach for
the Kleenex box, or I push the Kleenex box over, or I almost
always make sure there's water or tea in the room. I push the
tea. I just take a pause and let them collect themselves, and
then I go on. I did that with him. It was very, very hard. I

don't remember what we talked about, but he managed to
pull it together to a degree.

Later, the worker received an email from the wife about retriggering her husband's trauma, precisely what the oral historian attempted to guard against prior to and during the interview. "It was very, very, very painful because I didn't want to do the interview. I wanted to prevent the intensity." The worker bears the pain not only during the actual interview, but in her testimony reflecting upon the incident. Collecting traumatic histories thus exposes the oral historian to the uncontrollable in the human negotiation with pain.

The oral historian receives the transmission of a trauma story. She decides when, how, and under what auspices the transmission takes place, providing care during the interview. Ethical attunement to method and care demands discernment, alongside the maintenance of empathy for all involved.[28] Proficient care and empathy require alertness to subtle emotional cues and triggers, the ability to draw boundaries while maintaining safety, and attentiveness to logistics.

Practical demands of oral history include preparing for the interview, conducting the interview, properly preserving the recording, and creating access to the information the interview provides. Collecting traumatic oral histories pushes at the bounds of oral history practice.[29] The first rupture begins upon entrance into someone's home, where the structure and safety of a neutral environment cannot be ensured.

In Cambodia, homes in the fields and local villages situate the worker far from the office space. Both trained professionals and students hired as researchers capable of speaking the local language serve as oral historians. Students travel into the fields without training or forewarning about the challenges of listening to the trauma story. The exercise exposes one oral historian to precarious situations. She does her best to prepare: "I need to know in advance who I am going to interview, and some questions I should ask them, to be aware of any that are traumatic." She prepares herself to bear painful emotions, pain that is shared.

Collecting survivors' histories jeopardizes both the interviewee and the interviewer, opening both up to pain. The student understands this and examines the nature of the job, her exposure to the trauma story, and the well-being of the survivor.[30]

> *I need to protect myself when I am doing an interview, and I am asking a traumatic question. If the survivor does not answer immediately, it means that the question hit a difficult spot, and they cannot stop the sadness immediately. I try to talk about something else. I have one technique, when I am asking a question, and someone starts to feel uncomfortable, like when talking about rape during the regime, or forced marriage, or family members who lost their lives, I shift to talk about what their environment is like now. I ask "Right now, how many children do you have? Where are they now? Your house is so relaxed, beautiful." Something like that, to change the topic, to pull people back to the present and not let them stay in the past.*

This oral historian devised a strategy: she questions someone affected by past trauma about the present in order to locate the person in the here and now. The technique prevents retraumatization because the telling remains within the bounds of the tolerable.[31] The worker intuitively perceives that approaching traumatic memories without options for pain's containment can hurt the teller.[32] Emotional regulation and safety protect both teller and listener. Furthermore, the oral historian asks questions that recognize the teller's agency, and, by complimenting the home, she locates the survivor in the present, arresting the interview's detrimental effects.[33] Practiced therapists train extensively to develop such techniques here employed by a twenty-something-year-old.

But she says, dealing with a traumatized public takes a toll. "Emotions are immense, hard to deal with, stronger. It is hard to sit still, just to hear them survive, 'Oh, my father raped me, and then my mother reported it, and then my stepfather did something awful, now I live with a foster family,' and so on like that. Sometimes I am like, 'I cannot deal with this.'" But she remains, collecting stories and helping people bear the pain.

Bearing human suffering never ceases at a memorial museum. Obvious exposure to trauma through collecting oral histories represents one means of Pain-bearing, but not the only one. Working inside the exhibition areas, guarding the grounds of the memorial museum, or offering tours exposes these workers to pain. An academic and a communications officer in Cambodia operates a digitization project in commemoration of the survivors of the Khmer Rouge. She reflects:

> *People think that because you're working in a digital realm that it's not the same as when you're working in a museum. I don't think that's true. We also have experience dealing with testimony. My role as a communication officer means I'm the one who carries the organization's message, stories, how they work with the survivor to the public, but at the same time, I ensure confidentiality of the survivor.*

Dealing with the digital world spares workers neither from traumatic material nor survivors' painful memories. Communication officers work across every department in a memorial museum, connecting every public to the central history and mission of the space. They also associate with the survivor as an active participant in the organization. In Cambodia, the relationship results in a sensitivity to designation: "We don't use the terms 'survivor' or 'victims.' We say 'client.'" The terminology helps bear pain: "We don't want the victim to feel victimized, or to continue feeling like a victim. We raised the bar to call them clients, so they feel a little bit more special, and because they are really at a bad state." Again, the worker attunes to the need for agency in working through the trauma story: the victim/survivor becomes a client. The transformation of a term aids in Pain-bearing. But pain lingers to emerge elsewhere in the memorial museum setting.

Tour guides play a pivotal role in accompanying groups of people through the exhibition space, which tells the trauma story. They verbally perform the narrative in front of tourists, to balance an agonizing story and environment with education and empathy. A variety of emotional responses arise in the group. A guide at the Apartheid Museum discerns this: "With my visitors, with the school levels, I try to give myself time and see which ones are affected the most. I try to talk with them and have them point out exactly what is bothering them. It's more like I become a psychiatrist." He laughs. He concedes that emotional intelligence has helped him do his job alongside additional training:

> *There were a few courses that I've attended. Which I won't lie, they did give me some skills about how to handle people . . . the most difficult part is to talk to a person who is crying. You need to put yourself in that person's shoes. That's the best way to start off. Talk with that person. Make the person understand that you feel what he's feeling or she's feeling. I do have skills in that department, but I would be more than happy to have more.*

Visitors of all types visit the Apartheid Museum. They carry personal trauma narratives, painful memories, and conflicting sentiments toward the history in South Africa. The complicated exhibitions of history at the museum represent all members of society; local visitors thus see themselves in the displays; complex feelings and pain emerge. The guide bears the pain.

On one occasion, he mediates a conflict erupting between Black and white youth in the midst of a tour:

*One Black person in a group was angry and cursing. The
other [white] person says, "Okay, enough. We get where you
are coming from, and we hear you." It almost became a
physical situation. I had to interfere. My biggest challenge
was when they asked me which side of the fence I was on.
Do you understand? Between a South African white and a
South African Black. It was not easy for me to say I am civil
with the whole thing because one of the guys said: "We've
been talking about this. We've been trying to speak to them.
Perhaps since you're a guide, you can try to talk them out of
this crap that they're arguing." It was difficult for me because
as soon as I pay attention to the white guy, it's more like I'm
siding with him.*

The guide finds himself in a difficult position. But at the end of the
day, he recounts, the visitors realized they had a choice. "No one forced
them to fight. If they wanted to continue, they could." He let them
know that continuing would lead to security's interference and their
subsequent removal from the museum. "I had to be grounded for this
one. They started to relax though because they felt embarrassed." Then
he prayed silently.

*When you do such a job, you need to understand that skills
and expertise are not based on theory, but you need to pray
to God, asking for His assistance, because it's such a huge job.
A person can walk past and think, "Oh, he's a tour guide
and stuff," not knowing what being a tour guide in this
institution entails. I do pray, and I do pray for my job. I do
ask for wisdom. I believe on that day, wisdom was taking its
part.*

At the end of the conflict, the visitors apologized to him and each
other, nearly in tears, vulnerable to one another. The guide maintained

self-regulation and stayed calm while navigating exhibition space, political sentiments, and painful responses.[34]

Traumatic memory ignites pain and leads to intense interchanges between visitors and guides. An Australian tourist challenges a guide at the Galicia Museum in Kraków, on a tour of "Traces of Memory: A Contemporary Look at the Jewish Past in Poland." She argues about the executive decision in Poland to represent who died at landmarks located throughout the country as "Jews" or "Poles." The visitor presses the guide to offer a percentage of how many Poles (presumably Catholic and not Jewish) posed a danger to the Jewish population. Her question endangers the guide; Poland's laws about claiming Polish culpability in the Holocaust could lead to her being fired or fined. And yet, she exposes herself.

The guide answers: "I have no idea. It's very difficult to say." The woman inquires further, articulating that a representation of the victims versus the perpetrators is a question of "balance." The guide answers again: "We don't know about every event and plus during the Second World War, in Poland, sometimes not to do anything rather than to say anything was the best we could do." The visitor expresses the insufficiency of the answer, claiming that Polish Catholics were dangerous to the Polish Jews. Many survivors whom she knew in her community would attest to this, and she wanted the guide's affirmation.

Instead, the guide apologizes. She has access to no statistics: "I don't want to give you any number because I will be mistaken." The visitor answers: "Not numbers, I just want acknowledgment." The guide replies, "The personal story is one thing, and the history in general is something else. Some people can have one experience, and others have a different experience. So, I don't want to give you any number because . . ." The visitor cuts her off again asking for a proportion. This circuitous dialogue continues until another visitor on the tour intervenes.

Contentious encounters recur in memorial museums. Visitors confront guides with political questions, disputations of the historical narratives the memorial museum purports, and personal affronts. While they ask for their pain to be held, they also provoke. Tumultuous political atmospheres at any given site increases tensions, threatening the well-being of guests and guides. In Poland, recounting certain historical narratives can lead to fines or criminal offenses.

In Cambodia, the Ministry of Tourism influences the stories that workers recount. A tour guide in Cambodia reports: "As a tour guide, you have to know everything, the cultures, tradition, and the politics. We met with an authority from the Ministry of Tourism and were told that we didn't have freedom to express politics, especially if it was something bad about the government." The dynamics highlight the radical reality that the sufferer in pain can hardly be separated from the cause—evident in the original trauma and in the political aftermath.[35]

Collisions occur. Government policies, political positions, and personal agendas meet as the guides feel pain and bear it. They balance historical tensions as well, arbitrating conflicts between perceived perpetrators and victims, conflicts that do not simply dissipate with time.[36] A guide at Gallery 11/07/95 in Bosnia reflects on an assumption that people visiting from Serbia would be difficult. "No," she says, "Not once have I had a bad experience with people from Serbia. They're always humble and grateful, and they always have something to say, which is quite nice." However, "Once I had a Serbian girl from Sarajevo, who escaped as a refugee during the war, be quite offended by the exhibition. She told us, all of the Serbs are criminals, war criminals. I tried to talk to her, but she was so defensive that I couldn't reach her." The guide's rationale for the behavior the visitor represented was her distress in being associated with the perpetrating group. The intense emotional content of the gallery compounded that pain. "It can make you really tremble with emotions. Most people are crying, or they are shocked. Then you have people who are just opposite of that, angry." The worker meets the public at points of contention, riddled with fear, pain, and rage. Not a professional mediator but asked to mediate, and not a psychologist but asked to help people cope with difficult feelings, the guide persists. Each site requires different valences of Pain-bearing.

The Whitney Plantation workers navigate situations of refusal to hear the story, a denial of the shared pain of the ancestors represented there. Ali reports that one of the emotional challenges occurs when individuals simply walk off the tour. They say things like, "I don't want to hear that. Ain't none of that truth. This is revisionist."

> *That's an emotional low when you know you're out here giving your all with the best intention and someone still refuses to accept that information. They'd rather walk away from it and deny it. My antidote for that is like I said before, nothing defeats the truth. No matter how much we might consciously try to deny the truth, one thing about that good old subconscious, it's always working on its own.*

> *Once you plant those seeds, he can say whatever he wants out of his mouth, "Oh I don't believe that. That ain't true," but his subconscious is constantly mulling that over, and mulling that over, and mulling that over, looking for the answer that he wants. Eventually, may not be today, may not be next month, may not be five years from now, but one day his subconscious is going to say, "You know what? That guy was telling the truth." My antidote is knowing that if I plant the seed, eventually one day it's going to grow. One day their mind is going to tell them that they cannot deny that truth any longer; it is what it is.*

Ali develops a personal strategy to navigate hate, rage, defiance, and denial. One aspect of this strategy is to tell "the truth" of the trauma story, to proclaim it aloud, and to trust the telling ultimately evolves to higher levels of consciousness in the visitor. Like other guides in the field, such hope meets the reactivity to trauma, such as the refusal of its existence.

Extreme emotions as reactions or underlying denial indicate trauma. From a theological perspective, the tension emerges between the best and worst of humanity.[37] Human depravity and goodness emerge everywhere in the memorial museum. The worker opens himself to pain when he mediates the trauma narrative, created by human-on-human violence. The mediation entails Pain-bearing. People react and act out personal agony. These reactions take place on the grounds of the memorial museum, the space created for local communities to express divergent perspectives. The worker negotiates the differing perspectives and becomes a conduit for change. Trauma has the potential to transform events meant to divide and fragment memory, giving birth to lessons and meanings, or new life.[38]

Transforming Trauma

Memorial museum workers counter atrocity, the *tremendum*. They respond to the worst of humanity with the best that humanity can do.[39] That best emerges as honoring memory, with the intent that facing human pain and remembering produces a future good. The good manifests as teaching, communicating, and rebuilding to transform the effects of trauma.[40] Countering silence and fragmentation through reconstruction gives voice to the voiceless and connects death to meaning.

The enormity of the question of how to go on being alive, present, grateful, and joyous after mass atrocity looms in the memorial museum, and workers wrestle with helping others to keep living in the face of grievous wounds and collective trauma.[41] Living includes coming to terms with the meaning of trauma in the present; such meaning signifies a new way forward.[42] Recovery defines this new way forward, appearing differently in different contexts but representing a communal goal after mass trauma. Public health and well-being come into focus, as does the recognition of a community's strengths in the aftermath. As successful models of communal recovery show, workers acknowledge the trauma, create agency for the survivor group, encourage remembering to connect survivors to the experience and others, and reestablish support in order to foster hope; hope restored through meaning counteracts disrupted spiritualities.[43]

The people who do the work of memorialization, who encounter trauma and those who have endured trauma, model faith in the value and meaning of life.[44] Their actions provide Life-giving moments to the various publics. These moments transform trauma, arriving by way of education, on tours, and through public forums.

Educating about trauma acknowledges it, representing a position of standing on the side of the trauma dialectic that proclaims the truth of trauma aloud.[45] Education coheres with both the attestation to never forget, which makes a promise to the victims, and with the concept of prevention of a future atrocity with never again, which makes a promise to the living. Thus, education aligns with hope for the future, or hope for a future good.

At the Galicia Jewish Museum, a guide recounts how during her interview process, the head of education identified her passion for teaching others and likewise distinguished her potential as a tour guide. When the memorial museum hired her as a guide, she dedicated herself to "making sure every visitor that comes to the museum is aware of what each of the photographs in each exhibition in each section represent." This act of thoroughly recounting each photograph enlivens the Jewish past in Galicia in the mind of the visitor. She supports and creates a sense of community, one that survives after destruction, "and that gives me a sense of hope." She aims for each student, each visitor to "take just one small fact about the Holocaust or about Jewish life and culture in Galicia now or before the war and remember it." This goal engenders a "positive emotional toll because I realize how many people I'm talking to and hopefully making an impact upon." Education thus matures into the transformation of trauma, making a positive impact on the lives of others.

Educators develop unique ways of connecting lessons about past atrocity to survival in the present.[46] A guide at the History Museum of Bosnia in Sarajevo teaches children of survivors about their nation's history. Her inventiveness reflects commitment to her community. She works in a building that still has no funds to provide heating in the middle of December. Snowbanks cover the grounds, and she passionately conveys her belief that teaching contributes to communal well-being and lives full of meaning. She believes learning is crucial, that "nothing can keep an open mind from seeking after knowledge and finding a way to know," and she toils to positively transform the lives of those around her.[47]

> *When I work with kids, I don't like to tell them negative*
> *and pessimistic stories. I just encourage them to think about*
> *their lives, about just one day in their life without electricity,*
> *water, and the possibility to produce anything, and a day*
> *without the internet and vacations.*

She leads the children on an imaginative journey, using artifacts related to the Bosnian War to design a world without these luxuries. She asks the children what they would do with "just one day without pleasant things that they have in their life." Then, they imagine how they would warm up their apartment, find water, find food, and develop light. The lesson ends with showing them artifacts in the museum created during the war to achieve these ends.

> *Each object has its own story, its own specific contexts, and*
> *shows us how the human spirit is actually very beautiful*
> *and creative. This is something that, I think, provokes their*
> *brains. Teaching them that they can make a candle shows*
> *that they can think about possibilities to produce electricity. I*
> *also encourage them to learn more, to read more, because the*
> *knowledge of a foreign language, for instance, could save your*
> *life during the war.*

By focusing on the "beautiful and creative" aspects of the human spirit, the guide engenders a life-giving moment. She exercises the students' imaginative capacities while underscoring that during the war, education facilitated survival. An empowering exercise serves as a gift of possibility, and the guide harnesses a psychological reality: a child's imaginative capacity helps to alleviate stress and leads to greater resilience in the face of trauma.[48]

The guide in Bosnia respects students and the memories that she connects to the present. She envisions her role as a participant with them in a learning process that connects the memorial museum and pain to produce change. Learning generates possibilities for the future. Possibility emerges in Life-giving work performed together.

A guide from the Apartheid Museum identifies education as an exchange that produces change as well. The transformation happens internally, producing self-growth, as well as externally, in the compassion that shifts visitors' aggressive stances:

> *Number one, I've learned to accept many situations and*
> *have patience. Also, I've learned to listen a lot and talk less.*
> *I've been taught by this place to do so because sometimes as a*
> *tour guide you explain, and there's people that just take over.*
> *Not only because they want to steal your show, but they have*
> *something to say. Just by listening, you learn a lot. Sometimes*
> *it is people that were in the struggle themselves, and they feel*
> *they've got a lot to share with people; I allow them. That's one*
> *of the key ways that I have become a good tour guide.*

The process unfolds. Giving tours challenges the guide to develop sympathies and skills. Not every tour ends in consent, agreement, and hope. Strife also ensues. Committing to Life-giving moments does not free the worker from pain. The Apartheid Museum tour guide offers an example: "Say, I take white people on tour. Some of them, they still condescend and still indulge in their supremacies, status, and stuff. I have to deal with this." He responds by developing a sense of forgiveness.

> *If I didn't have a sense of forgiveness, I don't think I could*
> *do the job that I'm doing. I think I would carry that around*

with me. Forgiveness is the hardest thing to do. But without it, at the end of the day, you by yourself, you will be sitting with a heavy heart, so you need to have tactics in place to deal with such challenges.

Forgiveness means different things to different people. Different interpretations of the word bring sensitive issues to light when considering trauma of human betrayal. Engaged in too soon or refuted all together, forgiveness has repercussions for recovery after trauma.[49] Pumla Gobodo-Madikizela's work on forgiveness clarifies its risks in South Africa, risks that can be extrapolated to other communities recovering from mass trauma. Gobodo-Madikizela shifts the focus from forgiveness, which can be misconstrued as an agenda of the perpetrators, to a term that relates more to Swain's Life-giving: the work of repair that leads to solidarity.

> *[When forgiveness] is used often from the perspective of those who were perpetrators or those who benefited from the past, it's really to mean "let's forget the past, let's move on and forget the past." What I've found [in South Africa] rather is that the word actually tries to capture a sense that "I can live with my trauma, I can live side-by-side my trauma and I can tell a different narrative; now that I have encountered you as the perpetrator with your sense of remorse and your sense of recognition that what you have done has hurt and destroyed my family, I am able to take this step, the first step, to hold your hand into the future." It's really about that possibility, that the language is about the possibility. The rest of the work, as I say in my new work, is about repair; it's the work of repair.[50]*

Gobodo-Madikizela stresses the importance of coming together from different sides of history and the possibility of building a sense of solidarity, despite the past.

Inherent in efforts to live with or transform the past lies the desire to perform a good. The desire emerges in two acclamations that circulate in the field: "Never forget!"[51] and "Never again!"[52] The terms sustain institutional rhetoric across the globe.[53] Acts of commemoration align with "never forgetting" to prevent future atrocity captured in "never again." Public suffering—Pain-bearing—meets a future promise—Life-giving—in the space of the memorial museum. The words "never forget" and "never again" foster a framework with which to understand the value of memory, while fueling the capacity to act in the face of human horror. The worker internalizes the words. Never forget and never again, in positive iterations, motivate and structure the nature of the duties of commemoration as the phrases implicate the suffering public and make a promise that the memorialization of trauma will help to bear the pain.

Anita collected the stories of victims and survivors of the Bosnian War in the effort to never forget. As an activist and leader of the Youth Initiative for Human Rights, she worked closely with those who engage in memorialization to support them—with knowledge and emotional energy. "Too Young to Remember, Determined Not to Forget" reads the title of an article that describes her "memory activism," or her engagement in remembering as a form of citizenship.[54] The work benefits others.

Anita learned about the wars in Kosovo and Bosnia as a teenager. Prior to this, she had been unaware; she did not know the history because "this is something we don't talk about, not even with our parents. And the educational system doesn't teach us anything." Her first exposure to the wars occurred at the Srebrenica commemoration. When she saw the evidence of the trauma, she says, "I literally wanted to die because it was very difficult. I went to the laboratory when they did a postmortem identification of some of the victims. It was one of the hardest days of my life." She responded by immersing herself deeper into understanding, to teach herself, guided by an ethics of care, where care emerges as a matter of human interest.[55] Her efforts committed to pain-bearing and fostering community transformed the trauma.

*Youth Initiative saved my life. It made me who I am. I had the
opportunity to give back out of that. That is something that's
not ordinary. It doesn't happen to everyone. I was like, "I'm so
privileged to be able to speak and for people not just to listen to
me but what I'm saying, that it matters to them. It helps them."
And after 10 years, of doing this work, there's a lot of stories
that I can share, but I think that I came to the point I'm doing
the work because it is the right thing to do, simple as that. It's
simply just the right thing to do. It's not any kind of optimism
or it's any kind of wishful thinking. It's more like there's time
in history, and there's time in life when you just do the things
that are right, no matter what. Not thinking that your political
agenda will be fulfilled, not even thinking that you will win
because in these kinds of countries it's very unlikely that a person
like me will be well respected. I think it's very important that
you do it because it is the right thing to do for your country, for
your neighbors, for your region and for sometimes, and it stays
written that someone did resist this whole insanity.*[56]

Individuals like Anita comprise organizations and institutions
that commemorate. They care deeply about the mission of their institutions, and many view themselves as on the front line of remembering,
knowing, and teaching to promote prevention of future atrocities. The
work may adopt an idealistic undertone, but their contributions to the
lives of others indicate a practical approach that sees care of the individual, and memory, as transformative and preventative.

Prevention begins with self-examination and reflection at individual and institutional levels. In a 2018 conversation with the 9/11
Memorial & Museum, workers at the Apartheid Museum articulated
polarization as a risk of working toward prevention. One worker
comments:

*We have concerns about how that story gets told. We were just
talking earlier about the possible and expected consequences of*

having the case of further polarizing your audience
rather than the opposite effect, which is obviously part of our
mission, to bring those audiences closer together to encourage
understanding and reconciliation. That's a very complex
mission.

The mission though, she continued, entails saying the "the whole narrative" of apartheid intended racism and discrimination. The admission addresses a political system but also the individual. "We are all actually racists, whether we like it or not. We are all recovering racists at best. Let's admit that, and let's say this is something we are to work on in our own lives ongoing." The transformation of the trauma story thus extends from the institution to the community, and to the self.

Introspection and reflection constitute foundational aspects of work. The postures frame the belief that education, self-healing, and prevention intertwine. A tour guide in Soweto affirms the interrelationship: "I do this work for people to know, *yes.*" He paused. "Also, I do it for healing on my part and for people not to repeat the same mistake. If you forget the history, you are likely to repeat the same mistake." Teaching history to promote prevention thus conjoins with personal healing.

Personal healing exemplifies political resistance and the transformation of trauma for a digital archivist in Cambodia. Her education refutes the legacy of the Khmer Rouge, whose goals she articulated included eliminating the educated elite. She identifies her schooling as the pathway for "memory activism," for transformation of a painful reality into a future public good. For her, "scholarship must have a purpose," and the goal of her work is to transform her endowed education into contributions for future generations. A worker at the 9/11 Memorial & Museum feels similarly about giving back, framing the benefaction in terms of prevention. If prevention fails, then at least this worker will respond to others "with kindness or love." The assumption resonates; that worker's compassion and love will help visitors learn about pain and change. A worker in Cambodia echoes the sentiment:

the Tuol Sleng Genocide Museum provides learning, from the learning, "visitors return home and hopefully do something good."

A guide at Gallery 11/07/95 in Bosnia shapes Life-giving into "transferring knowledge." In the act of giving tours, she realizes how her story or the story of those who died changes the visitor. The possibility that sharing the knowledge of the war, along with her personal history, propels change energizes her work. Telling her life story and teaching visitors about the Srebrenica tragedy assumes new meaning in the potential to contribute to a greater good.

Commitments to communities and dedication to providing tools to support "never again" reflects in the work of commemoration. A worker at the 9/11 Memorial & Museum asserts,

> *we're not just these people in offices across the street fact checking and copyediting but we're part of this community of people that has been impacted. We are not part of this story in some bizarre offshoot way. The mission calls out the value of human life.*

The value of human life and the transformation of trauma comes to the fore in Ali's interpretation of his engagement at the Whitney Plantation.

> *Whitney for me has been a blessing twofold: it has helped me get my life together and advance myself, while at the same time being able to reach out to younger people and just people in general. I especially like reaching out to younger people and trying to set them on a path and project something positive to them. Especially for young African American children coming here to learn their history and learn about themselves, and to see an African American man in this job position. When I was an interpreter, they heard their history from somebody that looks like them, and talks like them.*

Once again, the process of transformation happens internally to the self and externally in the visitor. And once again, the negotiation of memory inherent in the promise to "never forget" manifests in the change implicit in "never again." "If we can change one of these young people's lives," the guide asserts,

> *if just one of them says, "You know what, after Whitney did that, I want to be a historian." If one says, "You know what, I ain't hanging with those guys over there no more because that ain't going to lead me to nothing but trouble, and I owe my ancestors better than that." If we have one person who's on the fence about how he feels about people of color, that leaves here and says, "You know what, I'm wrong. My feelings of unnecessary hate are wrong." If we just get one, then I feel like we've accomplished a lot. Of course, we're not going to settle for just one, but we know that if we get at least one, we are not out here in vain.*

Ali focuses on "just one" person, with the hope of making an impact on many more.

The Apartheid Museum intends to expand the impact of its institutional message on more than "just one" as well, but sees that extension emerging in what a worker calls "a transcendent message." In the conversation between staff from the Apartheid Museum and staff at the 9/11 Memorial & Museum, she stresses the importance of having a message that reaches beyond institutional goals: "One needs a transcendent message, doesn't one," describing how to inspire the visitors to internal reflection, communal reconstruction, and thus to the transformation of trauma. For the Apartheid Museum, the new construction of reality includes a future free of oppression, racism, and hate, a lofty goal but one that seeps into the ethos of the institution to emerge through the action of visitors. She continues to describe the last room of the museum:

One cathartic thing that we have at the end of the museum
is called the Constitutional Hall. You've [the visitor has]
come through the whole dark period of apartheid and the
transition to democracy, and then you walk through the
hall, and there is a pile of stones on the right-hand side.
You're invited to take a stone from the right-hand side and
to place it on a huge pile of stones on the left—they're quite
big stones—and to commit yourself to fighting against racism
and discrimination and prejudice in your own life wherever
you may encounter it. The South African national anthem is
playing, and the new flag is there. It's all about whipping up
a bit of feeling for this new post-apartheid state, but it's also
saying this is why we exist in the end.

Just as she completed the description, her colleague said to the group,
"never again."

Embedded into the ways in which memorials and/or museums
operate, the phrase "never again" is both an imperative and a speech
act, something intended by its very nature to influence the listener, to
ignite change, to give new life, and to transform trauma. The Apartheid Museum asks visitors to *do* something: to move a stone, using
their bodies to commit to a reflection on racism, and to work on this
racism in themselves. The starting point is the self, but the worker
models the action. The worker senses the importance of making space,
bearing pain, and transforming trauma, performing these out of love.

5

THE VOCATION OF MEMORY

The Memorial Museum Worker as a Wounded Healer

COMMEMORATING TRAUMA IMMERSES the worker in human suffering. Immersion includes a dialectical process where the person in need— the survivor, the family member, the community—and the person attending to the need—the worker as helper—exchange suffering. Availability and presence allow the worker as helper to absorb the suffering of the other. A replication of the therapeutic alliance embeds itself. In the collaborative exchange, the alliance co-acts to produce change.[1]

Attentive helpers usher those in need toward healing when they remain open to vulnerability and personal woundedness. Awareness of personal pain, and indeed, feeling personal pain, enables a deeper access to and with the other. The access informs care. A person engaged in care of another but aware of personal pain thus embodies the "wounded healer."[2] The wounded healer tends to the pain of the other from a place of compassion toward personal wounding. Wounding occurs due to loneliness, as a result of the human condition, or as a result of traumatic circumstances.[3] "Wounded healers" examine themselves, with attention to self-growth because that growth contributes to the growth of the other.[4] The wounded healer assumes responsibility for the suffering of the community to discover an answer for it.[5] In this framework, understanding personal inner turmoil leads to fulfillment and healing.

This wounded healer chooses to turn toward human suffering in order to be in communion with the one who suffers.[6] Walt Whitman's words describe this healer: "I do not ask the wounded person how he feels, I myself become the wounded person."[7] The posture exemplifies empathy as feeling *into* the other rather than compassion, feeling *for* another.[8] Empathy constitutes the "psycho-physical" and spiritual becoming of the self, who is in a continual process of growth or "unfolding."[9] This growth or unfolding happens amidst recognition of trauma and includes the perception of the other, and a projection of the self into the other.[10]

Memorial museum workers open their hearts to pain, and labor in the recognition of the sufferings of their time. Upon entering a dislocated world, the worker waits in the instability and tumult with confidence in the future: speaking to survivors and communities and honoring the dead. They testify to trauma daily. The memorial museum and the worker attend to a suffering world, speak to a suffering community, as a suffering servant aware of both personal wounding and public pain.[11]

The pain that exists after trauma begs to be acknowledged and accepted. Words and actions that deny, remove, eradicate, or, alternatively, promise a triumph over pain undermine practices of care. Such practices require reflection on pain in order to feel, process, and move through trauma toward its integration. Institutional and individual contemplation of the emotional and psychological costs of commemorating mass trauma allows woundedness to inform behavior. With understanding, the overwhelming nature of human atrocity can be modulated. Continual assessment accompanies woundedness, so that the worker can engage in the service of care and provide learning. The requirement of radical presence emerges. Being present to needs growing out of trauma—including the needs of the institution and the worker—means facilitating communication, training workers and leaders, coordinating departments, and most of all, acknowledging that exposure to trauma increases the stress of the work.

Intertwining Wounds: Survivors, Observing Witnesses, and Space

Personal stories, woundedness, and trauma intertwine in memorial museums. When the survivor memorializes, the process includes sharing of personal suffering. Parallels develop between individual memory and public mission. Jasmin Mešković survived torture and detention during the Bosnian War. To bring the reality of the Bosnian War into visitors' (especially other Bosnians') awareness, he and several other survivors built the Crimes Against Humanity and Genocide Museum in Sarajevo. They did so without an arbiter.[12] Jasmin also refused aid from any source. The memorial museum arose solely from the memories of the survivors. The exhibited stories lay bare testaments to trauma. Visitors encounter unfiltered wounds.

One exhibit visually represents personal torture. A life-size plaster of Paris reproduces Jasmin's experience: two soldiers beat a shackled, helpless inmate who has fallen to his knees. Representing horrific memories has value and meaning in its representation. For Jasmin, "all that matters is that the stories are not forgotten. And second," he asserts, "I think I did something meaningful with my life. At the end of the day, when I am no longer alive, I left a legacy. There's a legacy behind the museum." For Jasmin, the memorial museum, its mission, and the individual trauma story become one. Workers, in the empathic exchange, are always exposed to the other—both bear witness together.[13]

At the nearby War Childhood Museum in Sarajevo, survivors commemorate thousands of children's experiences during war, experiences the staff also endured. Personal narratives and institutional operation intertwine. The founding and building of the space assimilate with the working through of individual trauma. One of the founders reflects, "The museum evolved alongside personal processes of facing the war's details. We all had some personal experience with the war." At first, she resisted participating in such a project: "I was really honestly shocked that I managed to accept this as a topic that I would be working on on a daily basis, but now I'm really happy where I am. Also, in terms of personal dealings with survivors, I really feel okay and comfortable with it. Which I did not expect at all. This is really amazing, I think." At first, she resisted confronting personal wounds through the stories of others. But encountering personal wounds transformed to inform her interpretation of others' trauma and attentiveness to donors' needs.

Survivors' involvement emerges in every aspect of memorial museums' establishment. A worker at the 9/11 Memorial & Museum, a firefighter who participated in the recovery at Ground Zero, oversees fire safety at the space. His previous job and his service on 9/11 replicate themselves in his present role. He familiarizes other workers with evacuation plans in the case of an emergency. "I was looking for a job to keep myself busy for the next ten years. But little did I know I would end up here." He cannot visit some areas of the memorial museum due to the familiar sights and sounds that trigger his memories of 9/11. His words expose a personal process in his interpretation of others' contact with the space: when survivors and family members come to the space, "they are not going to have a good time. But they are going to face their fears . . . for survivors who work here, they are coping and getting closure. That is happening because of the museum." The survivor as worker has an immediate emotional connection to the organization—both bear the wound of the trauma commemorated—and sees the process of working through that wounding as a shared happening facilitated by the museum.

The worker who is not a survivor enters into the wounding of survivors and victims. People, narratives, artifacts, and environments provide the pathway. Sometimes the penetration happens by choice, sometimes as a result of intense engagement with content, and sometimes because of simply being in the space where the trauma occurred. In the case of collecting oral histories in Cambodia, language provides the vehicle for entrance into the trauma story and shared wounding. One worker travels the Cambodian countryside, taking oral histories because she speaks Khmer. She transcribes the interviews, and then translates them into English for international research and visitors. She enters the story three times: at the point of the retelling by the survivor, during the transcription, and then during the translation. She expresses the differences between taking the interviews while being exposed to traumatic content, and reading the trauma stories in a translated language:

> *Cambodian researchers get the direct trauma because the*
> *survivors talk to us in Khmer. The foreign researcher reads a*
> *translation. It's not direct but indirect trauma in translation.*
> *With the translation, I think we do not deliver the exact*
> *emotion that the interviewee uses [to help the witness]*
> *understand the trauma.*

The translation affords a barrier to the trauma story, an interpretation of it, but the collection of the story in Khmer grants direct access to the trauma the survivor conveys. The worker recounts the intensity in collecting the narratives. The repetitiveness provokes stress but also understanding. She says that the work enabled her to grasp the effects of the regime on her parents, who are survivors. Institutional work intertwines with another layer of personal narratives established by generational trauma.[14] Her parents' wounds come to light through her encounter with the woundedness of others, perpetuating the capability of understanding.

Workers at the 9/11 Memorial & Museum who have no direct experience of the event—although many witnessed it from classroom windows or on television—elect to remember, and in that remembering, enter woundedness. For one worker, initiation into another's pain occurs through the imagination and acquisition of knowledge. She dedicates each week to a specific victim, studying their lives and keeping them in mind daily to inspire her work. This activity enables her to connect to the trauma and the woundedness, to remind her where she works.

The choice to enter into the trauma undergirds a desire to be attuned, but also to validate one's professional and empathic capacity to do the task of supporting others through remembering and mourning. Workers choose to become "empathetically attuned" to a trauma victim or a survivor's stories by remining vulnerable, by opening themselves to pain and hurt.[15]

> *[Survivors] are just showing us they're emotional; they're not scared . . . I walk myself through [their memories] with them. If they start to cry, I am going to cry because it obviously was hard. It was something that that person really had to deal with and is still dealing with . . . I don't know how you get through that.*

In this case, the worker stands alongside the survivor and mirrors the survivor's affect. In others, the transmission of fear and sadness occurs through the assimilation of the narrative. The assimilation results in shared, even if imagined, feeling. For instance, workers dealing with trauma cases begin to experience symptoms like those found in the actual victim of trauma.[16] If the traumatic material has meaning or resonates with the worker's personal life and experiences, internalization in various forms intensifies. One worker at the 9/11 Memorial & Museum reports finding similarities between herself and a victim whose life she documents. She recounts that this happens about a dozen times per year:

> *There is one weird thing. Because I work with content so much, like if I am cataloging a family gift or something, and I read up on that person's life or I look through their family photos or whatever, I'll find similarities between that person's life and mine. It'll stick with me; then something else in my life will make me randomly think about that person. I have no connection to that person, but then I have*

this weird connection to them, so I feel haunted by some
victims in weird ways. Not that I've ever had a spirit visit
me or anything like that, but some of that. It'll depend on
where I'm at in my life at the moment. When it first started
happening, I'd only been working here for a little while, and
I would come across victims who had been in basically the
same stage of life that I was in at that time. Like the same
age as me: they came from some other state, and then they
moved to New York, and they're so excited to live there. They
got this awesome job, and it was so prestigious. That stuck
with me, that connection, and then dwelling on the fact
like, "Well, that person's life ended." Or, I was pregnant last
year, and I would sometimes think about the women who
were pregnant at the time, or I would think about women
who were evacuating and pregnant at the time. That kind of
thing. Or you know how you have a type that you're attracted
to? There was one victim who basically is similar to the type
of male that I'm attracted to. This was long before I was
dating or married. It was a weird connection because that
person would've been somebody that I would've wanted to
get to know, maybe date. Stuff like that. It's weird because
your brain processes it because you're looking at things
that they owned or family photos. It's like you're looking at
someone else's life, and they're still here, but it's a weird other
dimension where they're not here, and you've never met them.
You don't know them at all. It is this strange connection that
is no connection.

She enters the trauma or woundedness of the other. Work perpetuates
a connection that is "no connection." And yet the link is clear; fueled
by an imaginative capacity and a proximity to the details of a victim's
life, two lives overlap. Similar emotional and cognitive associations
form when the name or appearance of a trauma victim reflects that of

a close friend's. The worker may begin to experience distressing emotions, as though the trauma victim were a personal companion.

Another worker at the space intentionally enters the trauma story by placing herself where the emotional stimuli are high:

> *As part of the exhibition team, I do morning walk-throughs once every two weeks, but any time I'm in the museum space, I'm reminded of 9/11 and the victims; any time I'm on the plaza, I'm reminded of them. Usually, if I recognize that I'm losing my connection to the victims, I'll say to myself, "This is why you're here, and this is what you came here to do, and keep that as your guiding North star . . ." I keep that as my core personal mission. I try to keep the intensity at an eight to a ten. In moments where I'm working on the memorial exhibition object rotation and I'm deep in family member outreach and contact and research, then that's my core reason for being here. When I'm pulled to other things, that can fall to a five or a six.*

Entering the trauma story through institutional space entails changing levels of agency: choosing to go to particular spaces that have more emotional valence—the memorial pools of 9/11—or choosing to work in the space that commemorates mass trauma; the element of choice differs based on the job and based on institutional resources. Spaces matter. Place and space evoke feelings, memories of a victim, or intimate wounding. A guide at the Galicia Museum works from opening to close daily. "If I'm not there, I am going to a museum or synagogue." But Kraków itself provides little respite from the content, "When I go home to my apartment just across the river, I'm living in the former ghetto." She describes the town as a "bubble," because, she says, "everywhere you go or step, you know an atrocity happened."

Workers confront spaces that tax their emotional and psychological well-being. Tuol Sleng preserves its blood-stained floors and graffiti walls, and workers have their offices in the building. The situation evokes sadness according to a staff member working on a digitization project. "We are trying to get another new building to work as the office," he asserts. "It means finding a laboratory, a digitization room, an archive room, a storage room, and everything. We should have a separate building . . . but we have no choice but to work in this space." The same is true of Auschwitz, where workers sit daily in barracks, some built by prisoners, and at least one of which housed 700–1,200 prisoners during the Nazi occupation.[17]

Management at the 9/11 Memorial & Museum understands that some parts of the memorial museum contain more disturbing content than others. For instance, the Memorial or the Historical Exhibition display sensitive and emotionally intense material, so workers rarely find themselves stationed at these locations more than once a week. However, frequency depends on other workers' availability. A visitor services manager articulates her realization that some people have a harder time than others in particular locations. "I can think of one associate who was in the military. The historical exhibit was bringing back some memories, and so we decided that we were not going to put him in there until he was ready to go back." However, "there's only a certain number of places that we can move staff that don't have access to our artifacts or anything like that. The whole museum is about death. That's the difficulty."

Limiting confrontation with traumatic content grows exponentially more difficult during anniversary celebrations. The whole country pauses on Yom Ha Shoah, Israel's day of commemoration of the Holocaust. A worker at Yad Vashem reflects on the nature of the anniversary: "Every Remembrance Day you dive into these stories, and the [horror] is always there. There are people that are afraid, and I have friends that don't talk about it, don't want to hear about this day. They don't turn on the radio, or the television because it's hard for them. For me, it's not hard, but of course, some stories are more difficult than the others."

At some sites, the commemoration of an anniversary still includes the burial of human remains. Workers in Srebrenica and Prijedor, Bosnia and Herzegovina, still organize the events, and as one worker put it, "every single year there's some friend, or cousin, or father that you find. You have to be in contact with families who are crying, suffering, and tragedy is everywhere, and you are responsible for them."

Stress increases around anniversary celebrations when both workloads and emotional stimuli reach a peak. The biggest exposure to the content at the 9/11 Memorial & Museum, according to some workers, is on the anniversary. One worker asserts that around anniversaries: "You never know where the emotion is going to come out." Another independently concurs:

> *On 9/11 everything is more emotional. I should not be at my desk crying about this dog dying but still, it gets you. I think people dealing with traumatic occasions, all your emotions get magnified, so the anger is worse; the anxiety is worse; the crying, the weepiness is worse.*

Workers understand the difficulty, and they perceive the wounding, which illustrates a level of empathy. But sometimes empathy comes at a cost.[18] At the 9/11 Memorial & Museum, workers reflect on every act and attend to every word in the process of memorializing suffering. Their focus indicates a level of concern, or empathic attunement, about what behaviors demonstrate reverence for the dead. For instance, a security guard talks about how he changed his greeting when he welcomes visitors to the space: "At first, I said, 'enjoy your visit.' But this struck me as wrong somehow. Now I say, 'embrace your visit.' Because people come in, and they can embrace the memory of those who were lost on that fateful day." He took pleasure at what he asserts affected a compassionate stance. The focus also fosters doubts for workers: "There are a lot of questions here like, 'Can we have fun at work?' We can because we work here. But no, there's a limit of course. We are not supposed to have too much fun because we need to do our jobs." That job includes paying homage to the memories of victims of mass trauma.

Blurring the Boundaries

Trauma is characterized by extremes. In terms of opening oneself to the other, the extreme manifests as eradication of all boundaries. To close oneself off from the other manifests as the opposite, a state of nonfeeling or a rejection of woundedness. But clear boundaries resist traumatic symbolization and facilitate the address of human pain, psychologically and physiologically. Without clarity, confusion ensues. Blurred boundaries confound and distract from the processing of trauma.[19] Finding clarity and limits—around how much pain one can bear, how many stories one can hear, how to create safe space between and with someone in pain—becomes critical. Analysis and reflection at all levels of the institution uncovers the need for boundaries and keeps highly empathic workers safe.[20]

A prior child soldier working in memorialization in Africa articulates an important aspect of working with survivor narratives. He details how through psychological training he learned to create boundaries between the narrative being shared and his personal narrative by detaching himself a bit and becoming an observer. He asserts, "It is healthy to try to detach a bit, not to not listen, but not to emotionally go into their story and experiences because you would burn." He interprets a limit to his entering into wounding with the other. Exceeding that limit is to "burn."[21]

A Cambodian worker collecting oral histories in the fields shares her understanding of detachment and suggests a need for protection of the worker from embroilment with the trauma story through pre- and postcare that helps to establish "how to set a boundary between ourselves and the interviewee. I'm not underestimating their suffering;

I cannot measure the pain, but we should protect ourselves as well. Some people, they deliver their emotion. They always want us to understand, and they're crying." Sometimes the time demands of the survivor, she suggests, are too much for the worker. But no standard exists for what constitutes too much exposure to the trauma narrative in such settings. However, establishing boundaries maintains safety in the encounter with people who suffer.[22] A lack of stated boundaries threatens the protection of all parties involved in any given exchange.

Boundary crossing transpires in many subtle and not-so-subtle forms. A survivor or family member serves on a board or committee. The worker may be on the board or doing a job that requires interaction with the board, but in both cases, the family member/survivor assumes a dual role: an authority figure and part of the audience to which the memorial museum caters. In both cases, questions about roles and capacity evolve. Workers may interact in social activities outside of the confines of the memorial museum with family members or survivors. Such activities may be supported by the management or may directly follow events hosted by the memorial museum. The worker remains an employee in service to the larger body of the institution, but the survivor or family member then assumes another duality as a social acquaintance.

Boundaries shift when experience sharing exceeds that of collection or mediation of the trauma narrative. This crossing has potential to become a boundary violation. For instance, a worker may develop a sense of responsibility for a survivor's well-being after prolonged involvement with or excessive care of the survivor. Exposure occurs, for instance, when care is interpreted as an invitation to emotional or sexual intimacy. Survivors reach out to workers in such cases for continued contact or social engagement; access to emails and personal phone numbers exacerbates the risks.

A worker at the 9/11 Memorial & Museum reflects on a time when a 9/11 family member had access to her personal cell phone number. At one point, he texted and invited her out for a drink. She did not respond, but he persisted, calling her office phone and emailing.

*I felt like I was being somewhat harassed, so I did tell
someone about it. I don't think that anybody felt like they
could say anything to him, but at least when he came to
record his oral history and donate stuff to the collection, the
meetings took place offsite.*

This worker's job requires her to have close contact with survivors,
many of whom she identifies as traumatized. She reflects that the work
often creates a "complex, strange and unusual dynamic with a traumatized man."[23] People in need sometimes confuse nurturing with
more intimate interest or involvement. This curator had no access
to institutional provisions for education about the potential for such
confusion, which led to the violation of boundaries. "I have had no
support whatsoever from the institution in even recognizing that that's
something that we might have to deal with from time to time."

Workers' personal wounds also blur boundaries. As trauma
conflates with trauma, past traumas are triggered, even when that
trigger does not relate to the original wound. Similarly, when home life
presents distress, and workers' performance rests on confronting traumatic content at work, work transforms from being a place of escape
from personal life into a debilitative activity that exacerbates personal
pain. A worker at the 9/11 Memorial & Museum had just returned
from her father's funeral. This and the recent anguish inspired by a
neighbor's suicide left her vulnerable.

*There was a cop that got killed in the line of duty, so they were
having a ceremony downstairs for him. I knew I just couldn't go.
I knew that I would be a mess down there. I couldn't deal with
that at that moment. Bagpipes, anything like that was just too
much. Why do they use bagpipes? They are the most emotional
sound ever. Seriously. Rip your heart out every time . . .
When you get to work after something like that, you feel
better, then you hear something like this [the mark of some*

> *memorial event]: "We're going downstairs for this, and we all*
> *need to go," but I am like, "I can't. I can't do it."*

She reports this to her boss. He responds by giving her the freedom to leave early, to not participate in memorial activities, and to do whatever she needs to employ self-care. Management in this case provides boundaries and protection for the worker from the woundedness of others, what she needs to create personal safety and limits.

The sensory nature of the work, such as the sound of bagpipes and the tears of grieving visitors intrude, as trauma does, on everyday circumstances. The intrusion evidences the nature of the work and evidences a blurring of boundaries between past and present, between safety and danger, between the self and the other. One worker at the 9/11 Memorial & Museum arrived at her desk one morning to see a victim's ID card, which she described as carrying a horrible smell. She perceived the smell to be of burnt human flesh. After cataloging and preserving the card, she recalls being unable to rid herself of the smell of death for days. Other staff report that encountering human flesh on objects is unlikely due to extensive protocols forbidding the collection of human remains.[24] However, this implausibility fails to weaken the effects of an unexpected confrontation with a personal artifact. The worker experiences an impact on her sensory system that leaves her feeling surprised and disturbed. Boundary crossing surfaces in this anecdote in the element of surprise: the worker has no preparation for what she encounters.[25] A lack of preparedness intensifies intrusion, an exceeding of boundaries, but the experience lays the foundation for future stress. Anticipation of such exposure in itself can be stressful and can affect job performance.[26]

Workers learn over time that the content arouses their stress systems, and they intuitively build up defenses or boundaries:

> *I didn't realize until somebody told me that simply looking at*
> *photographs from the day can be stressful. You then have to*
> *remember to stop by people's desk and say, "How's it going? I see*
> *you've been cataloging those particular collection of photos, why*

don't you put that aside for a little bit and work on something else?" They say, "But I have to get it done." I'm like, "No, I'm telling you, take a little break from those photos, do something else." Departmentally we agree that it's probably a problem that we should address. Institutionally there's not been anything that's happened. I'm sure it's partly because we're very new, and the emphasis was to get the place open, and so taking care of the staff goes on the back burner. That's just the reality of life.

The same person reports two disparate experiences: on the one hand, someone tells them to take care of themselves, and on the other, the institution prioritizes the museum's opening so well-being "goes on the back burner." That this is the "reality of life" highlights that institutions that commemorate mass trauma often neglect boundaries in the name of production. The neglect has costs, including personal frustration and lowered capacity for job performance.

Workers both welcome assistance from others in exploring personal wounding and gaining assistance in creating boundaries that protect them from the most disturbing content, and they reject it.[27] Perceptions that such consultation would jeopardize employment status, engage the employee in future litigation, or result in being derided by fellow workers motivate resistance or refusal of professional care.[28] Often such care is also cost-prohibitive. Many workers assume counseling would not be beneficial, preferring instead brief talks or debriefing facilitated internally and that confer time and space to processing disruptive experiences or negative emotions. Some workers even wish such talks be mandatory.[29] Such attentiveness helps in jobs where what's happening next is unpredictable: survivors' stories startle when shared at unexpected times, and images of trauma catch marketers and archivists unawares.

Modeling Reflection

In their book, *Verunsichernde Orte: Selbstverständnis und Weiterbildung in der Gedenkstättenpädagogik* (Disconcerting Sites: Self-Understanding and

Capacity Building on Education at Memorial Sites), Barbara Thimm, Gottfried Koßler, and Susanne Ulrich emphasize that educational mediation at disconcerting sites be present for visitors and workers alike.[30] As part of the federal model project "Memorial Site Education and Relevance to the Present," educators from twelve memorial sites in Germany, Austria, and Poland developed a modern protocol for memorial site education, which, together with exercises for self-reflection, intended to qualify and further train people in contemporary memorial work.

From her current context at the Tuol Sleng Genocide Museum in Cambodia, Barbara Thimm discusses five years of experience with seminars offered at disconcerting places.[31] She describes the practical suitability of the seminars, and how they evolved in the field, with staff doing the daily work rather than emerging from removed, academic research. The evolution provided Thimm with an awareness of several issues around what staff need at sites that commemorate mass trauma. An educational approach unfolded, with pedagogy commercialized and established for visitors, but which also incorporated a concern for the well-being of the worker. The concern focuses on those engaged in the educational aspect of memorial museums; however, Thimm asserts that the observations apply to anyone who negotiates the trauma narrative, specifically in the work of translating or teaching traumatic content to others.

In the beginning of the project, participants asked Thimm and her colleagues if the training replicated therapy. Although a great part of the process includes personal reflection, Thimm stresses that the service operates more like consultancy or coaching: "In Germany, it's more like a team coach. If there's a problem in a group, you could call this coach to help to understand what is happening, to look at the group dynamics, but not act as a therapist. Nobody needs to be a psychologist to join the trainings or to give the trainings."[32]

Part of the logic in distinguishing the training from therapy relates to an underlying assumption that reacting to or having stress as a result of working at a site of mass trauma is expected. As a result, staff spend time contemplating personal histories and what earlier experiences or biases affect engagement with traumatic content. This reflective process includes reviewing how staff frame the trauma stories in the act of telling them to others. Thimm models this reflection: "I had times working in Buchenwald where I was crying in the morning under the shower, and I didn't want to go out there again. This can be one out of many reactions. I don't have to go into therapy just because of that. So, we tell people, 'We are dealing with such difficult history. What are you expecting? What should be normal related to this?'"

Aware of the challenges, Thimm recommends that staff develop resources. Emotional content pushes staff to the boundaries, and management can access only so many tools in response. Sometimes during the training, intense emotions erupt when participants realize that their personal story, or woundedness, interconnects with their work at the disconcerting sites. Coaches address the heightened affect by first helping participants identify limits, then suggesting group support and, if needed, external resources. Sometimes the limits suggest that a participant no longer work in the field.

Personal reflection expands into an examination about how one tells the trauma narrative to others, in teaching for instance, and then broadens to examine the relationship between the site or trauma story and the staff member. Thimm summarizes the process:

> *The training is in three parts; the first part is to reflect your own historical narrative. Where does it come from, and what is your personal relation to this history? The second part is to reflect on your relationship to the educational piece—your relation to the students or to anybody you are talking to. The third is to question how you involve the site, the exhibition, the survivors and perhaps, the objects, into your educational work?*[33]

Thimm recommends that training last two to three days. "It is so intensive that after three days, people say 'Okay, I've had enough now; I have enough to think about.'" The coaches work primarily with educators, but sometimes the museums are so small, all the staff join. "Even the accountant joined at one site. It's good, because sometimes family members of a victim would come to the accountant and talk and talk. Everybody working at a memorial site, especially if it's a small one, everybody is involved and has issues."

The training attends to power dynamics within any given institution, and thus speaks to the question of whether directors should join or not: "In the beginning we were very much like, 'No, the director should not join because everybody should be able to really talk openly,' but then so many directors said, 'Please, I want to join. I want to have this reflection with my staff.' They were curious and they said, 'We really want this.' They were happy that this kind of training helped them as a team to come in the deeper dialogue on the issues." In most of the cases, the coaches approved of director involvement, but with caveats: in some situations, and in advance, directors were asked to leave the group at certain points.

The project aims to encourage and support workers in reflecting on their personal narratives, and their woundedness. The examination leads to clearer communication with students and visitors to the sites. The training also helps staff be patient with visitors' mixed responses to the traumatic content:

> *Often the educators will say, "Yes, but these young people, they were only standing in the corner, and they were laughing." They interpret laughing as being disrespectful. I try to say, "Okay, first of all it's our interpretation of this laughing. Perhaps this laughing was something totally else. Perhaps it was simply that they felt totally helpless, because how do you react if you're standing in front of a former gas chamber? What is an adequate reaction? Who would be the one of us saying this or that is adequate?"*

Thimm's work, along with the needs articulated by the interviewees, serves as a model for training within the memorial museum setting that considers both the emotional responses of staff to the content of trauma and the need for staff to do their jobs well.

Thimm and her colleagues offer a framework through which to think about the global phenomenon of working at unsettling places of mass trauma. Her work supports the notion that attending to trauma first requires acknowledgment. Admitting the reality that working with and through the wounding of trauma is hard creates a pathway toward shared awareness, important to the formation of resiliency in an organization born out of trauma.[34]

For memorial museums, acknowledgment means recognizing that a majority of the people who come to work each day face disturbing content and various, inconsistent stressors. Addressing this normalizes reactions to the content, empowering people to name issues that emerge in the work and to gain access to resources. A worker in upper management at the Apartheid Museum emphasizes the responsibility of the institution to recognize the traumatic element of the work. The act of admitting that personal memories and trauma stories intertwine with the political world of the museum and the human rights issues it represents models responsibility:

> *The thing is that if our institutions can't acknowledge the interplay between the personal and the political, then which institutions are going to? We're sites that are dealing with traumatic events. We are representing, we are showcasing trauma.*

In *Verunsichernde Orte*, Thimm and her colleagues create a model that can advise institutions born out of trauma. A more generalized and clinical approach to dealing with the content of trauma in many locations has been to consult psychologists. For instance, the War Childhood Museum partnered with a psychological association to be more efficient at soliciting survivor stories. The 9/11 Memorial & Museum intermittently recruits speakers to deal with health and wellness in the staff and had the Red Cross, including chaplains and psychologists, present every day at the opening of the memorial plaza. The institution directed primary efforts at psychological and spiritual care toward family members and survivors. When approached by emotional visitors, workers directed the visitors to professionals trained to help. One worker recalls the atmosphere on the plaza:

> *We definitely had chaplains. I don't remember a specific*
> *psychologist; I think that they were mixed in with the*
> *Red Cross team. They just were able to sit down and talk*
> *to [survivors on the plaza]. I remember because I would*
> *ask them about how their day was and if a lot of people*
> *approached them. We were taught as the staff not to do that*
> *unless somebody was in danger. They needed help, and we*
> *could tell that they were emotional. But we were supposed*
> *to let them come to us because they might need that time.*
> *If they come to you, we were told, you should definitely give*
> *them your time. The Red Cross would actually approach*
> *people. They would talk about how they would just sit and*
> *listen. That's what they did. They just sat there and listened to*
> *people.*

In both cases, the institutions support the stakeholders in the trauma story, but not the workers. And in both cases, the worker serves as a mediator of the trauma story: collecting survivor testimony or identifying and being available to emotional visitors. Not recognizing workers' service incurs a risk. When institutions discourage workers from offering help to those in need, workers become vulnerable to the effects of vicarious trauma and the phenomenon of "getting without giving."[35]

Shifting the Lens

The *Verunsichernde Orte* (Disconcerting Sites) project models self and institutional reflection, shifting the lens from the visitor to the worker and moving into a mode of shared reflection and coaching. The training emphasizes that a one-size-fits-all approach does not work, and each institution's needs differ according to its situation: institutional operations, trauma history, access to resources, and the number of workers. Failure at reflection invites the trauma story deeper into the lives of the institution and the individuals who work there. The unacknowledged circulation of trauma invades boundaries and perpetuates emotional distress. The distress provokes repression, denial, and an increased likelihood of biased judgment.[36]

A lack of adequate reflection inhibits the institution's charge of giving meaning to emotional experiences of loss, linking present emotions to past events, or gaining access to new perspectives in the process of rebuilding.[37] Difficulties with processing emotions ensues. The individual feels depressed, uneasy, dissatisfied, or may erupt in an outburst of tears or anger; the institution experiences communication problems, reactive management, and uncomfortable power struggles.[38] Exploring the worker's experience illuminates correlations between individual and organizational responses to trauma. Clarity about the interrelationship underscores that responsibility, and response lies in the hands of both.

Although the strategies of reflection may be similar, implementation requires consideration of individual needs and the facilitation of specific capacities at the level of the institution to promote resiliency. The capacities include: bolstering interpersonal relationships; having effective leadership; creating adaptability, for instance by providing training and education; fostering community and connection; and, again, promoting emotional awareness about the dynamics of working in places born out of trauma.[39]

Velma Sariç reflects on memorialization in Bosnia, summarizing some of the key needs for those in the industry. First, "it's just necessary for us to be asked, 'How do you feel about what is going on? Do you need any help?'" She indicates the dual importance of interpersonal relationships offering support and shared awareness. She demonstrates further the importance of being acknowledged. "People in United States, ordinary people, they would just be nice and say to me, 'What you do its important. Someone cares and thank you for it.'" The acknowledgment creates, she asserts, a feeling of connectedness. She recognizes that going to a psychologist may also help, but that this requires economic resources, and she thinks the industry itself needs a "network" of support. "To be honest," she says, "there's a deep, deep, deep necessity for people who do this kind of work to get some support or at least to be exposed to the larger network of people who do similar things, and maybe they can talk to each other."

Her assertion reflects the concept of solidarity among the workers. But she adds that the work also draws out solidarity within the larger community of people who respond to mass trauma through memorialization; people who need acknowledgment.

> *It's about giving these [workers] a certain [status] by saying this person exists . . . I do exist. People know about it, and I can see how hard it is. I can talk about my hardship, and someone will listen . . . Genocide survivors who work in museums, I know that every single time they talk about their experience, they do with passion. But I also know how tired and exhausted and stressed they are. If they are connected, they can [share experience]. I'm sure if someone from Srebrenica connects with someone from wherever, Auschwitz, this person can say it's difficult for me. People have certain responses which they can share. Maybe we will have a manual. Someone will say like, okay this is how you can protect yourself. This is how you do this work. Then from there is a community. It's about solidarity. It's about support and encouragement that we keep going.*

Velma refers to internal support, essential to the work. She envisions this support as exceeding permitters: geographic and content related.

Connections and communication between people doing the work of memorialization across the globe serve an additional role by providing a platform for conversation for a group of people who generally refrain from discussing what they do beyond the confines of work.

For instance, workers often do not share their experiences with friends and family so as not to bring the wounds from traumatic content home. Reticence to bring sadness and horror into private life extends across continents. To help avoid exposing family and friends to the horrors of trauma workers confront daily, most underscore the critical need for support among colleagues. An oral historian from the 9/11 Memorial & Museum echoes the theme, articulating the assistance that he received from colleagues—not management—in negotiating tough interviews. He said he didn't need to necessarily process the interview, but to "just joke around, and that would help." He added, "I try not to go home and tell my wife stuff that is difficult—not that she wouldn't make herself available and listen and be compassionate, but it's just that never was really appealing to me."

Another oral historian from Cambodia reports that the stress and pressure of working in the field is alleviated by her relationships with her colleagues:

> *We understand each other. We discuss things; we are open-minded, and then after work, we always share about what we experienced during the fieldwork. We talk about that specific interviewee that was hard, like if someone's story was distressing. It's more like teamwork, team bonding; we support each other. We are family.*

She says that the environment on returning to the Tuol Sleng Genocide Museum shifts because she feels less understood by male executive leadership. So, while the content of the fieldwork is often more emotionally challenging than the museum work, the experience at the museum, in the absence of a sense of community, can be more draining. Comradery with young people in the field provides a sense of comfort and support: "We know how it feels. We have the same background as well. We are from the city; we share the same interests and the same suffering."

The words of a 9/11 Memorial & Museum worker summarize this sense of shared suffering that contributes to the community in the memorial museum setting: "Any group of people who has been through any challenging circumstance, that unique bond really can form if people let it." She reports that her ability to do the job for twelve years rests on the fact that she has a strong support system internally. "I think that without that support network, I probably would have maybe done the year here and moved on . . . it's such a specific experience working here, and the intensity is just so unique, that a shared experience with someone's being here in this environment creates a connection."

The interpretive guides at the 9/11 Memorial & Museum build a close network of support. One observes that "one of the few things that helps us get through the day is each other because we all understand what we're going through. If we have a bad interaction, or before we start a tour, if there's a visitor that's giving one of us a hard time, we all immediately have each other's back. I think it's a testament to the strength of this program."

Guides at all memorial museums encounter a wide variety of visitors with assumptions, feelings, and politics that emerge during tours. Executive director of the Whitney Plantation Museum, Ashley Rogers, discusses some means of support for interpretive guides. First, they have access to a break room, where they convene after tours. The 9/11 Memorial & Museum provides a room for the guides as well, but in both cases, the spaces are neither always assured nor always private. Second, and perhaps more importantly, Rogers states that when guides bring problems forward, "The number one thing we can do is believe them." She expresses the concern that all too often management at memorial museums minimize the experiences of the guides or workers in general, but the Whitney takes a different approach. The reaction workers get when they come to a manager is, "I am so sorry that happened to you. What do you need?"[40] Or she asserts, a manager will be in place to listen. Most recently, the Whitney enacted a policy where the guides carry radios. "They're supposed to let us know if something is happening, and they don't feel comfortable on the tour so that somebody can come and at least walk behind and support them and see what the dynamic is, maybe pull that person off to the side so they don't have to be the one doing it."

Rogers models good leadership. She acknowledges the challenges workers face and creates safety so that workers have some control over their experiences.[41] Implementing training and education that target preparation for encounters with traumatic content bolsters good leadership. Velma asserts that those who work in memorialization "are working with the most traumatized victims. We should have training." Psychoeducation—didactic learning about trauma that mitigates surprise and anticipates the possibility of arousal—provides one means of response. Systematic and structured processes increasing knowledge decrease the negative impact of dealing with traumatic content.[42] When workers experience intense affects, those affects felt and released, rather than being repressed, ignored, or even considered pathological, bolsters the work. For instance, crying in the shower to release the sadness about working at Buchenwald helped Thimm release emotions, establish regulation, and then proceed with her job and training.

The risks of not having training include hyperarousal, crossed boundaries, impeded communication, and additional wounding. Once affect becomes dysregulated, safety vanishes; the risk of traumatization, secondary or otherwise, emerges, and the ability to be self-aware diminishes. Self-understanding relies on the notion of safety—states of arousal can only be adjusted in a safe environment. Thimm and her colleagues recognize the need for safety in the dilemma of whether or not to allow directors into the groups. A question emerges: does the director's presence debilitate safety or pose a threat—to working environments, to the ability to talk freely, and to promotions? While open and uncensored conversations provide value, they may require insulation.

Communication facilitates awareness, endurance, and resilience. Providing an outlet for stress through dialogue decompresses heightened arousal and offers an opportunity for bonding. Open conversations about traumatic content and its effects reveals to workers the shared experience of the work; they are not alone, not as individuals, institutions, or countries. Three workers from across the globe express this need for communication from their varied positions and contexts.

> Bosnia: *I constantly think, "Okay," that is a place where there is a mass grave. That is a place where they were holding women, because everything is so fresh, and it's around us. If you have a deeper knowledge, you cannot stop thinking about it. It's like hearing the mortar shelling, when someone hits the door of a car but much stronger. I do see that this reflects a lot in other people's lives, and honestly, for me, it's necessary to talk about this.*

> New York: *I think it would be nice to be able to have an opportunity to talk about what I experienced and what triggered it, and for someone to be able to say what that is. To know that there are other people who have felt that way. And to know how to troubleshoot. I don't feel morbid or anything, but just to have that chance to say, "This is something that happened, and it kind of threw me off for a while."*

> South Africa: *Sometimes I regret speaking to people personally. I feel sometimes I have overexplained my sentiments about something. I watch my mouth, but at the same time, it helps me to speak freely, to express myself with you for instance. To speak the way that I see things.*

My perspective. I mean sharing my perspective and getting
yours, is what I want to say. I enjoy getting other people's
perspectives, and I enjoy when other people listen to my
perspective.

The need to talk not only emphasizes the importance of a community but also highlights that the verbal processing of trauma enables learning because workers move from the affective realm (i.e., triggered negative emotion) to the cognitive realm (making sense of the event). Building community serves as a source of support and a source of strength in the process of rebuilding after trauma—both external to and internal to the commemorative institution. The communal and communicative framework needs repetitive attention. Intermittent or singular responses to trauma highlight stressors instead of tempering them, whereas continuous or repeated attention to trauma's effects decreases stressors.

Persisting Challenges

The memorial museum field faces a challenge to acknowledge what workers bear daily. Effective acknowledgment requires both verbal recognition and action. Action takes many forms. To understand active effort in the facing of trauma, look to the workers, bearing the burden of constant exposure to human pain. Their woundedness reveals possibilities for both healing and learning. Workers listen without judgment. They open themselves to receiving memories, sometimes incoherent, sometimes factually incorrect, sometimes embodied and wordless. The memories carry pain that the workers bear. Workers enter the pain. They immerse themselves in the field, the home, the site of torture; they look at graphic pictures and vet these for public viewing; they work in the places that sensorily trigger trauma and face histories that engender helplessness and anger. They expose vulnerability and personal wounding to allow for meaning to emerge in the lives of the people they touch and who touch them. They tolerate ambiguity in this regard, and instead of demanding total explanations, allow themselves to be disrupted and shaped by the suffering they encounter.

These qualities emerged from nearly every person interviewed. Each approached the work of commemoration of mass trauma open to wounding with a desire to help. Perhaps not all workers can be touted as great listeners or as having the capacity to successfully navigate the effects of dealing with the trauma narrative, but institutions can help them. They need recognition, guidance, and training on self-care and how to keep oneself safe while working every day at the source of extreme pain. Rapid decision-making by management, feedback, and interpersonal relationships can also increase trust and safety within an institution.

Psychoeducation, boundary setting, and conflict resolution techniques enable personal responsibility in these regards. Workers also need affirmation and safe space—as a place for decompression or an alternative working space, away from the intensity or frequency of trauma exposure. They need support: people, upper management, executive, and donors who are willing to reflect together with workers on what they encounter, to empathize and form best practices. For instance, reinforcement and increased interpersonal engagement are essential around anniversaries and high-stakes events that enact professional pressure without any alleviation of the emotional burden of commemorating mass trauma. And last, these wounded healers can do their jobs better when the institution functions as a community, perhaps reaching out to and partnering with other institutions of its kind, whose workers have similar needs.

The Work Continues

Alongside the long, often ambiguous grieving process, burns the desire and necessity for the survivor of mass trauma to speak, to proclaim the trauma aloud, to combat silence and denial. Telling trauma has goals:

to verify it to the self and others—from other social groups to following generations—in the hope of some future good.[43] The memorial museum worker listens, entering into the situation. The worker bears wounding and pain, while witnessing human suffering. The worker enters into communion with wounding to help the other. The oral historian in Cambodia, Barbara Thimm, the curators at Yad Vashem and the 9/11 Memorial & Museum, Sudba and Velma, the guide at the Apartheid Museum, Teresa Klimowicz, Ashley Rogers, Ali, and Dr. Seck, and every other worker represented in these pages all remain vulnerable, empathic, and loving, attentive to human pain and demonstrating companionship.[44]

Obstacles materialize. Denial haunts communities in the aftermath. Boundaries blur. Confronting trauma hurts. Unspeakable pain confronts the worker at every turn. Barbed wire fencing encircles Auschwitz. Human skulls fill the memorial stupa at the Killing Fields in Cambodia. Sniper shots crack from a video at the entrance of the Museum of Crimes against Humanity and Genocide in Sarajevo: citizens run through the city streets as targets. Recorded goodbyes play in alcoves at the 9/11 Memorial & Museum as those stuck in the towers called their loved ones just before they died. A statue depicts a Black angel carrying a baby to heaven on the Whitney Plantation, memorializing the local deaths of 2,200 enslaved children between 1820 and 1860. The displays and restitutions—all created, composed, and cared for by workers—communicate trauma in sensations and emotions.[45] Feelings emerge, but no words can express the horror. The depths of suffering escape understanding and inspire questions about meaning, trust in God, and the depravity of human betrayal.

Does humankind have the capacity to be good? What happens after death? Where do we find meaning after trauma and loss? Where is God, and why? The questions resonate across the globe, in every tradition, and in every memorial museum. Encountering these questions requires immersion in the situation. The answers emerge tarnished with ambiguity, demanding a wrestling with the reality of mass atrocity. The worker tolerates the ambiguity of having no precise answer, running the risk of exposure to and disruption by the other. Any attempt at encountering the other or immersing oneself in the crises that perpetuate the human community must involve an acceptance of disruption to refute indifference: moral neutrality is not an option.[46]

Workers stand with the other in a confrontation with meaninglessness and extreme dislocation. They go to the "open wounds" of trauma—signified by places and internal to people. Memorial museum workers endeavor to heal fragmentation. They interpret suffering to give it meaning, and then rebuild. Attuned to the "big" questions asked after trauma, alongside the sensory, nonmaterial, unspeakable, and unexplainable aspects of ordinary experience, the worker becomes willing to risk an interpretation of how meaning emerges after suffering. What is the risk for the worker? Not having an answer, to what happens after death, where a body is, how a person died, where to seek comfort. They continue to face suffering.

Each battles denial that haunts communities in the aftermath. Their voices challenge the minimization of trauma and its vestiges. They speak to fragmentation, of the self and of the group after trauma, through rebuilding and reconstituting order, control, connections, and symbolization. They offer places for the disappeared to rest, even if symbolically, taking all who come there on "a journey to the awareness of loss."[47]

Human-to-human violence on individual and mass scales continues. And workers endure oppressive political situations, complications in funding, critiques of their work from outsiders, censure from insiders, and a lack of support from institutions. And still, they create and interpret to recollect (re-collect) and restore meaning.[48] Interpretation for restoration leads to faith.[49] From a theological lens, faith is in a revelation, a final truth, or a good God. The memorial museum worker models this faith on their own terms: faith that their work produces a good; faith that telling trauma will help people; faith in hope after mass tragedy; and faith in humankind.

NOTES

Preface

1 Their work resembles the burden of theology to, as in Shelly Rambo's words, "account for the excess, or remainder, of death in life that is central to trauma"; see Shelly Rambo, "Spirit and Trauma," *Interpretation: A Journal of Bible and Theology* 69, no. 9 (January 2015): 12.

2 The ratios of interview participants are as follows: survivors 35 percent, family members and friends 30 percent, community members 35 percent.

3 See Lila Petar Vrklevski and John Franklin, "Vicarious Trauma: The Impact on Solicitors of Exposure to Traumatic Material," *Traumatology* 14, no. 1 (2008): 1106–18. The study illustrates the prevalence of a trauma history in people's lives: 30 percent of respondents report no trauma history, 15 percent report one event, and 55 percent report multiple events (20 percent sexual abuse, 23 percent physical abuse, 15 percent neglect, 36 percent emotional abuse). These statistics concur with other studies: see Laura J. Schauben and Patricia A. Frazier, "Vicarious Trauma: The Effects on Female Counselors of Working with Sexual Violence Survivors," *Psychology of Women Quarterly* 19, no. 1 (1995): 49–64. In reference to higher stress levels related to trauma histories when dealing with traumatic content, see Elana Newman, Roger Simpson, and David Handschuh, "Trauma Exposure and Post-Traumatic Stress Disorder among Photojournalists," *Visual Communications Quarterly* 10, no. 1 (2003): 4–13.

4 See Maurice Halbwachs, *On Collective Memory*, trans. Lewis A. Coser (Chicago: University of Chicago Press, 1992).

5 Vilashini Coopan offers an envisioning of the worker as "connective tissue" in "Connective Tissue: Memory's Weave and the Entanglements of Diasporic Ethnicity," *Qui Parle* 28, no. 2 (2019): 282–306.

6 The attentive interview of Katherine Hite with Jordi Huguet illustrates the dilemmas and dynamics of his work. This interview inspired the testimonies and questions employed in this study; see Katherine Hite, *Politics and the Art of Commemoration: Memorials to Struggle in Latin America and Spain* (New York: Routledge, 2012), 44. Her research represents a creative approach to what remains a highly critical attitude toward memorial museums. See research on the violence portrayed in the memorial museum setting, perpetuating what has been called "dark tourism," as well as critiques about the investment of America in its own innocence through its commemoration of trauma; for example, Duncan Light, "Progress in Dark Tourism and Thanatourism Research: An Uneasy Relationship with Heritage Tourism," *Tourism Management* 61 (2017): 275–301, and Marita Sturken, *Tourists of History: Memory, Kitsch, and Consumerism from Oklahoma City to Ground Zero* (Durham: Duke University Press, 2007). Beyond Hite, little has been said about those working between debates on the contemporary commodification of death at sites that mark or commemorate mass trauma and the cultural condition of societies and groups grieving trauma. Two other debates circulate in the field. The first relates to the qualification, even commodification, of trauma itself that leads to the sweeping argument that everything is trauma, and, therefore, nothing is trauma. Lost or undervalued in this line of thinking are the real felt reverberations of a traumatic event, see Will Self, "A Posthumous Shock: How Everything Became Trauma," *Harpers*, December 2021, https://harpers.org/archive/2021/12/a-posthumous-shock-trauma-studies-modernity-how-everything-became-trauma/. The second relates to whether the field of commemoration will contribute to the eradication of genocide or at least inhibit it through creating empathic responses to trauma; all of this is encapsulated in the phrase "never again"; see for instance Dara Horn, *People Love Dead Jews: Reports from a Haunted Present* (New York: W. W. Norton, 2022).

7 See Harry F. Wolcott, *The Art of Fieldwork*, 2nd ed. (Lanham: AltaMira Press, 2004); also see Arthur Kleinman, "Moral Experience and Ethical Reflection: Can Ethnography Reconcile Them? A Quandary for 'The New Bioethics,'" *Daedalus* 128, no. 4 (1999): 69–97.

8 Analysis of places that commemorate mass trauma sometimes ignores the reality that people, real live human people with feelings and personal experiences, do the communal work of healing after trauma, work frequently regarded as commercial, even harmful. The critiques abound. Two examples are Nitasha Sharma, "Dark Tourism and Moral Disengagement in Liminal Spaces," *Tourism Geographies* 22, no. 2 (2020): 273–97, and Magdalena Hodalska, "Selfies at Horror Sites: Dark Tourism, Ghoulish Souvenirs and Digital Narcissism," *Zeszyty Prasoznawcze* 60, no. 2 (2017): 405–23.

9 Jeffrey Andrew Barash, *Collective Memory and the Historical Past* (Chicago: University of Chicago Press, 2016), 67.

10 Jonathan Huener, *Auschwitz, Poland, and the Politics of Commemoration, 1945–1979* (Athens: Ohio University Press, 2004). See also Pierre Nora, "Between History and Memory: Lieu de Memoire," *Representations* 26 (1989): 7–24, and Marek Kucia, "The Meanings of Auschwitz in Poland, 1945 to the Present," *Holocaust Studies* 25, no. 3 (2019): 220–47.

11 "Memorial Timeline," Auschwitz-Birkenau Memorial Museum, accessed August 3, 2022, http://www.auschwitz.org/en/museum/history-of-the-memorial/memorial-timeline/.

12 "Auschwitz I, Auschwitz II-Birkenau, Auschwitz III-Monowitz," Auschwitz-Birkenau Memorial Museum, accessed August 3, 2022, http://70.auschwitz.org/index.php?option=com_content&view=article&id=87&Itemid=173&lang=en.

13 "Memorial Timeline," Auschwitz-Birkenau Memorial Museum, accessed August 3, 2022, http://www.auschwitz.org/en/museum/history-of-the-memorial/memorial-timeline/.

14 "Mission Statement," Auschwitz-Birkenau Memorial Museum, accessed August 3, 2022, http://www.auschwitz.org/en/education/iceah-general-information/mission-statement/.

15 Cnaan Liphshiz, "In Poland, Plans to Build a Museum on Schindler Survivors' Former Camp Spark Environmental Protest," Jewish Telegraphic Agency, November 26, 2021, https://www.jta.org/2021/11/26/global/in-poland-plans-to-build-a-museum-on-schindler-survivors-former-camp-spark-environmental-protest.

16 "KL Płaszów Concentration Camp in Kraków," In Your Pocket Essential City Guide, accessed August 6, 2022,

https://www.inyourpocket.com/krakow/kl-plaszow-concentration-camp-in-krakow_73759f.

17 "About the Museum," Muzeum KL Płaszkow, accessed August 6, 2022, https://plaszow.org/en/about-the-museum/mission-and-strategy.

18 Galicia represents a geopolitical region comprising parts of Poland and Ukraine, once united under the Austro-Hungarian Empire (prior to 1918) as its largest province. Andrew J. Drummond and Jacek Lubecki, "Reconstructing Galicia: Mapping the Cultural and Civic Traditions of the Former Austrian Galicia in Poland and Ukraine," *Europe-Asia Studies* 62, no. 8 (2010): 1312.

19 Galicia Jewish Museum, "About Us," https://galiciajewishmuseum.org/en/museum/.

20 "Galicia Jewish Museum," Krakow Museums, accessed August 3, 2022, http://www.museums.krakow.travel/en/muzea/id,72,trail,15,t,galicia-jewish-museum.html.

21 "Martyrs; and Heroes Remembrance (Yad Vashem) Law 5713-1953," Yad Vashem, accessed August 6, 2022, https://www.yadvashem.org/about/yad-vashem-law.html.

22 "Mission Statement," Yad Vashem, accessed August 6, 2022, https://www.yadvashem.org/about/mission-statement.html.

23 "Mission Statement," Yad Vashem, accessed August 6, 2022, https://www.yadvashem.org/about/mission-statement.html.

24 Israel established a unique date in the Hebrew calendar observed for the global Jewish community, Israel, and the Jewish Diaspora called Yom HaShoah. It coincides with the 27th of Nisan (on the Hebrew calendar) to mark the beginning of the Warsaw Ghetto Uprising of 1943, when Jewish resistance fighters defied the Nazis and fought for freedom and dignity. January 27 marks the liberation of Auschwitz concentration camp by the Red Army in 1945; see "Jewish Holidays: Yom HaShoah-Holocaust Memorial Day," Jewish Virtual Library, accessed September 5, 2022, https://www.jewishvirtuallibrary.org/yom-ha-shoah-holocaust-memorial-day. The United Nations General Assembly designated the date in 2005 and encourages the world population to recognize the anniversary; see International Holocaust Remembrance Day," United States Holocaust Memorial Museum, accessed September 5, 2022, https://encyclopedia.ushmm.org/content/en/article/international-holocaust-remembrance-day.

25 Amnesty International, "Poland: The Law on the Institute of National Remembrance contravenes the right to freedom of expression" (2018), 1, accessed March 8, 2021, https://www.amnesty.org/download/Documents/EUR3778582018 ENGLISH.pdf.

26 Isabel Kershner, "Yad Vashem Rebukes Israeli and Polish Governments over Holocaust Law," *The New York Times*, July 5, 2018, https://www.nytimes.com/2018/07/05/world/middleeast/israel-poland-holocaust.html.

27 Sam Sokol, "Top Polish Institute Accused of Firing Historians over Holocaust-Era Research," *Haaretz*, November 21, 2021, https://www.haaretz.com/world-news/europe/.premium.HIGHLIGHT-top-polish-institute-accused-of-firing-historians-over-holocaust-research-1.10398136. The trend continues in Poland.

28 Adam Barnes, "Antisemitic Graffiti Discovered at Auschwitz-Birkenau," The Hill, October 5, 2021, https://thehill.com/changing-america/respect/equality/575385-antisemitic-graffiti-discovered-at-auschwitz-birkenau/.

29 "Polish Official Fired after Calling Holocaust Law 'Stupid,'" Aljazeera, January 10, 2022, https://www.aljazeera.com/news/2022/1/10/polish-official-fired-after-calling-holocaust-law-stupid.

30 See Suryia Chindawongse, "Pol Pot's Strategy of Survival," *The Fletcher Forum of World Affairs* 15, no. 1 (1991): 127–45, in which Chindawongse articulates the conditions of warfare in Cambodia with more military forces of South Vietnam using Cambodia as a sanctuary, which prompted the US to initiate bombing in Cambodia. The destruction of the bombing campaigns from 1970 to 1973 "hardened Khmer will and accelerated popular support for Pol Pot's strategy of revolutionary warfare," 134–35.

31 Chindawongse, "Pol Pot's Strategy of Survival," and Taylor Owen, "Bombs over Cambodia," *The Walrus*, October 12, 2007, https://thewalrus.ca/2006-10-history/.

32 Owen, "Bombs over Cambodia."

33 Bullfrog Films, "Documentaries That Changed the World— Year Zero: The Silent Death of Cambodia (Bullfrog Films clip),"

YouTube video, August 19, 2009, 2:58, https://www.youtube.com/watch?v=CGSuE7_HdeE.

34 Francois Ponchaud, *Cambodia: Year Zero* (New York: Henry Holt, 1978).

35 Terence Duffy, "The Peace Museum Concept," *Museum International* 45, no. 1 (1993): 4–8.

36 "Tuol Sleng Genocide Museum Archives Preservation and Digitization Project," UNESCO, accessed August 3, 2022, https://en.unesco.org/themes/holocaust-genocide-education/tuol-sleng-genocide-museum-archives.

37 "Support Us," Tuol Sleng Genocide Museum, accessed August 3, 2022, https://tuolsleng.gov.kh/en/collections/archive-research/support-us/.

38 Cindy Co, "US to Fund Project Preserving Cloths of S-21 Victims," *The Phnom Penh Post*, December 12, 2017, https://www.phnompenhpost.com/national/us-fund-project-preserving-clothes-s-21-victims.

39 "Tuol Sleng Genocide Museum," #Memoriassituadas, accessed August 3, 2022, https://www.cipdh.gob.ar/memorias-situadas/en/lugar-de-memoria/museo-del-genocidio-tuol-sleng/.

40 NGO worker, Cambodia, personal conversation, July 2019.

41 Duffy, "The Peace Museum Concept," 1.

42 Caroline Bennett, "Living with the Dead in the Killing Fields of Cambodia," *Journal of Southeast Asian Studies* 49, no. 2 (2018): 199.

43 Sopheng Cheang, "Anti-Tank Mine Kills 3 Demining Experts in Cambodia," *Associated Press*, January 10, 2022, https://apnews.com/article/cambodia-land-mines-89e03ac2902e4ff1e8e628f5d1f07fa5.

44 "Cambodia," Limbs International, accessed August 3, 2022, https://www.limbsinternational.org/cambodia.html.

45 Frank Hayes, "South Africa's Departure from the Commonwealth, 1960–1961," *The International History Review* 2, no. 3 (1980): 492.

46 Hayes, "South Africa's Departure from the Commonwealth, 1960–1961," 476.

47 In accordance with the Gauteng Gambling Act (4 of 1995), Akani Egoli submitted a successful bid that included the commitment

to social responsibility by building a museum. The Gold Reef City Casino was built and an adjacent piece of land given for the construction of a museum paid for by the entity but registered as a Public Benefit Company (incorporated not for gain) with an independent board of trustees; see "The Apartheid Museum's Genesis," Apartheid Museum, accessed August 3, 2022, https://www.apartheidmuseum.org/about-the-museum.

48 Holocaust Museum Houston, "Virtual Lecture with Apartheid Museum Director Christopher Till," YouTube video, October 13, 2020, 57:35, https://www.youtube.com/watch?v=dsL8QtXPfSA.

49 "The New Constitution," Apartheid Museum, accessed August 3, 2022, https://www.apartheidmuseum.org/exhibitions/the-new-constitution.

50 Thabisani Ndlovu, "Shuttling between the Suburbs and the Township; The New Black Middle Class(es) Negotiating Class and Post-Apartheid Blackness in South Africa," *Africa* 90, no. 3 (2020): 568.

51 Lucille Davie, "Hector Pieterson Gets His Memorial," Joburg, October 24, 2001, https://web.archive.org/web/200705190 61318/http://www.joburg.org.za/october/hector.stm.

52 "Our Purpose," Mandela House, accessed November 1, 2022, https://www.mandelahouse.com.

53 Nelson Mandela, *Long Walk to Freedom* (Boston: Back Bay Books, 1994), 340.

54 "RIM Establishment," Robben Island Museum, accessed August 3, 2022, https://www.robben-island.org.za/organisation.

55 Freedom Park, Brochure, January 2019.

56 Alma Diamond, "Burying the Past and Building the Future in Post-Apartheid South Africa," The Conversation, February 20, 2022, https://theconversation.com/burying-the-past-and-building-the-future-in-post-apartheid-south-africa-174010.

57 For an in-depth history of the prelude to the war, see Leonard J. Cohen, *Broken Bonds: The Disintegration of Yugoslavia* (Boulder: Westview Press, 1993).

58 See David Rieff, who calls the siege of Sarajevo beginning on this day not a war but a "slaughter"; *Slaughterhouse: Bosnia and the Failure of the West* (New York: Simon & Schuster, 1996). For

information about the Hilton Shooting, see Kenneth Morrison, "Crossing the Rubicon: The Outbreak of War in Sarajevo," in *Sarajevo's Holiday Inn on the Frontline of Politics and War* (London: Palgrave Macmillan, 2016), 103–16.

59 Rieff, *Slaughterhouse*, 17. Serbian forces are represented by the following leaders at the time: the Serbian president Slobodan Milošević; Radovan Karadžić, leader of the Serb Democratic Party; and Ratko Mladić, Bosnian Serb general of the Army of Republika Srpska. See Cohen, *Broken Bonds*, and Reiff, *Slaughterhouse*, 17 and 30.

60 Barbara Demick, *Logavina Street: Life and Death in a Sarajevo Neighborhood* (New York: Random House, 2012), 153.

61 "Historical Museum of Bosnia and Herzegovina," Museums of the World, accessed August 3, 2022, https://museu.ms/museum/details/278/historical-museum-of-bosnia-and-herzegovina.

62 Elma Hašimbegović, "The History Museum of Bosnia and Herzegovina in Sarajevo," *Observing Memories*, December 2019, https://europeanmemories.net/magazine/the-history-museum-of-bosnia-and-herzegovina-in-sarajevo/.

63 Hašimbegović, "The History Museum of Bosnia and Herzegovina in Sarajevo."

64 "About," Galerija 11/07/95, accessed March 15, 2022, https://galerija110795.ba/about-gallery-110795/.

65 "The Idea, Mission and Vision," War Childhood Museum, accessed August 3, 2022, https://warchildhood.org/the-idea-mission-and-vision/.

66 Vesna Besic, Lejla Biogradlija, and Sanela Crnovrsanin, "Coffins of 19 Srebrenica Genocide Victims Carried to Potocari Cemetery," Anadolu Agency, July 11, 2021, https://www.aa.com.tr/en/europe/coffins-of-19-srebrenica-genocide-victims-carried-to-potocari-cemetery/2300728.

67 "The Srebrenica-Potočari Memorial Centre and Cemetery to the Victims of the 1995 Genocide," Holocaust Memorial Day Trust, accessed August 10, 2022, https://www.hmd.org.uk/wp-content/uploads/2014/04/Life-Story-Srebrenica-Genocide-Memorial.pdf, and "UK National Srebrenica Memorial Day Programme and Annual Report," Remembering Srebrenica, accessed August 10, 2022, https://srebrenica.org.uk/wp-content/

uploads/2021/07/2021-Programme-Annual-Report-WEB-01.
pdf.

68 Filip Rudic, "Hague Court Chief Criticizes Serbian PM's Genocide Denial," Balkan Insight, November 20, 2018, https://
balkaninsight.com/2018/11/20/hague-tribunal-chief-criticises-
serbian-pm-s-genocide-denial-11-20-2018/. On November 14,
2018, in an interview with Deutche Welle, Brnabić denied the
massacres of Bosniaks by Bosnian Serb forces in Srebrenica as
being an act of genocide; "Serbian PM Ana Brnabic: Srebrenica
'A Terrible Crime,' not Genocide," Deutche Welle, November
15, 2018, https://www.dw.com/en/serbian-pm-ana-brnabic-
srebrenica-a-terrible-crime-not-genocide/a-46307925.

69 Beta, "Vucic: Serbia Will Not Adopt a Resolution on Srebrenica While I Am President," N1, June 6, 2021, https://rs.n1info.
com/english/news/vucic-serbia-will-not-adopt-a-resolution-on-
srebrenica-while-i-am-president/.

70 Sudba Musić, personal conversation, December 2017.

71 "Bijela Traka Nije naš Izbor, Nego Njihovo Djelo," Radio
Slobodna Evropa, trans. Armin Halilović, May 31, 2022,
https://www.slobodnaevropa.org/a/prijedor-dan-bijelih-traka-
zlocin/31877209.html?fbclid=IwAR0p7rR4hPnAM4vHlA6cQ
jYsrJwMT-PEMp4-aU6sniexlfQRA0vxWVbElPU.

72 "1993 World Trade Center Bombing," Bureau of Diplomatic
Security, accessed August 3, 2022, https://www.state.gov/
1993-world-trade-center-bombing/.

73 "9/11 Memorial & Museum Mission," 9/11 Memorial &
Museum, accessed February 2, 2021, https://www.911memorial.
org/about.

74 Andrew Rafferty, "$700 Million and Counting: 9/11 Museum
Opens with Money Worries," NBC News, May 15, 2014, https://
www.nbcnews.com/news/us-news/700-million-counting-9-11-
museum-opens-money-worries-n106536.

75 No national memorial exists for loss endured by Native American populations; however, the National Native American Veterans Memorial at the Smithsonian honors Native Americans in
the military. It opened in 2020. Several smaller local memorials,
along with cultural heritage sties, recognize the egregious loss of
Native Americans. See for instance, "Wounded Knee Memorial,"

Migration Memorials Project, accessed August 9, 2022, https://migrationmemorials.trinity.duke.edu/items/wounded-knee-memorial, and "Trail of Tears," National Park Service, accessed August 9, 2022, https://www.nps.gov/trte/index.htm.

76 See Jeanette Haynes Writer, "Terrorism in Native America: Interrogating the Past, Examining the Present, and Constructing a Liberatory Future," *Anthropology & Education Quarterly* 33, no. 3 (2002): 317–30; Haynes analyzes the term "terror" and the interpretation of the mass slaughter of Native Americans; see also Saidiya Hartman's negotiation of terror in its mundane forms in *Scenes of Subjection: Terror, Slavery, and Self-Making in Nineteenth Century America* (Oxford: Oxford University Press, 1997).

77 Oliva B. Waxman, "The First Africans in Virginia Landed in 1619: It Was a Turning Point for Slavery in American History—But Not the Beginning," *Time Magazine*, August 20, 2019, https://time.com/5653369/august-1619-jamestown-history/.

78 Equal Justice Initiative, "Slavery in America: The Montgomery Slave Trade," 2018, 10, https://eji.org/report/slavery-in-america/montgomery-slave-trade/.

79 P. R. Lockhart, "How Slavery Became America's First Big Business," *Vox*, August 16, 2019, https://www.vox.com/identities/2019/8/16/20806069/slavery-economy-capitalism-violence-cotton-edward-baptist.

80 "Plantation Owners," Whitney Plantation, accessed July 17, 2022, https://www.whitneyplantation.org/history/plantation-owners/#:~:text=Jean%20Jacques%20did%20more%20than,1820%2C%20Jean%20Jacques%20Haydel%20Sr.

81 "Whitney Plantation History," Whitney Plantation, accessed July 17, 2022, https://www.whitneyplantation.org/history/.

82 Allison Keyes, "In This Quiet Space for Contemplation, a Fountain Rains Down Calming Water," *Smithsonian Magazine*, September 21, 2017, https://www.smithsonianmag.com/smithsonian-institution/quiet-space-contemplation-fountain-rains-down-calming-waters-180964981/.

83 Four Raleigh Charter High School students, personal conversation, summer 2020, see their project: "The Freedom Struggle Committee," Raleigh Charter High School, accessed August 9, 2022, https://www.raleighcharterhs.org/fsc/.

84 The use of the word "situation" alludes to both Paul Tillich and David Tracy's use of the term; see Paul Tillich, *The World Situation* (Philadelphia: Fortress Press, 1965), and David Tracy, *Fragments: The Existential Situation of Our Time* (Chicago: University of Chicago Press, 2019). See a more extended discussion of this in the Introduction and chapter 1 on theology.

85 See Laura E. Captari, Joshua N. Hook, Jamie D. Aten, Edward B. Davis, and Theresa Clement Tisdale, "Embodied Spirituality Following Disaster: Exploring Intersections of Religious and Place Attachment in Resilience and Meaning-Making," in *The Psychology of Religion and Place*, ed. Victor Counted and Fraser Watts (Palgrave Macmillan: London, 2019), 49–79.

Introduction

1 Philip Gourevitch writes a moving piece in "After the Genocide," *The New Yorker*, December 10, 1995, https://www.newyorker.com/magazine/1995/12/18/after-the-genocide, where he addresses the Rwandan Genocide and in a section entitled "Why Am I Alive? Living Came to Seem an Accident of Fate," a phenomenon of mass trauma articulated by a Tutsi priest, Abbé Modeste Mungwararora, "Every survivor wonders why he is alive."

2 See Janina Fisher, *Healing the Fragmented Selves of Trauma Survivors: Overcoming Internal Self-Alienation* (London: Routledge, 2017). Throughout the text, Fisher addresses fragmentation or splitting off parts of the self to preserve a belief in internal goodness, or good parts of the self, and to facilitate rejection of badness, the bad abused/victimized parts of the self. Traumatic pasts, along with present stimuli, trigger the splitting. She focuses acutely on this topic in chapter 1, "The Neurobiological Legacy of Trauma: How We Become Fragmented."

3 The introduction and pages 1–3 of Ann Ulanov's *The Unshuttered Heart: Opening Aliveness/Deadness in the Self* (Nashville: Abingdon Press, 2007), as well as her teaching, influence the thought behind the ideas in this paragraph. Ulanov expresses the concept of enduring after trauma in terms of "aliveness," a process that instead of being captured, is symbolized. Psychology and religion

facilitate the process, providing guiding questions. Two are significant here: (1) What makes for aliveness in the therapeutic endeavor that leads to healing?; and (2) What do "we believe of the reality our symbols point to that makes us feel connected to the source of aliveness?," x.

4 Judith Herman introduces this as the "central dialectic of trauma" in *Trauma and Recovery* (New York: Basic Books, 1997), 1.

5 Specific definitions and functions of each institution—memorial or museum—vary, and the interpretations of what constitutes history and memory change according to the country and organizational bodies within countries that establish the definitions. For instance, in the United States, the American Association of Museums defines a museum's central role as education, while in Australia, the International Council for Museums defines the spaces according to what they contain, not their intention; see "Core Standards for Museums," American Alliance of Museums, accessed August 20, 2022, https://www.aam-us.org/programs/ethics-standards-and-professional-practices/core-standards-for-museums/, and chapter 2 of K. F. Lehman, "Museums and Marketing in an Electronic Age," PhD thesis (University of Tasmania, 2008).

6 Ashley Rogers, Executive Director of the Whitney Plantation, conversation for podcast series *Bearing Witness*, July 15, 2022.

7 See Alon Confino and his discussion on the "politics of memory" in "Collective Memory and Cultural History: Problems of Method," *The American Historical Review* 102, no. 5 (1997): 1386–403, and his reference on p. 1393 to Peter Burke, who, Confino states, poses such questions in relation to social amnesia. Peter Burke, "History as a Social Memory," in *Memory: History, Culture and the Mind*, ed. Thomas Butler (New York: Blackwell, 1989), 108.

8 See James E. Young, "The Memorial's Vernacular Arc," in *The Stages of Memory: Reflections on Memorial Art, Loss and the Spaces Between* (Amherst: University of Massachusetts Press, 2017). Young differentiates between "collective memory" and "collected memory," preferring the latter in his observation that "we recognize that we never really shared each other's actual memory of past or even recent events, but that in sharing common spaces in

which we collect our disparate and competing memories, we find common (even a national) understanding of very disparate experiences and our very reasons for recalling them," 15. Young also deals with the differentiation in collective and collected memories in "The Memorial's Arc: Between Berlin's *Denkmal* and New York City's 9/11 Memorial," *Memory Studies* 9, no. 3 (July 2016): 325–31.

9 Jeffrey Barash, personal email exchange, June 2022.

10 Images serve as languages, as bearers of "iconographic signs." Images are also capable of overstepping "the confines of the contexts in which they emerge . . . to spontaneously communicate a sensuous meaning that written language can only indirectly convey"; see Jeffery Andrew Barash, *Collective Memory and the Historical Past* (Chicago: University of Chicago Press, 2016), 124.

11 Avishai Margalit, *Ethics of Memory* (Cambridge, MA: Harvard University Press, 2002), 155. See also Shelly Rambo, *Spirit and Trauma: A Theology of Remaining* (Louisville, KY: Westminster John Knox Press, 2010), 22–26, where Rambo offers a thorough account of the witness related to trauma, memory, and theology.

12 See Margalit, *Ethics of Memory*, 148–51, and what he calls the "moral witness."

13 Herman, *Trauma and Recovery*, 1–3.

14 Herman, *Trauma and Recovery*, 2.

15 Herman, *Trauma and Recovery*, 8.

16 Herman, *Trauma and Recovery*, 7.

17 Richard Gillett starts his inquiry with a question regarding the significance of the worker in globalization's distancing economics from theology. He argues that theology be brought "under the same tent" as the economy. For him, the whole capitalist system relies on the worker, requiring a theology of work that takes seriously the dignity of the worker. The workers matter in his estimation, and he presses engagement from interfaith communities in the lives of workers everywhere. Questions I ask in parallel to his insistence on considering the workers alongside the imbrication of theology and the economy: What is the significance of the memorial museum worker in recovery from trauma? And where does religion/theology emerge in secular space where faith claims are either obscured or not welcomed? See Richard

Gillett, "Workers: A Missing Link in the Theology–Economics Debate," *ATR* 92, no. 4 (October 2010): 753–60.

18 See Henry Greenspan, Sara R. Horowitz, Éva Kovács, Berel Lang, Dori Laub, Kenneth Waltzer, and Annette Wieviorka, "Engaging Survivors: Assessing 'Testimony' and 'Trauma' as Foundational Concepts," *Dapim: Studies on the Holocaust* 28, no. 3 (2014): 205. The authors frame testimony further, as "testifying to God's presence and conferring an easy, because uncontested, meaning on suffering."

19 See David Tracy, *Fragments*, including his discussion of the hermeneutic nature of Paul Tillich's correlational method, which correlates the message with the situation, 214; see also the chapter that details his conception of the situation: "The Situation: The Emergence of the Uncanny," in *The Analogical Imagination: Christian Theology and the Question of Pluralism* (New York: The Crossroad Publishing Company, 1981), 19–33. A more robust discussion of the situation can be found in chapter 1 of this text.

20 Tracy contends that theology constitutes public theology, participating in public discourse. Each theologian accordingly "addresses three distinct and related social realities: the wider society, the academy, and the church"; see Tracy, *The Analogical Imagination*, 5.

21 Tracy, *Fragments*, 11–15.

22 The traditional form of wrestling with suffering appears as theodicy. Theodicy asks: How do people and communities maintain belief in a good God in the face of human evil? Shelly Rambo states an important reality that emerges in the conflict of questions inherent in memorialization: "While theodicies might provide explanation [of human suffering], the degree to which explanations are helpful to the healing process is unclear"; see *Spirit and Trauma*, 5.

23 William T. Cavanaugh, *Torture and Eucharist* (Oxford: Blackwell, 1998). Cavanaugh's assertion relates to the malleability of terms like "politics" and "religion"—I add memorialization as a means of responding to political evidence of death and torture. Cavanaugh states that the real theoretical mistake lies in treating politics and religion "as two essentially distinct activities

occupying distinct 'spaces' which can be either mixed or kept separate," 86–87.

24 Paul Ricoeur, *Figuring the Sacred* (Minneapolis: Fortress Press, 1995), 28.

25 See Bessel van der Kolk, *The Body Keeps the Score* (New York: Penguin, 2015), in which he addresses a central experience of survivors in the aftermath, having reactions that feel "incomprehensible and overwhelming. Feeling out of control, survivors of trauma often begin to fear that they are damaged to the core and beyond redemption," 2.

26 Gillett, "Workers," offers the words and concerns that I apply to the memorial museum worker.

27 Johann Baptist Metz, "The Future in the Memory of Suffering," in *New Questions on God,* ed. Johannes Baptist Metz (New York: Herder & Herder, 1972), 15.

28 See Sharon Welch, "Dangerous Memory and Alternate Knowledges," in *On Violence,* ed. Bruce B. Lawrence and Aisha Karim (Durham: Duke University Press, 2007), 362–76.

29 Carrie Doehring, *The Practice of Pastoral Care: A Postmodern Approach* (Louisville, KY: John Knox Press, 2015), xxiv.

30 This retrieval can be commonly understood through Carl Jung's work on the archetypes, specifically on the wounded healer; see Carl Jung, *The Practice of Psychotherapy: Essays on the Psychology of the Transference and Other Subjects* (New York: Pantheon Books, 1966).

31 bell hooks, *Wounds of Passion* (New York: Macmillan, 1999), 157.

Chapter 1

1 Michael Arad, "Finalists Statements," *The New York Times,* November 19, 2003, https://www.nytimes.com/2003/11/19/nyregion/finalists-statements.html.

2 Pope Francis, "Speech at the 9/11 Memorial & Museum," *Catholic News Agency,* https://www.catholicnewsagency.com/news/32701/full-text-pope-francis-speech-at-the-911-memorial-and-museum.

3 "9/11 Memorial & Museum Mission," 9/11 Memorial & Museum, accessed February 2, 2021, https://www.911memorial. org/about.

4 Tracy, *Fragments*, "Every theology lives in its own situation," 339. Tracy revises Paul Tillich's method of correlation between the "situation" and the "message"; see Paul Tillich, *Systematic Theology* (Chicago: University of Chicago Press, 1967). Tracy also departs from Tillich in the interpretation of the human condition at the time of the question: Tracy redefines Tillich's existential question in the face of "conflictual pluralism," 342. The situation as presented here builds on Tracy's formulation, taking that formulation as a framework for analysis of the memorial museum and its situation. Tillich establishes the definition of the situation "as one pole of all theological work," which "does not refer to the psychological or sociological state in which individuals or groups live. It refers to the scientific and artistic, the economic, political, and ethical forms in which they express their interpretation of existence," (3–4). Although Tillich seeks to correlate the situation with the tradition, what he does with it is therefore different than Tracy. Tillich still wants to avoid the totalizing of it, "The 'situation' to which theology must respond is the totality of man's creative self-interpretation in a special period. Fundamentalism and orthodoxy reject this task, and, in doing so, they miss the meaning of theology," 4.

5 Tracy, *Fragments*, 346. His lens draws into juxtaposition unconscious/conscious, and individual/communal. This underscores that although the particular way doing memorialization is culturally bounded, consideration of the workers from different countries reveals shared behaviors, responses to trauma, and experiences.

6 This idea of entering into another's pain that I use throughout the texts has its psychological roots in empathy; see my chapter on empathy in *Shame, Affect Theory, and Christian Formation* (London: Palgrave, 2016) and other notes where I talk about empathy throughout this text. Theologically, I reference Henri Nouwen in *Out of Solitude: Three Meditations on the Christian Life* (Notre Dame: Ave Maria Press, 2004). See, specifically, his attention to Kierkegaard, Sartre, Camus, Hammarskjöld, and

Merton: "none of them have ever offered solutions. Yet many of us who have read their works have found new strength to pursue our own search. Their courage to enter so deeply into human suffering and to become present to their own pain gave them the power to speak healing words," 39. For more on the theological concept of entering in communion that I draw from, see John D. Zizioulas, *Being as Communion* (Yonkers: St. Vladimir's Seminary Press, 1997), and *Communion and Otherness* (Edinburgh: A&C Black, 2006).

7 Tracy, *Analogical Imagination,* 47, "If the social portrait of the theologian is marked by a recognition of complexity, the more personal portrait is marked by a recognition of that mixture of good and evil, light and darkness named ambiguity."

8 Ambiguity and its tolerance emerge as theological categories in response to ambiguous circumstances characteristic of the domain of trauma. A combat veteran asserts that in war, "The only certainty is overwhelming ambiguity"; see Herman, *Trauma and Recovery,* 53. Herman also refers to ambiguity in the therapeutic encounter of confronting trauma that both therapist and patient "must learn to live with," in the exploration of traumatic memory, 180. Tolerating ambiguity represents resilience for Pauline Boss; see "Resilience as Tolerance for Ambiguity," in *Handbook of Family Resilience,* ed. Dorothy S. Becvar (New York: Springer, 2013), 285–97. Theologically the tolerance of ambiguity emerges readily in situations characteristic of trauma. Cheryl A. Kirk-Duggan explores how African American spirituals document slavery and racism to compose a "cosmological faith" that "tolerated ambiguities and contradictions," the faith evident in the spirituals exists amidst "incongruity, absurdity and frustration"; see Cheryl A. Kirk-Duggan, "African-American Spirituals: Confronting and Exercising Evil through Song," in *A Troubling in My Soul: Womanist Perspectives on Evil and Suffering,* ed. Emile M. Townes (New York: Orbis, 1993), 157. Theologian Susan A. Ross explores and develops the characteristic nature of sacramental theology—ambiguous in itself—showing how ambiguity is a meaningful theological concept, drawing from David Tracy to do so; see Susan A. Ross, *Extravagant Affections: A Feminist Sacramental Theology* (New York: Continuum, 2001).

9 From Lois Malcom, "An Interview with David Tracy," *The Christian Century*, February 13–20, 2002, in which Tracy articulates the two things that matter to him most in postmodern thinking: (1) breaking the totality systems, especially triumphalist ones, which Christianity is always tempted to be; and (2) attending, both intellectually and spiritually, not to the self but to the other.

10 Behind the idea of plurality lies Hannah Arendt's discussion of the human condition, or the conditions of human existence in *The Human Condition* (Chicago: University of Chicago Press, 1989); plurality is one among life, natality, mortality, worldliness, and the earth, 11. Her assertion of this condition lies at the heart of understanding the testimonies in this text as distinct but yet unveiling some common phenomenon related to memorialization: "Plurality is the condition of human action because we are all the same, that is, human, in such a way, that nobody is ever the same as anyone else who ever lived, lives or will live," 8. Bonnie Mann and Jean Keller interpret Arendt, when she writes that "Pluralism . . . is nothing short of an affirmation of a shared world that is necessary for meaning to emerge between us at all. At the same time, pluralism affirms the distinctness of the perspectives through which a shared world is constituted"; see Bonnie Mann and Jean Keller, "Why a Feminist Volume on Pluralism?" *Philosophical Topics* 41, no. 2 (2013): 4.

11 Tracy expands on the difficult task of discernment in *Fragments* in an evaluation of the theologian who has fled "into the less pressing demands upon the human spirit where the visions of other theologians can be reduced to curiosities and labels, where the risk of asking the questions which constitute religions and theologies can be replaced by the less arduous, more respectable task of asking about the curious questions which other people seem to ask," 345.

12 Tracy, *Fragments*, 351. This use of "porous" facilitates Tracy's description of what is "uncanny." His interpretation, alongside Freud's use of the term, inform this idea of how trauma and new meaning emerge in the memorial museum; see Sigmund Freud, *The Uncanny* (London: Penguin, 2003). Freud elaborates the uncanny as that which was meant to be hidden away and now has come into the open, that which is unexplainable, such as the

confirmation of an old, discarded belief; that which is mysterious (154); and that which indicates that the boundary of reality and fantasy has been blurred (150).

13 This notion of numinous appears in Paul Ricoeur's use of the term in his construction of a phenomenology of the sacred; see Ricoeur, *Refiguring the Sacred*. In the text, Ricoeur constructs the sacred as having five traits briefly articulated here and cited throughout the chapter. The traits consist of (1) having the character of provoking *tremendum*, of being overwhelming, (2) eliding description itself but manifesting—this manifestation can be described, (3) revealing itself in behavior, (4) possessing a function of cosmic polarities, (5) and following a law of correspondence.

14 These words derive from David Tracy's quote above. It is worth also citing dangerous memories, as they reflect a theme throughout this text in terms of what the memorial museum affects or does: disrupt the status quo and inspire oppressed groups to resist and redefine their lives and identities. See Metz, "The Future in the Memory of Suffering," 9–20; Michalinos Zembylas and Zvi Bekerman, "Education and the Dangerous Memories of Historical Trauma: Narratives of Pain, Narratives of Hope," *Curriculum Inquiry* 38, no. 2 (2008): 125–54.

15 See Mary Daly, *Beyond God the Father* (Boston: Beacon Press, 1993). I draw attention to two points in her argument about method, which she initially distinguishes from Paul Tillich's "correlation," "the method is not one of correlation but of *liberation*," specifically of language, 8. The first is that the method should emerge from the problems a person faces, here trauma at the memorial museum. The second is that method is a "reclaiming of the right to name," important as a response to trauma, related to both achieving agency (the right) and identifying the trauma at all, proclaiming it aloud, or acknowledging it.

16 My use of the concept of public theology straddles two methods articulated by E. Harold Breitenberg Jr., "To Tell the Truth: Will the Real Public Theology Please Stand Up?" *Journal of the Society of Christian Ethics* 23, no. 2 (2003): 55–96. The first is informed by the work of David Tracy, used extensively in this chapter, that defines the three publics—society, the academy, and the church

(see Tracy, *Analogical Imagination*)—and focuses on how public theology should be carried out. The second underscores concerns that are of interest and importance to both the church and the larger societies. Breitenberg's essay is dense, and the field has since expanded, but some of his critical points underlie assumptions made about theology in this book. I note a few: public theology lies at the intersection of theology and ethics (65); "public theology addresses issues that bear upon a religious community but also pertain to the larger society, including people of other faith traditions or who claim none," (57); public theology relies heavily on resources, research, and methods that are available to the general public and are not necessarily Christian; public theology provides theologically informed interpretations; public theology communicates how Christian authorship and practice informs public life and the common good, persuades both Christians and non-Christians to action, 65–66; public theology "gives interpretations of and guidance to society's various sectors, institutions, and interactions, and possibly to evaluate between religious beliefs and practices as they bear on matters of public concern," 67.

17 See Robert McAfee Brown, *Kairos: Three Prophetic Challenges to the Church* (Grand Rapids, MI: Eerdmans, 1990), 5–7.

18 Katy Day and Sebastian Kim, "Introduction," in *A Companion to Public Theology*, ed. Katy Day and Sebastian Kim (Leiden: Brill, 2017), assert that E. Harold Breitenberg's definition of public theology captures a fundamental essence of public theology that distinguishes it from other forms of theology and ethics, that it is as much about process as content, where the process of construction is "socially interactive," 5–6.

19 The Archbishop of Canterbury, "Archbishop of Canterbury and Chief Rabbi Visit Yad Vashem," The Archbishop of Canterbury, March 5, 2017, https://www.archbishopofcanterbury .org/speaking-and-writing/latest-news/archbishop-canterbury- and-chief-rabbi-visit-yad-vashem.

20 "Khmer New Year Blessing Ceremony," Tuol Sleng Genocide Museum, accessed October 1, 2022, https://tuolsleng.gov.kh/ en/2016/05/16/khmer-new-year-blessing-ceremony/, and The

Associated Press, "Cambodia Inaugurates Memorial at Khmer Rouge Genocide Museum," KSL.com, March 26, 2015.

21 This conjoinment can be further clarified by Ricoeur's understanding of the relationship between ritual and cosmic paradigms, which evidences the sacred. Ricoeur writes, "The work of agriculture, in other words, more than any other expresses this relation between ritual and the cosmic paradigms." Agriculture parallels the work of memorialization in its transportation to the cosmic, reflected in myths for instance about trauma, life, and death; see Ricoeur, *Figuring the Sacred*, 52.

22 Annie Rogers, *The Unsayable: The Hidden Language of Trauma* (New York: Ballantine Books, 2007).

23 David Tracy, *Plurality and Ambiguity: Hermeneutics, Religion, and Hope* (Chicago: University of Chicago Press, 1987), 70.

24 David Tracy, "The Role of Theology in Public Life: Some Reflections," *Word & World* 4, no. 3 (1984) 230–39, in which Tracy writes, "Theology is substantially precarious by trying to think the seemingly impossible." His ultimate thesis is that "theology should play a role in the public realm because theology helps us all to ask the kinds of questions which all reflective human beings ask," 231–32.

25 See Rogers, *The Unsayable*.

26 See Edward Linenthal, *Preserving Memory: The Struggle to Create America's Holocaust Museum* (New York: Columbia University Press, 2001), in which the author discusses Elie Wiesel's position that the United States Holocaust Memorial Museum needed to be a place where the impossibility of knowing existed alongside the traditional ways of knowing in a museum, 122.

27 See Judith Butler, *Precarious Life: The Powers of Mourning and Violence* (New York: Verso, 2006), where we are undone by the other in desire and grief: "one is undone in the face of the other, by the touch, by the scent, by the feel, by the prospect of touch, by the memory of the feel," 23–24. Butler describes the process more fully on page 32: "For if I am confounded by you, then you are already of me, and I am nowhere without you. I cannot muster the 'we' except by finding the way in which I am tied to 'you,' by trying to translate but finding that my own language must break up and yield if I am to know you. You are what I

gain through this disorientation and loss. This is how the human comes into being, again and again, as that which we have yet to know." Xochitl Alvizo, in "Being Undone by the Other: Feminisms, Blogs, and Critique," in *Feminism and Religion in the 21st Century: Utilizing Technology to Expand Borders*, 67–81, ed. Gina Messina-Dysert and Rosemary Radford Ruether (New York: Routledge, 2015), picks up the notion of the undone in Butler and expands to consider the work of Saba Mahmood as open to being undone or "remade" by another's point of view. From another angle, see also James Cone, *The Cross and the Lynching Tree* (Ossining: Orbis Books, 2013), 102, in which Cone discusses how W. E. B. Du Bois uses Jesus's presence and values in his stories as disruptive because he showed solidarity to poor Blacks.

28 See Tracy, *Fragments*, 239, for a theological posture that replicates this approach.

29 Johannes Kritzinger and Martin Mande, "Theology Disrupted by the Challenge of Refugee Children," *HTS: Theological Studies* 72, no. 1 (2016): 1–10.

30 Tracy, *Fragments*, 343.

31 Desmond Tutu, *God Has a Dream: A Vision of Hope for Our Time* (New York: Doubleday, 2003), vii.

32 Tutu, *God Has a Dream*, vii.

33 Judges 19:30, *National Revised Standard Version*. See Daisy Machado, "The Undocumented Woman in Aquino," in *A Reader in Latina Feminist Theology: Religion and Justice*, ed. Maria Pilar, Daisy Machado, and Jeanette Rodriguez (New York: University of Texas Press, 2021), 161–76: "While we in the theological academy enjoy the luxury of time in which to research and write, and while we have available to us a space in which to share our ideas, the urgency of the reality of the unnamed women of the border challenges us to rethink what our task is about. Elena's disfigured face is a witness to the violence, vulnerability, powerlessness so many women experience. She is no longer a statistic. You know her story. You have seen her face. You have heard her voice. The biblical imperative calls to us: consider what you have seen, take counsel on what action to take, and speak."

34 "Conflict is the situation, conversation is the hope"; Tracy, *Fragments*, 363.

35 Emma Justes, *Hearing Beyond the Words: How to Become a Listening Pastor* (Nashville: Abingdon Press, 2006): "The feeling content in what is spoken and what we hear may be more important than the words used for speaking," xiii.

36 I am marked in this sentiment again by Daisy Machado, "The Unnamed Woman," about going to the borderlands. Machado meets Elena—who, likened to the unnamed women in Judges 19, has no control over her fate—at the borderlands, introduced by a previous concentration camp survivor in Cuba who is now a minister, Reverend F. Feliberto Pereira. Here I underscore Machado's immersion in another social location, into the area of what Gloria Anzaldúa calls "an open wound"; see Gloria E. Anzaldúa, *Borderlands/La Frontera: The New Mestiza*, 3rd ed. (San Francisco: Aunt Lute Books, 2006).

37 Doehring, *The Practice of Pastoral Care*, vvii. Doehring articulates this sense of hospitality for pastoral care that addresses a pluralistic world: "We must embody compassionate respect, step over the threshold, and enter into another's religious or spiritual world, not knowing when we will encounter sacred images, meanings, and places within the narrative worlds of care seekers."

38 Shelly Rambo complicates the notion of a quick or stable solution in the theological response to suffering throughout her work; see *Spirit and Trauma*, and *Resurrecting Wounds: Living in the Aftermath of Trauma* (Waco: Baylor University Press, 2017). For this reference specifically, see Shelly Rambo, "Spirit and Trauma," *Interpretation: A Journal of Bible and Theology* 69, no. 9 (January 2015): 13: "Theology, in its narration of death and life, can fuel the 'get over it already' statements that Deacon Lee and others heard in the aftermath of Hurricane Katrina."

39 See Dietrich Bonhoeffer, *Letters and Papers from Prison* (New York: Macmillan, 1972) and his explication of what faith is, 369–70.

40 See Edward Farley, *Divine Empathy: A Theology of God* (Minneapolis: Fortress Press, 1996), and his discussion of trust in the I–Thou relationship, 90–93.

41 See Eric Fromm, *The Art of Listening* (London: Continuum, 1998).

42 See Joan Halifax, *Standing at the Edge: Finding Freedom Where Fear and Courage Meet* (New York: Flatiron Books, 2018). She conceives of compassion as never running out and thus complicating a diagnosis of "compassion fatigue."

43 These two terms came from independent interviews. The first took place in New York in 2018 in a conversation at the 9/11 Memorial & Museum between workers there and from the Apartheid Museum. "Guardians of memory" was a phrase used by a researcher from South Africa. This phrase, "guardians of memory," is also displayed on the Srebrenica Memorial Center website. An independent interview with a worker from the 9/11 Memorial & Museum included an additional expression reflective of being a "guardian": "I think when you work for museums, you know you are never going to get a million dollars, but you feel like you are a steward of history."

44 See Henri Nouwen, *The Wounded Healer* (New York: Doubleday, 1979): "Indeed, the paradox of Christian leadership is that the way out is the way in, that only by entering into communion with human suffering can relief be found," 78.

45 Ricoeur defines this alongside Freud as nothing other than a continual narration; see Paul Ricoeur, *On Psychoanalysis: Writings and Lectures* (Cambridge: Polity, 2012), 43.

46 C. S. Lewis, *The Problem of Pain* (Grand Rapids, MI: Zondervan, 2001), in which he describes at length his notion of the uncanny and the numinous.

47 Deirdre Colgan, "Visiting Sacred Spaces: A "How-To" Guide with Tips & Suggestions for Groups & Individuals" (Sacred Space International, 2010), https://www-tc.pbs.org/godinamerica/art/VisitingSacredSpaces.pdf.

48 Many of the sites include designated areas for contemplation, reflection, or processing. The African American History Museum, the 9/11 Memorial & Museum, and the Apartheid Museum have spaces for reflection at their sites, and Freedom Park has an area for accessing ancestors where one removes shoes.

49 Deirdre Colgan, *Visiting Sacred Spaces*, asserts, "We believe that religion should be part of the discussion, relying upon people who use the particular space to help. We view it as an opportunity, a teachable moment, otherwise, the function of the sacred space just sits there—like an 800-pound gorilla in the room."

50 Deirdre Colgan, *Visiting Sacred Spaces*. The authors use Emile Durkheim's definition of sacred, see Emile Durkheim, *The Elementary Forms of Religious Life*, trans. Karen E. Fields (New York: The Free Press, 1995). Furthermore, the word "conscience" evokes the International Coalition of Sites of Conscience, a coalition of places of memory that provide *safe* spaces to remember and preserve tragedy. Many but not all sites identified in this study are members of the coalition. The coalition supports grieving, casting a positive moral valence in its rejection of indifference and support of political action even as it endeavors to be pluralistic. In the guide and the coalition, memory rests in the sphere of the sacred or moral, a sphere that protects mourning; see International Coalition of Sites of Conscience, https://www.sitesof conscience.org/en/home/.

51 Linenthal, *Preserving Memory*. Linenthal comments on the erecting of the United States National Holocaust Memorial Museum on "the nation's most sacred soil—home of the monumental expressions of core national narratives—that would now be ceremonially commingled with 'holy soils' from European concentration and death camps and venerated cemeteries: Auschwitz, Bergen-Belsen, Dachau, Theresienstadt, Treblinka, and the Warsaw Jewish Cemetery," 57.

52 Fred Schwartz, "Reflecting on the Essence of Auschwitz," *The New York Times*, February 26, 2011, https://www.nytimes.com/2011/02/27/opinion/l27auschwitz.html.

53 Yad Vashem, "Newsletter no. 29, May 2013," accessed March 10, 2021, https://www.yadvashem.org/yv/en/newsletters/general/newsletter_print.asp?cid=1052013.

54 "Tuol Sleng Genocide Museum," Tuol Sleng Genocide Museum, accessed October 1, 2022, https://tuolsleng.gov.kh/en/museum/.

55 Tom Baxter, "South Africa: The Roller Coaster, The Casino, and Sacred Memory," SaportaReport, September 25, 2017,

https://saportareport.com/south-africa-roller-coaster-casino-sacred-memory/.

56 "Remembering Srebrenica Comment on the Desecration of the Srebrenica Genocide Memorial," Remembering Srebrenica, accessed October 1, 2022, https://srebrenica.org.uk/news/remembering-srebrenica-comment-desecration.

57 "9/11 Memorial & Museum Mission," 9/11 Memorial & Museum, accessed February 2, 2021, https://www.911memorial.org/about.

58 Durkheim, *The Elementary Forms of Religious Life*.

59 For Ricoeur, to describe what is numinous, we must describe how it manifests. Very few interviews I conducted, if any, failed to use the word "sacred" to describe either the space of the memorial museum or its function to remember lost lives and human suffering; see Ricoeur, *Figuring the Sacred*, 49. Linenthal, *Preserving Memory*, 82, asserts this directly related to the building of the United States Holocaust Memorial Museum: "the whole museum building was a secret environment, and it was inconceivable to them that any part of a building devoted to Holocaust memory could be characterized as non-sacred."

60 Linenthal, *Preserving Memory*, 122, discusses the museum, specifically the United States Holocaust Memorial Museum, the place where "the sacred mystery that was the Holocaust would stamp itself on individual psyches, and visitors would, ideally, emerge with a new appreciation of mystery."

61 Ben Anderson, "Affective Atmospheres," *Emotion, Space and Society* 2, no. 2 (2009): 77–81. Anderson references affectivity and subsequent ambiguity. Ricoeur, *Figuring the Sacred*, 54–55, frames the structure of the sacred as emerging from correspondences, between creation and natural appearances for instance. At the root of the law of correspondences lies the capacity of the cosmos to signify something other than itself.

62 To approach the "Uncanny at the fringes of the Numinous" derives from C. S. Lewis, *The Problem of Pain*, 6. See also Catherine Wanner, "An Affective Atmosphere of Religiosity: Animated Places, Public Spaces, and the Politics of Attachment in the Ukraine and Beyond," *Comparative Studies* 62, no. 1 (2020): 68–105. Wanner critiques the evolution of religion

into religious nationalism. She envisions the process beginning, in part, when religious institutions engage the secular in public forums affecting religiosity. In the memorial museum, I see a similar trajectory—although the spaces are secular institutions assuming a sacred role—with a different end. Memorial museums foster an affective atmosphere of religiosity, based on their assumption of sacred space. The atmosphere "has motivational power," for believers and for nonbelievers, as it accesses and shapes—affectively and sensorially—those who visit the public space.

63 Larry Kent Graham, "Pastoral Theology and Catastrophic Disaster," *Journal of Pastoral Theology* 16, no. 2 (2006): 1–17.

64 Rudolph Otto, *The Idea of the Holy*, trans. John W. Harvey (Oxford: Oxford University Press, 1923; 2nd ed., 1950), in which Otto defines the *mysterium tremendum* as a designation of the numinous constituting an emotional response of dread and awe and having the character of provoking shaking. Ricoeur, *Figuring the Sacred*, 49, where he discusses the character of "shaking" before Rudolph Otto's *tremendum*. See also Arthur A. Cohen, *The Tremendum: A Theological Interpretation of the Holocaust* (New York: Continuum, 1993). Cohen retrieves Otto's language for the holy as the uncanny *mysterium tremendum*, defining the Holocaust as *tremendum* that goes beyond—as in beyond below—thought and action. These words from Cohen depict the wake of the *tremendum,* for Cohen the Holocaust, to which the memorial museum speaks: "We are in the fourth decade. The distance between ourselves and the event of the *tremendum* has grown. The survivors persist, most in private communication with their memories, most silent; others, vigorously, often desperately trying to bridge the chasm which opened beneath them, then, nearly 40 years ago, talking to us well and badly, convincingly and truly, patiently and irritably, superior to us and supercilious, guarding as they do a body of images and imaginings; or else vaguely and mystically, floating beyond us, palpable ghosts and spectres of a world we never knew. To the side of the survivors have come, however, in recent years, other aids and interpreters, the thinkers," 5. The memorial museum enters as an aid.

65 Ricoeur, *Figuring the Sacred*, 51, on how the ritual as a modality of acting reveals the sacred in behavior.

66 "Day of Reconciliation," SouthAfrica.co.za, accessed October 1, 2022, https://southafrica.co.za/day-of-reconciliation.html.

67 Katarina Panić, "The White Armband Day: Activism at Its Best," Fair Planet, June 6, 2020, https://www.fairplanet.org/editors-pick/the-white-armband-day-activism-at-its-best/.

68 Durkheim, *The Elementary Forms of Religious Life*, 285.

69 Doris Francis, "Cemeteries as Cultural Landscapes," *Mortality* 8, no. 2 (2003): 57–69, specifically 223, where she fosters an understanding of the memorial museum as a cemetery, "The cemetery is the appropriate sacred space where the living and the dead are separated and symbolically joined as one people through the performance of transition and memorial rites. The annual Memorial Day rituals, a modern cult of the dead, integrate the various faiths, associations, ethnic and class groups of the city into a unified community; and as a sacred collectivity they confront and triumph over anxieties about death through common action." See also William D. Haglund, Melissa Connor, and Douglas D. Scott, "The Archaeology of Contemporary Mass Graves," *Historical Archaeology* 35, no. 1 (2001): 57–69.

70 See Arthur Kleinman, Paul E. Brodwin, Byron J. Good, and Mary-Jo Delvecchio Good, "Introduction," in *Pain as a Human Experience: An Anthropological Perspective*, ed. Mary-Jo Delvecchio Good, Paul E. Brodwin, Byron J. Good, and Arthur Kleinman (Berkeley: University of California Press, 1992), 13. "What is so impressive about current forms of suffering is the relative weakening in the modern era of moral and religious vocabularies, both in collective representations and the language of experts. In their place we see the proliferation of rational-technical professional argots that express and constitute suffering in physiological, public health, clinical, psychological, and policy terms . . . for example, talk of yearning, misery, aspirations, and transcendence [is replaced] with the much more systematic, routinized, quantified talk about biomedical and psychiatric and legal and policy issues. The transformation of language is notable, even within the social sciences, for leaving out the human spirit and the sacred."

71 Pope Francis, "Speech at the 9/11 Memorial & Museum," *Catholic News Agency*, https://www.catholicnewsagency.com/news/32701/full-text-pope-francis-speech-at-the-911-memorial-and-museum.

72 Pope Francis, "Speech at the 9/11 Memorial & Museum."

Chapter 2

1 See "Antisemitism Explained," Horwitz-Wasserman Holocaust Memorial Plaza, accessed July 17, 2022, https://www.philaho locaustmemorial.org/antisemitism-explained/; cartoons exhibit ideological messages and serve as persuasive forms of propaganda, facilitating anti-Semitism prior to World War II; see "Propaganda and the Visual Arts in the Third Reich," Yad Vashem, accessed August 19, 2022, https://www.yadvashem.org/education/educational-materials/lesson-plans/germanys-sculptor.html, and Dominic Williams, "*Punch* and the Pogroms: Eastern Atrocities in John Tenniel's Political Cartoons, 1876–1896," *Canadian Art Review* 42, no. 1 (2017): 32–47.

2 Rare Historical Photos, "The Racist Signs of Apartheid Seen through Rare Photographs, 1950–1990," Photos, December 12, 2021, https://rarehistoricalphotos.com/signs-apartheid-south-africa-1950-1990/.

3 Religion played a central role in Afrikaner identity. Most Afrikaners were members of the Dutch Reformed Church in South Africa, a strict and conservative Calvinist church that promoted the belief that the Afrikaners were a new "chosen people" to whom God had given South Africa. As a result of the religious claim of identity, Afrikaners saw themselves as a select group whose right to the land was greater than any other group's. Journalist Terry Bell explains the role of religion in the outlook of those who supported the National Party: "Afrikaners [saw themselves] as players in the unfolding of the Book of Revelations, upholding the light of Christian civilization against an advancing wall of darkness . . . It was God's will that the 'Afrikaner nation' . . . linked by language and a narrow Calvinism . . . had been placed on the southern tip of the African continent"; see *Unfinished Business: South Africa, Apartheid and Truth* (London: Verso, 2003), 23. This quote

appeared first in Barbra Brown and Timothy Longman, "Confronting Apartheid," *Facing History and Ourselves* (blog), 2018, https://www.facinghistory.org/confronting-apartheid/chapter-2/introduction.

4 John Marston, "Khmer Rouge Songs," *Crossroads: An Interdisciplinary Journal of Southeast Asian Studies* 16, no. 1 (2002): 105.

5 See James Cone's *The Cross and the Lynching Tree* (Ossining: Orbis Books, 2013), 15–16. Cone discusses Thomas Dixon's *The Leopard's Spots: A Romance of the White Man's Burden—1865–1900* (New York: Doubleday, 1903), *The Clansman: An Historical Romance of the Ku Klux Klan* (New York: Grosset & Dunlap, 1905), and the film *directed* by D. W. Griffith, *Birth of a Nation* (Los Angeles, CA: Triangle Film Corp., 1915). Furthermore, lynching has at its roots the history of slavery in the United States. Religious, biblical, and historical sanctions supporting slavery mobilize in writing and rhetoric in the early 1800s; see Larry E. Tise, *Proslavery: A History of the Defense of Slavery in America, 1701–1840* (Athens: University of Georgia Press, 1987).

6 Arnaud Siad, "The 'Butcher of Bosnia' Radovan Karadzic Will Serve His Genocide Sentence in a UK Prison," CNN, May 12, 2021, https://www.cnn.com/2021/05/12/europe/radovan-karadzic-uk-prison-genocide-sentence-intl/index.html. Western media outlets have also called Ratko Mladić by the same name. See The Week Staff, "'Butcher of Bosnia': Why War Criminal Ratko Mladic Has Hero Status Among Some in the Balkans," *The Week,* June 9, 2021, https://www.theweek.co.uk/news/world-news/europe/953073/why-ratko-mladic-butcher-of-bosnia-still-hero-balkans.

7 Gabrijela Kišiček, "The Rhetoric of War—Former Yugoslavia Example," *Journal of Arts and Humanities* 2, no. 8 (2013): 81.

8 John Miller, "Greetings America, My Name Is Osama Bin Laden . . .," Frontline, February 1, 1999, https://www.pbs.org/wgbh/pages/frontline/shows/binladen/who/miller.html.

9 David Adler, "Story of Cities #19: Johannesburg's Apartheid Purge of Vibrant Sophiatown," *The Guardian*, April 11, 2016, https://www.theguardian.com/cities/2016/apr/11/story-cities-19-johannesburg-south-africa-apartheid-purge-sophiatown.

10 Albert J. Raboteau, *Slave Religion: The "Invisible Institution" in the Antebellum South* (Oxford: Oxford University Press, 2004), 154.

11 Anthony B. Pinn and Anne H. Pinn, *Fortress Introduction to Black Church History* (Minneapolis: Fortress Press, 2002), 4.

12 Pinn and Pinn, *Fortress Introduction to Black Church History,* 4–5.

13 212 Brdska Brigada Srebrenik, "Serbs Demolition of a Mosque in Bijeljina, and Ethnic Cleansing 17.3.93," YouTube video, January 30, 2012, 6:35, https://www.youtube.com/watch?v=Vze9v9GrO5w; András J. Riedlmayer, *"Destruction of Cultural Heritage in Bosnia-Herzegovina, 1992–1996: A Post-War Survey Of Selected Municipalities"* (Cambridge: International Criminal Tribunal for the Former Yugoslavia, 2002), accessed August 17, 2022, http://heritage.sensecentar.org/assets/sarajevo-national-library/sg-3-01-destruction-culturale-en.pdf.

14 Signs erected by Roma Sendyka and her students indicate small portions of the camp. The signs had been up for less than a year upon my visit in spring 2018.

15 Linenthal discusses this dynamic in *Preserving Memory,* see specifically the Preface, x.

16 Shoshana Felman and Dori Laub, *Testimony: Crisis of Witnessing in Literature, Psychoanalysis, and History* (New York: Routledge, 1992), 64.

17 Thomas Lynch on burying babies, from *The Undertaking: Life Studies from the Dismal Trade* (New York: W. W. Norton, 2010), 50–51.

18 Reports on numbers of those finally murdered and liberated vary. The statistics shown here derive from "The Number of Victims," Auschwitz-Birkenau Memorial Museum, accessed August 19, 2022, https://www.auschwitz.org/en/history/auschwitz-and-shoah/the-number-of-victims/. See also Natasha Frost, "Horrors of Auschwitz: The Numbers Behind WWII's Deadliest Concentration Camp," History, January 21, 2020, https://www.history.com/news/auschwitz-concentration-camp-numbers.

19 "Death March from Auschwitz," United States Holocaust Museum, accessed July 17, 2022, https://www.ushmm.org/learn/timeline-of-events/1942-1945/death-march-from-auschwitz.

20 "Auchwitz-Birkenau Extermination Camp," Yad Vashem, accessed July 17, 2022, https://www.yadvashem.org/holocaust/about/final-solution/auschwitz.html.

21 Companies with specialties in disaster management attend to uncovering mass graves. "Mass Grave Exhumation and Identification," Kenyon Emergency Services, accessed July 17, 2022, https://www.kenyoninternational.com/Our-Services/Disaster-Recovery-Services/mass-grave-exhumation-and-identification/.

22 "Mass Grave Exhumation and Identification," Kenyon Emergency Services.

23 The Documentation Center of Cambodia, "Mapping Project," accessed August 18, 2022, http://d.dccam.org/Projects/Maps/Mapping.htm.

24 Katherine Gruspier and Michael S. Pollanen, "Forensic Legacy of the Khmer Rouge: The Cambodian Genocide," *Academic Forensic Pathology* 7, no. 3 (2017): 415–33.

25 In 2005, the site's sale to the Japanese management company JC Royal Company eliminated the walk upon natural ground as the new owners added boardwalks and wooden walkways; Seth Mydans, "Cambodia Profits from Killing Fields and Other Symbols," *The New York Times,* November 6, 2005, https://www.nytimes.com/2005/11/06/world/asia/cambodia-profits-from-killing-fields-and-other-symbols.html.

26 This juxtaposition concretizes Choeung Ek as a cemetery viewed in light of Foucault's heterotopia; see Michel Foucault and J. Miskowiec, "On Other Spaces," *Diacritics* 16, no. 1 (1986): 22–27.

27 Nicky Rosseou, Riedwaan Moosage, and Ciraj Rassool, "Missing and Missed: Rehumanisation, the Nation and Missing-Ness," *Kronos* 44 (2018): 10.

28 Death squads operated throughout the country from 1969 to 1994, removing civilians, sometimes in cooperation but often vying for political and territorial power in the killing of those perceived as enemies of the state. Binckes, who spent several days with me in South Africa, on tours and history lessons, names some of these agencies: BOSS (Bureau of State Security), Military Intelligence, the Security Police, the Regional Security Police, Vlakplaas, South African Medical Services, and Civil Cooperation Bureau (CCB); see Robin Binckes, *Vlakplaas:*

Apartheid Death Squads, 1979–1994 (Barnsley: Pen & Sword Books, 2018).

29 Africa Watch Committee, "The Killings in South Africa: The Role of Security Forces and the Response of the State" (New York: Human Rights Watch, 1991), https://www.hrw.org/reports/1991/southafrica1/5.htm#_ftn7.

30 John Aitchison, "The Pietermaritzburg Conflict: Experience and Analysis," Centre for Adult Education, University of Natal, Pietermaritzburg, 8, quoted in Africa Watch Committee, "The Killings in South Africa: The Role of Security Forces and the Response of the State."

31 Apartheid Museum SA, "Pumla Gobodo Madikazela," YouTube video, April 4, 2019, 10:41, https://www.youtube.com/watch?v=SlJS0i64EA.

32 Mersiha Gadzo, "Can Aircraft Technology Uncover Mass Graves in Bosnia?," Aljazeera, February 23, 2021, https://www.aljazeera.com/features/2021/2/23/could-lidar-help-uncover-clandestine-mass-graves-in-bosnia.

33 Priests in Louisiana insisted that all bodies receive a proper burial, including enslaved people. Elizabeth Shown Mills and Gary B. Mills, "Missionaries Compromised: Early Evangelization of Slaves and Free People of Color in North Louisiana," in *Cross, Crozier, and Crucible*, ed. Glenn R. Conrad (New Orleans: Archdiocese of New Orleans and the Center for Louisiana Studies, 1993), 33.

34 Greg Allen, "'Thank God You Found Me': Florida Officials Unearth a Fourth Forgotten Black Cemetery," NPR, December 20, 2021, accessed August 1, 2022, https://www.npr.org/2021/12/20/1065178753/florida-fourth-black-cemetery-discovered.

35 Greg Garrison, "Slave Trade to Mass Incarceration, Museum Tells Grim Truth," *Al.com*, October 1, 2021, https://www.al.com/life/2021/10/slave-trade-to-mass-incarceration-museum-tells-grim-truth.html.

36 Corey Kilgannon, "'Reopening Old Wounds': When 9/11 Remains Are Identified, 20 Years Later," *The New York Times*, September 6, 2021, https://www.nytimes.com/2021/09/06/nyregion/9-11-ground-zero-victims-remains.html.

37 W. Lloyd Warner, *The Living and the Dead: A Study in the Symbolic Representations of Americans* (New Haven, CT: Yale University Press, 1959).

38 Thomas G. Long and Thomas Lynch, "Preface," in *The Good Funeral: Death, Grief, and the Community of Care,* ed. Thomas G. Long and Thomas Lynch, xxiii–xxiv (Louisville, KY: Westminster John Knox Press, 2013). The quote reads, "A society that is unsure about how to care for the dead and is confused about what to do with grief and loss is a society that is also uncertain about life," xxiv.

39 See Christopher Isherwood, Chester Kallman, and Wystan Hugh Auden, *The Completed Works of W. H. Auden: 1969–1973* (Princeton, NJ: Princeton University Press, 1988), 644; Auden's exact quote reads: "Without communication with the dead, a fully human life is not possible."

40 Pauline Boss developed the concept of ambiguous loss, designing interventions for the families of the missing after 9/11 who struggled with an ongoing recovery process and an absence of bodies, which obscured the fact that likely their loved one suffered incineration; see *Ambiguous Loss: Learning to Live with Unresolved Grief* (Cambridge, MA: Harvard University Press, 1999).

41 Boss, *Ambiguous Loss*, 6.

42 Boss, *Ambiguous Loss*, 5. This type of ambiguous loss represents one aspect of the loss itself: a person is dead or missing but no verification exists in either case. The other type of ambiguous loss, Boss indicates, emerges when a person remains physically present but psychologically absent, as in Alzheimer's or after certain incidences of stroke.

43 See Boss, *Ambiguous Loss*. Throughout the text Boss discusses different types of atrocities and their intersection at the point of ambiguous loss.

44 Boss, *Ambiguous Loss*, 1.

45 Boss, *Ambiguous Loss*, 3.

46 Boss, *Ambiguous Loss*, 4.

47 See Thomas G. Long, who asserts that undertaking "turns out to not merely be a job, but an act of faith, as ancient as the priesthood"; "Habeas Corpus . . . Not," in *The Good Funeral: Death,*

Grief, and the Community of Care, ed. Thomas G. Long and Thomas Lynch (Louisville, KY: Westminster John Knox Press, 2013), 92.

48 Boss, *Ambiguous Loss*, xviii.

49 James Young, *The Texture of Memory: Holocaust Memorials and Meaning* (New Haven, CT: Yale University Press, 1993), x.

50 In Cambodia, the use of tombstones is not common. Instead, bodies are cremated. Some bones may be retained and either kept in family members' homes or buried at a special place on temple grounds, close to the Buddha.

51 For a discussion of the sacred as removed from the profane, see Emile Durkheim, *The Elementary Forms of Religious Life.* Insofar as cemeteries and tombstones are sacred, see Richard A. Etlin, *The Architecture of Death: The Transformation of the Cemetery in Eighteenth-Century Paris* (Cambridge, MA: MIT Press, 1984).

52 See Marianne Hirsch's conceptualization of "Holocaust Photographs" in "Family Pictures: *Maus*, Mourning, and Post-Memory," *Discourse* 15, no. 2 (Winter 1992–93): 7.

53 See Marianne Hirsch, "Surviving Images: Holocaust Photographs and the Work of Postmemory," *The Yale Journal of Criticism* 14, no. 1 (2001): 5–37.

54 Hirsh, "Family Pictures," 7.

55 Hirsh, "Family Pictures," 6.

56 See Sharon Jackson, Kathryn Backett-Milburn, and Elinor Newall, "Researching Distressing Topics: Emotional Reflexivity and Emotional Labor in the Secondary Analysis of Children and Young People's Narratives of Abuse," *SAGE Open* (April 2013). The authors discuss the potential for an empathic and long-lasting connection with victims of sexual abuse that entails no personal encounters but rather interaction with stories and data, substantiating the claim that researching the lives of victims of trauma can lead to an emotional attachment to the victim.

57 David R. Unruh, "Death and Personal History: Strategies of Identity Preservation," *Social Problems* 30, no. 3 (1983): 345.

58 In "Ethical Space: Ethics and Propriety in Trauma Tourism," Laurie Beth Clark recognizes the different rules, how they adjust culturally, how the spaces engage in different types of consumerism, and how architecture reinforces comportment. Her

observations reinforce the concept that spaces shape visitors, and—in my research—workers, at varying degrees. See this essay and others in *Death Tourism: Disaster Sites as Recreational Landscape*, ed. Brigitte Sion (Seagull: Calcutta, 2014), 9–35. From the perspective of the workers, the phrase "recreational landscapes" captures some aspect of some of the sites but fails to encompass and address, instead minimizing, the difficulty the workers encounter daily related to the other words of the subtitle: disaster sites.

59 In *Hermeneutics and the Human Sciences* (Cambridge: Cambridge University Press, 1981), Paul Ricoeur asks and answers a question that underscores this assertion: "But what is it to remember? It is not just to recall certain isolated events, but to become capable of forming meaningful sequences and ordered connections. In short, it is to be able to constitute one's own existence in the form of a story where a memory as such is only a fragment of the story. It is the narrative structure of such life stories that make a case a case history," 153.

60 Jeffrey Alexander, "Cultural Trauma, Morality, and Solidarity: The Social Construction of 'Holocaust' and Other Mass Murders," *Thesis Eleven* 132, no. 1 (2015): 14. Alexander discusses the expansion of trauma from the individual to the collective. He differentiates traumatic processing of the two groups on the basis of the symbolic construction and framing—of creating stories and characters—needed by the "we" constructed through narrative and coding. Alexander's more general theory of cultural trauma applies to the analysis of the memorial museum; see also Jeffrey Alexander, "Toward a Theory of Cultural Trauma," in *Cultural Trauma and Collective Identity*, ed. Jeffrey C. Alexander, Ron Eyerman, Bernard Giesen, Neil J. Smelser, and Piotr Sztompka (Los Angeles: University of California Press 2004), 1–16.

61 See Herman, in her chapter in *Trauma and Recovery* on remembrance and mourning, where telling the trauma story includes understanding the circumstances leading up to the event, an assembled and detailed verbal account of the event, and a systematic review of the meaning of the event, 175–79.

62 Three hundred skulls of victims originally covered a 129-square-foot wall of bones in the form of a map at the memorial museum, but now they rest, enclosed in glass cases, near a Buddhist altar.

63 Linenthal quotes Elie Wiesel at the official groundbreaking for the United States Holocaust Memorial Museum in Washington, DC on October 16, 1985, in *Preserving Memory*, 57.

64 Melissa Meyer, *Blood Is Thicker Than Water: The Origins of Blood as Symbol and Ritual* (New York: Routledge, 2005), 5. Meyer asserts, "humans have imposed more symbolic and metaphorical meanings on blood in more ritualized contacts than any other substance. Blood symbolizes life most extensively, death secondarily. All other connotations pale in comparison to these two dominant metaphors."

65 Black in Appalachia, "Lynching Site Soil Collection: David Hurst, Kent Junction, VA," YouTube video, November 19, 2021, 1:00, https://www.youtube.com/watch?v=fndfuNJBQ4o.

66 "Up to today" signifies December 18, 2018, the date of his interview.

67 "The Freedom Park Garden of Remembrance," GREENinc, accessed September 18, 2022, https://www.greeninc.co.za/the-freedom-park-garden-of-remembrance. Visitors traverse the five key elements of the IKS: *hapo* or "dream" (the museum), *Isivivane*, *S'khumbuto*, *Moshate* and *Tiva*, linked by the *Vhuwaelo*. Visitors remove their shoes when traversing the *Isivivane*, which symbolizes the spiritual resting place for those who died in the struggle for the freedom and liberation of South Africa. The *S'khumbuto* is the central monument including the names of victims, the gallery of heroes, an amphitheater for large gatherings commemorating important events in the country's history, a sanctuary for meditation, an eternal flame for the heroes who helped shape South Africa, and a large reed sculpture visible across the capital, which signifies rebirth. The *Moshate* is a stone building that hosts dignitaries and other guests of the state in honor of traditional African leadership structures. The *Tiva* is the large body of water at the park symbolizing peace and tranquility. These elements are connected by the *Vhuwaelo*, the contemplative pathway that spirals up the hill.

Chapter 3

1 In *Trauma and Recovery*, Judith Herman addresses this phenomenon as the "central dialectic of psychological trauma," see 1–2 and 47–50.

2 See Elie Wiesel's Nobel Peace Prize acceptance speech, where he articulates the source of Job's hope as memory: "The source of his hope was memory, as it must be ours. Because I remember, I despair. Because I remember, I have the duty to reject despair. I remember the killers, I remember the victims, even as I struggle to invent a thousand and one reasons to hope," ("Nobel Peace Prize Acceptance Speech," Oslo, December 10, 1986), https://www.nobelprize.org/prizes/peace/1986/wiesel/acceptance-speech/.

3 Elie Wiesel asserts this in a short piece for *Moment Magazine*, "40th Anniversary Symposium: Wisdom for the Next Generation," May–June 2015. He had said the same previously in the past tense in his "Nobel Lecture," given the day after the peace prize was awarded; The Nobel Prize (December 11, 1986), https://www.nobelprize.org/prizes/peace/1986/wiesel/lecture/.

4 Wiesel, "Nobel Peace Prize Acceptance Speech."

5 The responses can be described as intrusion and constriction. The former indicates abnormal forms of memory that break into consciousness and the present, arresting development and recovery. The latter indicates a form of self-defense where trauma inspires a complete shutting down of the nervous system or state of detachment; see Herman, *Trauma and Recovery*, 37–47.

6 Maria is an anonymized name for the supervisor who hired this worker.

7 Herman, *Trauma and Recovery*, 176.

8 Carla Joinson's "Coping with Compassion Fatigue," *Nursing* 22, no. 4 (1992): 116–21, introduces what she and fellow nurses experienced on the job as "compassion fatigue." A later publication by Charles Figley popularized the term, relating it to Secondary Traumatic Stress (STS), a term that indicates what happens when a caregiver, such as a therapist, deals with someone diagnosed with post-traumatic stress disorder. "Vicarious traumatization" is a term sometimes used interchangeably with STS. All the terms describe the negative transformation in the self as a result of working with traumatized clients and reports

of traumatic circumstances; see Charles Figley, *Encyclopedia of Trauma: An Interdisciplinary Guide* (Thousand Oaks, CA: Sage, 2012), 137–38. See also Christina Maslach and Wilmar B. Schaufeli, "Historical and Conceptual Development of Burnout," in *Professional Burnout: Recent Developments in Theory and Research*, ed. Wilmar B. Schaufeli, Cristina Maslach, and Tadeusz Marek (Philadelphia: Taylor & Francis, 1993), 1–18; Christina Maslach, "Burnout: A Multidimensional Perspective," in Schaufeli, Maslach, and Marek, eds., *Professional Burnout*, 19–32; Charles Figley, *Compassion Fatigue: Coping with Secondary Traumatic Stress Disorder in Those Who Treat the Traumatized* (New York: Brunner/Mazel, 1995); Charles Figley, "Compassion Fatigue: Toward a New Understanding of the Costs of Caring," in *Secondary Traumatic Stress: Self-Care Issues for Clinicians, Researchers, and Educators*, ed. B. H. Stamm (Lutherville, MD: Sidran Press, 1995), 3–28.

9 See Christina Maslach and S. E. Jackson, *Maslach Burnout Inventory Manual*, 2nd ed. (Palo Alto: Consulting Psychologists Press, 1986). See also Karen W. Saakvitne and Laurie Anne Pearlman, *Transforming the Pain: A Workbook on Vicarious Traumatization* (New York: W. W. Norton, 1996). To discern whether an occupation includes facing trauma, Saakvitne and Pearlman ask: "In your profession, do you help or work with people who have been traumatized? Do you listen to stories of abuse, suffering, or trauma from your clients every day?" In their estimation, if the answer to these questions is "yes," then the trauma story has an effect.

10 See Figley, *Encyclopedia of Trauma*; Figley, *Compassion Fatigue*; Stamm, *Secondary Traumatic Stress*.

11 Ezra Klein, "Interview with Bessel van der Kolk," *The Ezra Klein Show*, podcast audio, August 24, 2021, https://www.nytimes.com/2021/08/24/podcasts/transcript-ezra-klein-interviews-bessel-van-der-kolk.html.

12 "What *Is* The Neshoma Project?," The Neshoma Project, accessed February 15, 2022, https://neshomaproject.org/about.

13 See van der Kolk, *The Body Keeps the Score*, 1–4, but also see his more specific discussion on the brain and the thalamus shutting down, 68–71. See also Oprah Winfrey and Bruce Perry, *What*

Happened to You? Conversations on Trauma, Resilience, and Healing (London: Boxtree, 2021). Perry discusses brain mechanisms throughout the text in clear and understandable terms, growing more specific in chapter 8, "Our Brains, Our Biases, Our Systems."

14 In *Trauma and Recovery*, Herman discusses the concept of reconstructing the trauma story to "integrate" it into the new reality. Although I will argue later that memorial museums achieve integration, the preservation aspect of trauma threatens what Herman calls "The work of reconstruction," which "actually transforms the traumatic memory so that it can be integrated into the survivor's life," 174. She articulates the aim: "The goal of recounting the traumatic experience is integration not exorcism," 181. The memorial museum enacts this retelling and reconstructing of the trauma narrative on a macroscopic scale to integrate atrocity into a community's new reality.

15 Barbara Thimm's broader project and writing involves what she calls "dealing with the burdened past." The project assists educators at historical sites to reflect on the beliefs and assumptions they have about teaching history; see Barbara Thimm, Gottfried Kößler, and Susanne Ulrich, eds., *Verunsichernde Orte: Selbstverständnis und Weiterbildung in der Gedenkstättenpädagogik* (Frankfurt am Main: Brandes & Apsel Verlag, 2010).

16 See Barbara Thimm and Chhay Visoth, "Displaying New Reprints at Tuol Sleng Genocide Museum Obtains New Information and Further Questions," *DK Memosis*, June 6, 2018, https://dkmemosis.wordpress.com/2018/06/26/displaying-new-reprints-at-tuol-sleng-genocide-museum-obtains-new-information-and-further-questions/.

17 "Home," Tuol Sleng Genocide Museum, accessed September 25, 2021, https://tuolsleng.gov.kh/en/.

18 Herman, *Trauma and Recovery*, describes poor sleep as an aspect of hyperarousal, 35, and the occurrence of nightmares that invade sleep as intrusion, 37. The frozen "wordlessness" of trauma is also characteristic of intrusion, see 37 and 189. Also, Thimm's work, referred to extensively in chapter 5 of this text, presses museum educators to reflect on personal biases and affective responses to connect these to the telling of the trauma in order to add

dimension to workers' processing their experiences. The training helps workers both to manage the suffering portrayed in memorialization and understand that what they are feeling is a normal reaction to an extreme circumstance.

19 Patricia A. Frazier and Laura J. Schauben, "Vicarious Trauma: The Effects on Female Counselors of Working with Sexual Violence Survivors," *Psychology of Women Quarterly* 19, no. 1 (1995): 49–64. The article references women psychologists and sexual violence counselors who report better adjustment to symptoms from the work after training and education. Also, interestingly, symptomatology related to vicarious trauma and disrupted beliefs had no correlation with prior trauma. Trauma-specific education, especially ongoing, also reduces the potential of vicarious trauma in part because it offers a framework for understanding the experience of encountering trauma at work; see Holly Bell, Shanti Kulkarni, and Lisa Dalton, "Organizational Prevention of Vicarious Trauma," *Families in Society* 84, no. 4 (2003): 463–70. For support related to regular ongoing training, see C. Regehr and S. Cadell, "Secondary Trauma in Sexual Assault Crisis Work: Implications for Therapists and Therapy," *Canadian Social Work* 1, no. 1 (1999): 56–63.

20 This list is not exhaustive but exemplary.

21 See Inger Agger, "Calming the Mind: Healing after Mass Atrocity in Cambodia," *Transcultural Psychiatry* 52, no. 4 (August 2015): 543–60.

22 Patrice Ladwig and Paul Williams, "Introduction," in *Buddhist Funeral Cultures of Southeast Asia and China,* ed. Patrice Ladwig and Paul Williams (Cambridge: Cambridge University Press, 2012), 13–14. In "Giving Up Ghosts: Notes on Trauma and the Possibility of the Political from Southeast Asia," *East Asia Cultures Critique* 16, no. 1 (2008): 229–58, Rosalind Morris asserts, "It is widely believed throughout Southeast Asia that a premature death—a death experienced 'before its time,' and especially a violent death for which no preparation has been possible—generates an unhappy ghost. Such ghosts tend to linger in the place of death and, in fits of vindictive melancholy, are apt to trouble the living, making them ill or even causing their deaths in jealous efforts to obtain companionship," 230.

23 See Heonik Kwon, *Ghosts of War in Vietnam* (Cambridge: Cambridge University Press, 2013).

24 Inger Agger and Søren Buus Jensen explore the testimony method within the lives of refugees who had been victims of violence. Their abstract captures the import of the article as well as its relevance here: "When political refugees give testimony to the torture to which they have been subjected, the trauma story can be given a meaning, can be reframed: private pain is transformed into political dignity. In the context of testimony, shame, and guilt connected with the trauma can be confessed by the victim and reframed"; see Inger Agger and Søren Buus Jensen, "Testimony as Ritual and Evidence in Psychotherapy for Political Refugees," *Journal of Traumatic Stress* 3, no. 1 (1990): 115–30.

25 Many resources confirm this, along with the guide at the museum who shared his narrative. See specifically, Clifford Shearing and Michael Kempa, "A Museum of Hope: A Story of Robben Island," *The Annals of the American Academy of Political and Social Science* 592, no. 1 (2004): 62–78, and Rulon Wood, Julia Berger, and Marouf Hasian, "Public Memory, Digital Media, and Prison Narratives at Robben Island," *ESSACHESS Journal for Communication Studies* 10, no. 1 (2017): 173–97.

26 The long-term effects of trauma, especially in the case of children, are still being studied. However, several factors make an impact on these effects and therefore on recovery: the severity of the stressor; genetic predisposition; the developmental phase a person or child is in at the time of the trauma; a person's social support system; having a prior history of trauma (early trauma or a history of trauma leads to more symptomatology if a trauma occurs later in life); and a preexisting condition or adaptation to prior life stressors; see Bessel A. van der Kolk, *Psychological Trauma* (Washington, DC: American Psychiatric Publishing, 1987), 10–13.

27 Van der Kolk, *The Body Keeps the Score*, 2–3.

28 See Herman, *Trauma and Recovery*, 37–47, where Herman discusses these mechanisms extensively.

29 See one such presentation: Apartheid Museum SA, "Pumla Gobodo Madikazela," YouTube video, April 4, 2019, 10:41, https://www.youtube.com/watch?v=SlJS0i_64EA.

30 Pulma Gobodo-Madikizela, "In Conversation with Pumla Gobodo-Madikizela," interview by Tamar Garb, University College London, https://www.ucl.ac.uk/racism-racialisation/transcript-conversation-pumla-gobodo-madikizela.

31 Julia Kristeva works extensively with the concept of the abject—that part of the self that is dejected or spit out, in *Powers of Horror: An Essay on Abjection*, trans. Leon S. Roudiez (New York: Columbia University Press, 1982).

32 Henry Krystal, *Integration and Self-Healing: Affect—Trauma and Alexithymia* (New York: Routledge, 1988), 79.

33 Herman, *Trauma and Recovery*, where part of the book's organization reflects her vision of the stages of recovery from trauma, articulated not as a linear process but as a continual one that advances as the trauma is integrated. The stages are safety, remembrance and mourning, and reconnection.

34 Emir Suljagić details denial as a form of memory particularly operative in Bosnia in "Denial of Genocide and Other War Crimes Committed in Bosnia as a Form of Collective Memory," *Bosnian Studies: Journal for Research of Bosnian Thought and Culture* 6, no. 1 (2022). On page four, he describes the process of denial: "Denial takes place within the context of the social identity construction of the victim group and is part of the processes of 'sanitizing' the national identity narrative of the perpetrators. Denial is thus the logical extension of the social construction of the victim group as a mortal threat; physical annihilation is followed by a process which aims to portray the victims as deserving of their fate, and to recast the perpetrators' actions as heroic deeds. The deliberate selection of which facts are to be remembered and which are to be forgotten is the underlying process which connects denial and national narrative construction. In order to preserve a coherent grand narrative of national identity, politicians/perpetrators omit certain facts from the collective historical memory, and regulate which topics are to be spoken about, and which are to be avoided. Denial, therefore, is a form of memory. It is a conscientious decision on how certain events are to be remembered."

35 Chico Harlan, "Bosnia Is Still Finding Bodies from a Genocide Some Leaders Claim Never Happened," *The Washington*

Post, February 21, 2022, https://www.washingtonpost.com/world/2022/02/21/bosnia-genocide-denial-crisis/.

36 Una Hajdari, "Bosnia's Peace Envoy Bans Genocide Denial," Politico, July 23, 2021, https://www.politico.eu/article/bosnia-peace-envoy-bans-genocide-denial/.

37 See The Observer, "'It's Getting Out of Hand': Genocide Denial Outlawed in Bosnia," *The Guardian*, July 24, 2001, https://www.theguardian.com/world/2021/jul/24/genocide-denial-outlawed-bosnia-srebrenica-office-high-representative.

38 Lamija Grebo, "Bosnian Serb War Criminal Rasoslav Brdjanin Released Early," Balkan Insight, September 5, 2022, https://balkaninsight.com/2022/09/05/bosnian-serb-war-criminal-radoslav-brdjanin-released-early/.

39 Denic Dzidic and Denis Dzidic, "100,000 Bones Exhibit to Open in Srebrenica," Balkan Insight, July 7, 2015, https://balkaninsight.com/2015/07/07/one-hundred-thousand-bones-to-open-in-srebrenica/.

40 Van der Kolk, *The Body Keeps the Score*, 44.

41 Herman, *Trauma and Recovery*, again referring to the concept of intrusion of traumatic memory, 37.

42 Center for Substance Abuse Treatment (US), "Understanding the Impact of Trauma," in *Trauma-Informed Care in Behavioral Health Services* (Rockville, MD: Substance Abuse and Mental Health Services Administration, 2014), chapter 3. Available from https://www.ncbi.nlm.nih.gov/books/NBK207191/.

43 In his book, *My Grandmother's Hands* (Las Vegas: Central Recovery Press, 2017), Resmaa Menakem calls this silence a "historical habit," 209. He also treats trauma, generational trauma, and racialized trauma. Especially poignant are his discussions about trauma as rapid, thus requiring the converse slow, steady address for recovery (see chapter 1, "Your Body and Blood," especially 13–14), and trauma as embodied ways of being in a racialized society (see chapter 1, "Your Body and Blood," and chapter 6, "Violating the Black Body").

44 The process that Ali undergoes in his own coming to the Whitney plantation reflects Shawn Copeland's theology of suffering. She discusses remembering, retelling, resisting, and redeeming evil and suffering. "A theology of suffering in womanist

perspective remembers and retells the lives and sufferings of those who 'came through' and those who have 'gone on to glory land.' This remembering honors the sufferings of the ancestors, known and unknown, victims of chattel slavery and its living legacy." The retelling constitutes testimony that recenters and "revives the living as well," 123; see M. Shawn Copeland, "Wading through Many Sorrows: Toward a Theology of Suffering in Womanist Perspective," in Townes, ed., *A Troubling in My Soul*, 109–29.

45 Joy DeGruy, *Post-Traumatic Slave Syndrome: America's Legacy of Enduring Injury and Healing* (Portland: Joy DeGruy Publications, 2017): "We rarely look to our history to understand how African-Americans adapted their behavior over centuries in order to survive the stifling effects of chattel slavery, effects which are evident today." She refers to examples throughout the introduction that illustrate how Black children grow up understanding that the world belongs to white children and how deference to power emerges in human behavior, relating these to "trans-generational adaptations associated with the past traumas of slavery and ongoing oppression." She terms this condition Post-Traumatic Slave Syndrome or PTSS, 13.

46 Rambo, *Resurrecting Wounds*, 78. The image of "invisible wounds," often used to represent trauma, must extend beyond the clinical framework to speak about the processes involved in rendering suffering invisible and of keeping those truths from coming to the surface. We can think of this in terms of the wider politics of trauma.

47 The memorial museum becomes a pedagogical place. Phillis Sheppard refers to pedagogical space as a theo-ethical-pastoral process, where "one notices and probes the reality of what is being wrought in the world"; see "Hegemonic Imagination, Historical Ethos, and Colonized Minds in the Pedagogical Space: Pastoral Ethics and Teaching as if Our Lives Depended on It," *Journal of Pastoral Theology* 27, no. 3 (2017): 191. Ashley learns concretely about embodied justice and injustice, as she says herself, "by doing." On the theo-ethical-pastoral process, see Phillis Sheppard, "Womanist-Lesbian Pastoral Ethics: A Post Election Perspective," *Journal of Pastoral Theology* 27, no. 1 (2017).

48 In "The Case for Reparations," Ta-Nehisi Coates refers to this expectation that racialized trauma is processed and resolved immediately—which constitutes part of the perpetrator's wish: "Indeed, in America there is a strange and powerful belief that if you stab a black person 10 times, the bleeding stops and the healing begins the moment the assailant drops the knife. We believe white dominance to be a fact of the inert past, a delinquent debt that can be made to disappear if only we don't look"; Ta-Nehisi Coates, "The Case for Reparations," *The Atlantic*, June 2014, https://www.theatlantic.com/magazine/archive/2014/06/the-case-for-reparations/361631/.

49 If silencing the victim doesn't work, denial and rationalizations ensue. Herman draws this reality out: "after every atrocity one can expect to hear the same predictable apologies: it never happened; the victim lies; the victim exaggerates; the victim brought it upon herself; and in any case *it is time to forget the past and move on*. The more powerful the perpetrator, the greater is his prerogative to name and define reality, and the more completely his arguments prevail"; *Trauma and Recovery*, 8, italics mine.

50 This worker made no report of initial trauma of the event of 9/11, or other trauma, so the level of reaction to sound as a result of direct trauma is unclear. The interaction with traumatic content made an impact nonetheless. Studies show that the brain responds to images or sounds related to trauma by activating the limbic system, and specifically the amygdala, which alerts the body to danger and increases stress impulses and nerve impulses; see van der Kolk, *The Body Keeps the Score*, 42.

51 J. Martin Daughtry addresses the two valences of sound in *Listening to War: Sound, Music, Trauma, and Survival in Wartime Iraq* (Oxford: Oxford University Press, 2015). Van der Kolk discusses the nature of sound as a trigger for reliving trauma throughout his text, delineating between remembering and reliving the trauma, initiated by sound, images, and other sensory stimuli; see van der Kolk, *The Body Keeps the Score*, 65–68.

Chapter 4

1 As mentioned and detailed in chapter 2, emotional demands at places of employment differ from those who do

people-work—defined as nurses, service workers, and caring professions—than those who do not employ care in any way. Here I add dimension to the concept using Céleste M. Brotheridge and Alicia A. Grandey, "Emotional Labor and Burnout: Comparing Two Perspectives of 'People Work,'" *Journal of Vocational Behavior* 60, no. 1 (2002): 17–39. Brotheridge and Grandey also discover that people-work may have unusual demands related to emotions, but that these act as both stressors and resources. When emotional demands are rewarding, those demands correspond with management styles. The article supports the concept of training around trauma to decrease stress and to uncover the rewards of the work that combats such stress. Christina Maslach, in "Burned-Out," *The Canadian Journal of Psychiatric Nursing* 20, no. 6 (1979): 5–9, explores the risks of the work, including the threat of detachment, the radical separation of personal and professional life (manifested in the memorial museum worker who does not talk about work at home or publicly), and the sharp distinctions between being "on the ground" with people as opposed to doing more administrative work. The author reports additionally that burnout will inspire workers to seek administrative jobs that have fewer encounters with people.

2 Herman, *Trauma and Recovery*, 178: "the traumatic event challenges an ordinary person to become a theologian, a philosopher, and a jurist."

3 Joan Tronto, *Moral Boundaries: A Political Argument for an Ethic of Care* (New York: Routledge, 1994), 125. In the book, Tronto argues that the moral and the political are not two separate spheres. Care serves as an example of the imbrication as a moral value, and as a basis for performing a good in society.

4 Joan Tronto, "Joan Tronto," interview by Ethics of Care, August 4, 2009, https://ethicsofcare.org/joan-tronto/. See also Tronto, *Moral Boundaries*, 104.

5 Storm Swain, *Trauma and Transformation at Ground Zero: A Pastoral Theology* (Minneapolis: Augsberg Fortress, 2011), 37. Each movement reflects language from Jim Cotter's Lord's Prayer, inspired by the Anglican Church in Aotearoa New Zealand, *New Zealand Prayer Book: He Karakia Mihinare o Aotearoa* (San Francisco: HarperOne, 1997).

6 Cast in the framework of pastoral care, the model emulates the *activity* of the ecclesiastical Trinity rather than its hierarchical order. Swain connects her model to D. W. Winnicott's relational model of psychotherapy—"Holding, Suffering, Transforming" throughout the text. Each chapter connects the theological model with the psychoanalytic one, working together to inform and ground pastoral care. See Swain's direct discussion on the parallels on pages 11–12.

7 See Swain, *Trauma and Transformation at Ground Zero*, 37, where she describes this imminent trinity. The model illuminates caregiving practices in the work of those who attend to mass trauma, and theologically reflects God's work in the world.

8 See Augustine of Hippo, *On the Trinity*, Book 15, chapter 36, trans. Patrick A. O'Boyle (Washington, DC: The Catholic University Press, 1963), where the gift is love. Augustine's chapter explores gift giving as it emerges in the following statement: "no subordination of the Gift, and no domination of the Givers, but concord between the Gift and the Givers." Thus, the exchange of the gift, as love, is modeled after the divine notion of the Holy Spirit as a gift given from God, not to dominate but to share in restoration of the soul.

9 Swain, *Trauma and Transformation at Ground Zero*, 42.

10 Swain put this in terms of an eschatological vision where one looks back at the creation narratives and forward to an understanding of what we are created for, while living in the present in terms of holding creation and being; *Trauma and Transformation at Ground Zero*, 41.

11 Swain, *Trauma and Transformation at Ground Zero*, sees bearing pain and holding pain as nearly interchangeable, referring to Donald Winnicott's "holding space," the uninterrupted space that replicates the caregiving relationship to a child, extrapolated to the life of an adult. A hypostatic union evidences itself "where the child may be held in its becoming," 54. Thomas H. Ogden provides an additional viewpoint on holding "an ontological concept that he uses to explore the specific qualities of the experience of being alive at different developmental stages as well as the changing intrapsychic-interpersonal means by which the sense of continuity of being is sustained over time"; see Thomas

H. Ogden, "On Holding and Containing, Being and Dreaming," *International Journal of Psychoanalysis* 85 (2004): 1350.

12 Swain, *Trauma and Transformation at Ground Zero*, 48. Of one chaplain's testimony after 9/11, Swain remarks, "Those at Ground Zero had to work constantly in an environment that not only contained the dead, but indeed at times, as this chaplain noted, even *was* the dead." This designation continues to hold value for those who work at the space.

13 The alliance indicates the therapeutic aspect in Swain's framework; see *Trauma and Transformation at Ground Zero*, 58. A more detailed exploration of the term and terms emerging from the idea of an alliance can be found in Adam O. Horvath and Lester Luborsky, "The Role of the Therapeutic Alliance in Psychotherapy," *Journal of Consulting and Clinical Psychology* 61, no. 4 (1993): 561–73.

14 Paul Ricoeur, on memory's location in *Memory, History, Forgetting*, trans. Kathleen Blamey and David Pellauer (Chicago: University of Chicago Press, 2004), 57.

15 Doehring, *The Practice of Pastoral Care*, xv.

16 Noted by Tom Hennes, in "Witnessing Each Other: An Intersubjective Stance for Exhibitions Related to Substance Use and Abuse," *Substance Use & Misuse* 50, nos. 8–9 (2015): 968–70.

17 In *Trauma and Transformation at Ground Zero*, Swain rightly points out the intertwining and high demand of cognitive activity and sensory/affective experience as a part of a job that people do well when they are highly empathic. She articulates some of the dangers posed by feeling another's pain, see 67–71.

18 Swain, *Trauma and Transformation at Ground Zero*, 55. Here Swain frames empathic attunement in relation to the caregiving dyad. See also my chapter on empathy, attachment, and attunement in Arel, *Shame, Affect Theory, and Christian Formation*.

19 Swain, *Trauma and Transformation at Ground Zero*, 67.

20 This approach qualifies as an ethics of care in Carol Gilligan's terms. Gilligan uses an example in *In a Different Voice: Psychological Theory and Women's Development* (Cambridge, MA: Harvard University Press, 2016), where she details, in her college student study, Amy's response to herself and "morality as arising from the recognition of relationship" alongside communication as conflict

.. ..x

---

resolution. Amy's judgments reflect, Gilligan asserts, "insights central to an ethic of care" and a belief in the "restorative activity of care," 30.

21 Brenda Cowan, Ross Laird, and Jason McKeown, "Mending the Mind and the Spirit: The Role of Objects and Exhibitions in Health and Healing," *Exhibition* 36, no. 1 (2017): 80–89. Giving and receiving make up one segment of the authors' three-part dynamics to objects as a means of healing; the other two are releasing/unburdening and composing.

22 See Tom Hennes, "Exhibitions: From a Perspective of Encounter," *Curator* 53, no. 1 (2010): 21–34. Tom Hennes also played a substantial role in supporting the original steps of research for this book, including connecting me to interviewees in South Africa.

23 Since I draw readily from Swain, it is important to note her caveat about using the term as a distancing technique; *Trauma and Transformation at Ground Zero*, 84: "I chose to use the word *pain*—because it is all encompassing but does not prescribe. It acknowledges that at times we do hold things in our body that we do not have the time, space, or resources to hold in our minds, and declinicalizes and humanizes what we will explore under the terms *trauma* and *stress*."

24 The "suffering space" delineates Winnicott's term corresponding to Swain's "pain-bearing"; *Trauma and Transformation at Ground Zero*.

25 "Who can take away suffering without entering it?" Henri Nouwen asks in *Creative Ministry* (New York: Doubleday, 2013), 73.

26 Swain supports this statement in her observance that fatigue and satisfaction occur in the caregiving relationship; see *Trauma and Transformation at Ground Zero*, 123.

27 The impact of the work increases because bearing the pain of the other opens oneself up to personal feelings and pain; see Swain, *Trauma and Transformation at Ground Zero*, 89.

28 Mark Klempner discusses the nature of the oral historian assuming the therapeutic role and the importance of discernment and empathy as guideposts to avoid traumatization; see "Navigating Life Review Interviews with Survivors of Trauma," *The Oral History Review* 27, no. 2, (2000): 71–72, where Klempner asserts,

"As oral historians we are not psychotherapists, yet we hear narratives as miasmic as any that might surface in a therapist's office. Our interview subjects may never visit a psychiatrist, yet they will talk to us, and, in some cases, disclose things they have never shared with another human being. Any attempt at carrying out a life review interview with a survivor of trauma puts the interviewer in a position where he or she may precipitate the externalization of the event."

29 Like Klempner, Lynn Abrams sees the role of the oral historian in trauma as expanding beyond the confines of tradition; see *Oral History Theory* (New York: Routledge, 2010). She uses the word "unfolding" to describe the way that a personal narrative emerges during an interview. I extend the term to address the question of interviewing people when the event is "unfolding." For situations where the mass trauma continues to present itself—in subtle and not so subtle ways—how does one assess "unfolding"? In Cambodia, many who live in the fields are surrounded by landmines and still suffering from the economic reverberations of the Khmer Rouge regime. Does this count as a trauma in process, or one that is resolved? See Jennifer K. Elek and Paula Hannaford-Agor, "First, Do No Harm: On Addressing the Problem of Implicit Bias in Juror Decision Making," *Court Review: The Journal of the American Judges Association* 49, no. 4 (2013): 190–98, for assistance in discerning the answer to this question.

30 Klempner articulates the dilemma and reflection, employing the word "Navigating" in his title, and beginning his essay with a description of the "what" of that navigation: "I'm sitting with a Holocaust survivor listening to her recount the murder of her entire family. To hear about such devastation is difficult. I go blank and numb, not knowing how to respond to suffering of such magnitude. I feel cheap somehow, that I am hearing these things so casually, that is, upon having just met her. In these few seconds, as the depth of her loss continues to sink in . . .," 67.

31 Herman discusses the framing of telling the trauma story in safety and control, discussing this extensively throughout *Trauma and Recovery*, but specifically on pages 175–76.

32 Herman insists that this balance is ethically critical in the protection of the survivor; *Trauma and Recovery*, 175.

33 See Herman, *Trauma and Recovery*, where she discusses how
helping a teller bear the pain of past trauma entails counteracting
the telling of the trauma story with recognition of autonomy and
empowering the survivor in confrontation with the horrors of
the past, 175.

34 Bessel van der Kolk includes four truths related to helping people
overcome trauma. They are worth repeating here because they go
beyond the brain-disease model, which the memorial museum
field also disrupts and in similar ways. The truths are: "1) our
capacity to destroy one another is matched by our capacity to
heal one another. Restoring relationships and community is central to restoring well-being; 2) language gives us the power to
change ourselves and others by communicating our experiences,
helping us to define what we know, and finding a common sense
of meaning; 3) we have the ability to regulate our own physi-
ology, including some of the so-called involuntary functions of
the body and brain, through such basic activities as breathing,
moving, and touching; and 4) we can change social conditions
to create environments in which children and adults can feel safe
and where they can thrive"; see *The Body Keeps the Score*, 38.

35 Swain, *Trauma and Transformation at Ground Zero*, 93. Of the
theology of the Trinity, Swain says it must "take into account
suffering but cannot do so by splitting off the sufferer and the
cause of the suffering."

36 See Vamik Volkan, *Killing in the Name of Identity: A Study of
Bloody Conflicts* (Durham: Pitchstone Publishing, 2006). Volkan's
unique body of work considers large group identities and mass
trauma in long-term processes where restoration takes time. In
this text, he considers what he calls a post–September 11 world
of violent conflict. He remains skeptical that large groups will
stop humiliating and killing others that belong to differing identity groups. However, he writes, "I have become optimistic about
using psychoanalytically informed insights and techniques to deal
with and modify certain specific and limited international problems and establish nonviolent coexistence between groups with
different identities. For this to happen, psychoanalysts must be
willing to work steadily over long periods of time with historians,
political scientists, diplomats, and others within an established

team and also in the trenches of troubled locations of the world";
see the "Introduction," specifically page 17. Memorial museums
all over the world respond to and interject themselves in such
conflicts, and may be one location where dialogue and long periods of research and work can take place.

37 Swain, *Trauma and Transformation at Ground Zero*, where she
shapes pain-bearing as "anthropologically and theologically
grounded in the tension between the best and worst of humanity," 89.

38 The idea of value related to lessons, purpose, and meaning is
internally imposed by most memorial museums, but it is also
externally imposed. For instance, Robben Island and Auschwitz
mark two memorial museums considered as World Heritage
sites, "due to the intangible symbolic value [they hold] for a
large community of direct or indirect victims, and also beyond
that for the world at large"; see Sabine Marschall, "Memory and
Identity in South Africa: Contradictions and Ambiguities in the
Process of Post-Apartheid Memorialization," *Visual Anthropology*
25, no. 3 (2012): 191. Marschall argues that intangible heritage
is community-defined, an assertion supported by my research,
and important to communities where remains of destruction are
absent: "Nothing tangible remains of these events, but memories and oral history, personal narratives, sometimes photos." She
speaks specifically to the Sharpeville Massacre and the Soweto
Uprising, but her argument holds for other events of mass
trauma. She continues to argue, "Not only do the living memories fade and gradually disappear with those who hold them, but
the physical places where these events happened are also often
threatened by development, such as by proposed shopping centers. The government supports the identification, safeguarding
and marking of these sites and events, usually through the placement of a commemorative monument, memorial, public statue
or sometimes a museum or interpretation center . . . Commemorative markers are hence purpose-built containers of memories
and intangible heritage values."

39 Swain, *Trauma and Transformation at Ground Zero*, 145.

40 Ann Belford Ulanov speaking to the global response to 9/11
in "The Space between Pastoral Care and Global Terrorism,"

Scottish Journal of Healthcare Chaplaincy 10, no. 2 (2007): 3–8. The chaplains brought goodness, as an opposition to suffering. She suggests the one way to articulate what is good in the face of loss is to make links. For the memorial museum, links emerge between tattered presents to both the past prior to the trauma and the future potential for hope in survival.

41 Ulanov, "The Space between Pastoral Care and Global Terrorism." "When loss strikes us, the great question is how to go on being alive, real, grateful, glad. How to keep loving alive in the face of this wounding hurt, and now in the face of collective trauma? The psychological and spiritual danger in the face of great loss is that we cease to make links to receive connections to our deeper selves, to our neighbours, and to God," 4.

42 Herman, *Trauma and Recovery*, 197.

43 The research on community recovery from mass violence derives from Laurie Anne Pearlman's work in Rwanda and what she calls the RICH (RIChE—in French) approach. I have selected aspects of this approach, which are included in the acronym for the essential elements of recovery: Respect, Information, Connection, and Hope. This is a philosophy or framework for treatment that can be adapted to a range of social/cultural contexts. See Laurie Anne Pearlman, "Restoring Self in Community: Collective Approaches to Psychological Trauma after Genocide," *Journal of Social Issues* 69, no. 1 (2013): 111–24. To note, Pearlman uses the term "victim group"; I have changed that to "survivor" or "surviving group," to stay consistent with the usages of the terms throughout the text, which utilizes "victim" to identify the dead.

44 Faith in the value and meaning of life is the second principle of Christian leadership; see Nouwen, *Creative Ministry*, 74.

45 I understand that there is critique about this, who is doing the telling, that the stories come from "elite" voices and places, but I would argue that what I saw from workers takes education and telling the story of those in their particular contexts seriously, and not without suspicion. Deep thinking and consideration characterize the work, rejecting blind following or random recall.

46 Educators in memorial museums often model a form of education that "enables us to confront feelings of loss and restore our sense of connection." bell hooks calls this "progressive

education," which "teaches us how to create community"; see bell hooks, *Teaching Community: A Pedagogy of Hope* (New York: Routledge, 2003), xv.

47 In many ways, this guide reflects the teacher that bell hooks understands herself to be, modeled in *Teaching Community*, xiv.

48 See Lenore Terr, *Too Scared to Cry: Psychic Trauma in Childhood* (New York: Basic Books, 1990), and Charlotte Reznick, *The Power of Your Child's Imagination: How to Transform Stress and Anxiety into Joy and Success* (Westminster: TarcherPerigee, 2009).

49 Herman discusses the problem of bypassing mourning and rage to move too quickly toward forgiveness, engaging in a "forgiveness fantasy"; see *Trauma and Recovery*, 189–91.

50 Pumla Gobodo-Madikizela, "In Conversation with Pumla Gobodo-Madikizela," interview by Tamar Garb, University College London, https://www.ucl.ac.uk/racism-racialisation/transcript-conversation-pumla-gobodo-madikizela.

51 This phrase aligns with remembrance of the Holocaust, and can be traced to a 1946 Austrian exhibition entitled "Niemals Vergessen" or "Never Forget," as articulated on a brochure from the exhibit on display at the United States Holocaust Memorial Museum. The artifacts gallery can be found here: "Brochure for an Austrian Exhibition Titled 'Never Forget,'" United States Holocaust Museum, accessed July 17, 2022, https://www.ushmm.org/propaganda/archive/never-forget-brochure/. The phrase became a part of a postwar lexicon, embedded in both the German psyche and the Jewish recovery of memory after the Holocaust, and which has been adopted and adapted by memorial museums since as a part of the fabric of commemorative activity.

52 The origins of "never again" can be traced to a translation of Ukrainian-born Hebrew poet Yitzhak Lamdan's 1926 poem "Masada," where the English reads: "Never shall Masada fall again," alluding to the conquest of the Romans of the Jewish holdouts at the place in the first century; Makom, "Second Conversation Chapter 4: Masada, 1942," Makom, November 8, 2013, https://makomisrael.org/second-conversation-chapter-four-masada-1942/. The translation in Hebrew from the poem implies but does not precisely capture this sense of never

again, and yet the phrase has achieved currency in English. In a 2008 speech at Israel's Knesset, President George W. Bush repeated the phrase, reflecting the sense of dominance it assumes along with a sense of solidarity: "At this historic site, Israeli soldiers swear an oath: 'Masada shall never fall again.' Citizens of Israel: Masada shall never fall again, and America will always stand with you"; Herb Keinon and Rebecca Anna Stoil, "Bush: Masada Will Never Fall Again," *The Jerusalem Post*, May 15, 2008, https://www.jpost.com/israel/bush-masada-will-never-fall-again.

53 The term is often critiqued as having no validity. Even Volcan cited in this chapter feels skeptical that mass atrocities will ever be arrested. But, I would argue, workers have internalized the message as having value and giving meaning to suffering in the light of prevention of any kind; see Martha Minow, "The Work of Re-Membering: After Genocide and Mass Atrocity," *Fordham International Law Journal* 23, no. 2 (1999): 429–39, in which Minow discusses how to remember in ways that do not make "never again" an empty phrase. Helen Fein challenges the term and its interpretation in "Remembering for the Present: Using the Holocaust to Misunderstand Genocide and to Segregate the 'Final Solution of the Jewish Question,'" in *Remembering the Future: The Holocaust in an Age of Genocide*, ed. John K. Roth, Elisabeth Maxwell, Margot Levy, and Wendy Whitworth (New York: Palgrave, 2001), where she calls "Never Again," "ever again," addressing the repetition of atrocity, 43.

54 Orli Fridman, "'Too Young to Remember Determined Not to Forget': Memory Activists Engaging with Returning ICTY Convicts," *International Criminal Justice Review* 28, no. 4 (December 2018): 423–37.

55 This practice of care emerges in Gilligan, *In a Different Voice*, and Joan Tronto's *Moral Boundaries*, where personal, political, and moral interests intertwine.

56 Personal interview, December 2018. More about Anita can be found here: Dafina Halili, "Anita Mitic—Living Life as an Activist," Kosovo 2.0, September 3, 2019, https://kosovotwopointzero.com/en/a-life-of-activism/.

Chapter 5

1 This use of alliance expands on the use of the term in chapter 4 as the dyad relates to psychoanalytic practice and pastoral care; see Carl Jung in the essay "Fundamental Questions of Psychotherapy," in *The Practice of Psychotherapy*, ed. Carl Jung (Princeton, NJ: Princeton University Press, 1951), 111–25, and Robert L. Hatcher, "Alliance Theory and Measurement," in *The Therapeutic Alliance: An Evidence-Based Guide to Practice*, ed. J. Christopher Muran and Jacques P. Barber (New York: Gilford Press, 2010), 7–28; Neil Pembroke, *The Art of Listening: Dialogue, Shame, and Pastoral Care* (Grand Rapids, MI: Wm. B. Eerdmans, 2002).

2 Nouwen, *The Wounded Healer*. The book articulates the condition of modern man and is extrapolated to the modern minister, "who is wounded by the suffering about which he speaks." The description of the wounded healer that follows derives primarily from Nouwen, but also Carl Jung, see note 4.

3 Nouwen, *The Wounded Healer*, 1.

4 See Jung, "Fundamental Questions of Psychotherapy," and Jung, *Memories, Dreams, Reflections* (New York: Pantheon Books, 1963): "Just as the wounder wounds himself," Jung writes, "the healer heals himself," 216.

5 This accounts for the expansion of the archetype Jung observes as the wounded healer, see Marie-Louise von Franz, *The Problem of the Puer Aeternus* (Ontario: Inner City Books, 2000), 111–12, and its emergence in other caretaking fields, see Cheryl Laskowski and Karen Pellicore, "The Wounded Healer Archetype: Applications to Palliative Care Practice," *American Journal of Hospice & Palliative Care* 19, no. 6 (November/December 2002): 403.

6 I return to this idea from first chapter, referring again to Nouwen's *Out of Solitude* and *The Wounded Healer*, and Zizioulas's *Being as Communion* and *Communion and Otherness*.

7 Walt Whitman, "Song of Myself," in *Leaves of Grass* (1855; reprint. Nashville: American Renaissance, 2009), 40.

8 Halifax, *Standing at the Edge*, 57.

9 Edith Stein, *On Empathy*, trans. Waltraut Stein (Washington, DC: ICS Publications, 1989), 111.

10 The empathetic connection serves as a dual introduction, of the self to the self and of the other to the self. "I see" the "sensing living body" of the foreign other and "empathically project myself into it." This develops a new image, a new understanding through the empathic projection that reveals something more about the self; see Stein, *On Empathy*, 61–69.

11 These are the four doors through which the wounded healer enters in order to engage in service as articulated in Nouwen, *The Wounded Healer*, xv.

12 The owners wanted to tell "the stories of people's lives and what they went through," with no professional interpretation or demands by exhibition designers about aesthetics; conversation with the owners, December 2018.

13 Stein, *On Empathy*, 41. For Stein, this connection also constitutes the union of the tactile and visual senses and is radically intimate.

14 The field of intergenerational trauma continues to expand. In reference to the scientific basis for intergenerational transmission of trauma, see Rachel Yehuda and Amy Lehrner, "Intergenerational Transmission of Trauma Effects: Putative Role of Epigenetic Mechanisms," *World Psychiatry* 17, no. 3 (2018): 243–57, and for a more specific reference related to the content in this book, see Rachel Yehuda, Stephanie Mulherin Engel, Sarah R. Brand, Jonathan Seckl, Sue M. Marcus, and Gertrud S. Berkowitz, "Transgenerational Effects of Posttraumatic Stress Disorder in Babies of Mothers Exposed to the World Trade Center Attacks During Pregnancy," *The Journal of Clinical Endocrinology & Metabolism* 90, no. 7 (2005): 4115–18; Joy DeGruy, *Post-Traumatic Slave Syndrome*; Marianne Hirsch, "The Generation of Postmemory," *Poetics Today* 29, no. 1 (2008): 103–28; Marianne Hirsch, "Family Pictures," 3–29; Yael Danieli, *International Handbook of Multigenerational Legacies of Trauma* (Berlin: Springer Science & Business Media, 1998).

15 J. P. Wilson and R. B. Thomas, *Empathy in the Treatment of Trauma and PTSD* (East Sussex: Brunner-Routledge, 2004).

16 Noreen Tehrani, "The Incidence of Secondary Traumatic Stress in Workers Dealing with Traumatising Materials, Victims and Perpetrators," in *Managing Trauma in the Workplace: Supporting*

Workers and Organisations, ed. Noreen Tehrani (New York: Routledge, 2010), 101.

17 This barrack was the location of one of the interviews that I conducted at Auschwitz in the summer of 2018. The office was located inside of the barrack; see "Life in the Camp," Auschwitz-Birkenau Museum, accessed August 25, 2022, https://www.auschwitz.org/en/history/life-in-the-camp/.

18 In *Standing at the Edge,* Joan Halifax challenges the conception of compassion fatigue, arguing that compassion, or too much of it, does not elicit fatigue. Instead, she says, it is empathy that causes fatigue, and too much of it can lead to withdrawal and moral apathy, 56–62. Her example for empathic distress is the 9/11 chaplain, but she also talks about hearing Holocaust survivor stories, and chaplaincy during Hurricane Katrina. Ultimately, too much empathy without attention to the self can lead to avoidance of instead of to serving those in need, 68–74.

19 The midpoint according to Robert Lifton, what he calls "an alternative" to the extremes is as follows: "boundaries can be viewed as neither permanent nor by definition false, but rather as essential and yet subject to the fundamental forces for change," that require "images of limit and restraint, if only to help us grasp what we are transcending"; see *Boundaries* (New York: Random House, 1969), xxi.

20 Halifax, *Standing at the Edge,* 46. Halifax considers setting boundaries another important interpersonal skill, which doesn't mean pushing people away. It means creating limits of exposure to suffering. Good boundaries protect from empathic distress and require remembering, of the person giving care, that they are not the suffering person. See also Klaus Blaser, "No Empathy without Self Boundaries: A New Spatial Attention Concept for Understanding Empathy," *Journal of Studies in Social Science* 12, no. 2 (2005): 219–34, who emphasizes that, for empathy to work well, the empathic person must be cognitively aware of where one person ends, and another begins.

21 This image can be reflected in a strategy of early intervention to differentiate pain and no-pain—or boundaries between those in pain and those not in pain, in Jean Decety, Chia-Yan Yang, and Yawei Cheng, "Physicians Down-Regulate Their Pain Empathy

---

Response: An Event-Related Brain Potential Study," *Neuroimage* 50, no. 4 (2010): 1676–82. Limits on empathy to free up cognitive processing have beneficial consequences when intervention begins early in the caregiving career.

22 See the section on "Compassionate and Transparent Boundaries," in Alex Shevrin Venet, "Role-Clarity and Boundaries for Trauma-Informed Teachers," *Educational Considerations* 44, no. 2 (2019): 1–9. The discussion applies to a classroom environment and pedagogical strategies, but it is applicable here.

23 Having worked in the field of caregiving in some capacity for years, I have repeatedly seen situations where male patients violate physical boundaries of women. This behavior has sometimes been aligned with sexual aggression, but sometimes it results from a confusion between intimacy and nurturing. The behavior rests as a violation, but training young women who work in the field about the risks of this occurring is critical. Stephen B. Levine, "Psychological Intimacy," *Journal of Sex & Marital Therapy* 17, no. 4 (1991): 259–67, helps to underscore the importance of reminding a speaker—if the listener is the caregiver—of psychological intimacy, differentiating it from physical intimacy. See also the very real risks of sexual harassment in the caregiving dyad: Sylvie Vincent-Höper, Mareike Adler, Maie Stein, Claudia Vaupel, and Albert Nienhaus, "Sexually Harassing Behaviors from Patients or Clients and Care Workers' Mental Health: Development and Validation of a Measure," *International Journal of Environmental Research and Public Health* 17, no. 7 (2020): 2570.

24 The protocols of the Memorial Museum, as detailed in the Collections Management Policy on its website, forbid the collection of any human remains. See 9/11 Memorial & Museum, "Collections Management Policy," 2018, https://www.911memorial.org/sites/default/files/inline-files/museum_collections_management_policy_full_1.pdf. An object containing anything suspected of being human remains would automatically be transferred to the Office of Chief Medical Examiner of the City of New York (the "OCME") for analysis. A cataloger would not proceed to document the item, unless the OCME had cleared it of any human remains. That said, working with artifacts of trauma and visual manifestations of death can be confusing and disturbing for workers who

are unaccustomed and untrained in handling such material. Those feelings could be further heightened when that material appears suddenly and without warning in someone's personal workspace.

25 The element of surprise can add extra distress to an already stressful situation. Training new workers to expect to be startled or shocked can reduce the impact of the negative effects of the shock itself; see James E. McCarroll, Robert J. Ursano, Kathleen M. Wright, and Carol S. Fullerton, "Handling Bodies after Violent Death: Strategies for Coping," *American Journal of Orthopsychiatry* 63, no. 2 (1993): 211–13.

26 McCarroll et al., "Handling Bodies after Violent Death," 210.

27 McCarroll et al., "Handling Bodies after Violent Death," 213.

28 McCarroll et al., "Handling Bodies after Violent Death," 213. This statement, directly put by the authors, reflects the same sentiment that many of my interviewees expressed.

29 McCarroll et al., "Handling Bodies after Violent Death," 213.

30 My translation of *Verunsichernde Orte* is "unsettling places"; see Barbara Thimm, Gottfried Koßler, and Susanne Ulrich, *Verunsichernde Orte.*

31 See Barbara Thimm's companion article, "Fragen sind geblieben: Aber es sind andere," *Gedenkstätten-Rundbrief* 180 (2015): 37–43.

32 In their essay, "The Impact of Trauma within Organisations," in *Managing Trauma in the Workplace*, ed. Tehrani, 137–58, Susan Klein and David Alexander write about four interventions for the workplace responding to traumatic events. The essay addresses incidents of trauma rather than an organization that responds to trauma daily, but in light of Thimm's work and the lack of evidence in the field that trained psychologists and mental health counselors should play active roles in institutional responses to trauma, I highlight their underscoring the following: The four interventions (peer support, critical incidents stress debriefing, trauma risk management, psychological first aid) "require some degree of training, particularly with regard to knowledge about normal and pathological reactions to trauma, at-risk factors for pathological ones and the normal trajectories of adjustment. Mental health professionals may help in their learning and training, but it would be wise for them not to lead the programme, as this may medicalize normal reactions," 135. The assessment

reflects a concern of mine related to pathologizing the feeling of pain—a normal response to the perception of human suffering.

33 Thimm continues: "We worked with some Austrian memorial sites, but we didn't manage to work closely with Polish memorial sites, because we said we really need Polish-speaking staff who would first be trained and work together with us, because it is so important that the participants be able to express themselves in their own language, and that the training is not happening in English. At that time their English level might have been not so good and so on"; personal conversation, July 2019.

34 See Tehrani, "The Incidence of Secondary Traumatic Stress in Workers Dealing with Traumatising Materials, Victims and Perpetrators."

35 Jan Coles, Jill Astbury, Elizabeth Dartnall, and Shazneen Limjerwala, "A Qualitative Exploration of Researcher Trauma and Researchers' Responses to Investigating Sexual Violence," *Violence Against Women* 20, no. 1 (January 2014): 96. Coles et al. quote Kate Connolly and Rosemary C. Reilly's conception of "getting without giving"; Kate Connolly and Rosemary C. Reilly, "Emergent Issues When Researching Trauma: A Confessional Tale," *Qualitative Inquiry* 13, no. 4 (May 2007): 536.

36 In terms of distress provoking bias, see Joseph Ciarrochi and Joseph P. Forgas, "The Pleasure of Possessions: Affective Influences and Personality in the Evaluation of Consumer Items," *European Journal of Social Psychology* 30, no. 5 (September/October 2000): 631–49.

37 Ana Nunes da Silva, António Branco Vasco, and Jeanne C. Watson, "Alexithymia and Emotional Processing: A Longitudinal Mixed Methods Research," *Research in Psychotherapy: Psychopathology, Process, and Outcome* 21, no. 1 (2018): 40–54. Alexithymia may be one explanation for the failure to process or reflect on difficult emotions, which here inhibits meaning making and linking emotions to events.

38 Francisco López-Muñoz and Francisco Pérez-Fernández, "A History of the Alexithymia Concept and Its Explanatory Models: An Epistemological Perspective," *Frontiers* 10 (January 31, 2020): 1–8. See also: Graeme J. Taylor, *Psychosomatic Medicine and Contemporary Psychoanalysis* (Madison, CT: International

Universities Press, 1987); Daniel Stern, *The Interpersonal World of the Infant: A View from Psychoanalysis and Developmental Psychology* (New York: Basic Books, 1985). Noreen Tehrani asserts that an organizations' response to traumatic stress mirrors that of the individual; see Noreen Tehrani, "Building Resilient Organisations in a Complex World," in *Managing Trauma in the Workplace: Supporting Workers and Organisations,* ed. Noreen Tehrani (New York: Routledge, 2010), 298–313.

39 This my brief summation of some qualities Tehrani names as building resilient organizations or organizations that "maintain the ability to function, relate and grow in the presence of significant disturbances and challenges"; see Tehrani, "Building Resilient Organisations in a Complex World," 298 and 305–9.

40 In a pastoral care framework, confirmation precedes empathy and acceptance; see Pembroke, *The Art of Listening: Dialogue, Shame, and Pastoral Care,* 4. Rogers also references a potential response to unreasonable or unruly workers, one that confirms their experiences and communicates that management stands behind them.

41 See Herman, *Trauma and Recovery,* 166. Herman spends time describing and outlining safety, what she describes as the first and critical step in trauma recovery. The fundamentals of creating external safety and providing education on internal safety would benefit the working environments at memorial museums, see 155–74.

42 Literature about psychoeducation around trauma and vicarious trauma abound. Most studies report that education and training alleviate distressing symptoms, create opportunities for community and communication, and increase spirituality or a sense of purpose in the world; see, for instance, Michael J. Rice and Mary D. Moller, "Wellness Outcomes of Trauma Psychoeducation," *Archives of Psychiatric Nursing* 20, no. 2 (2006): 94–102. McCarroll et al. also address training in "Handling Bodies after Violent Death," observing that training works but that long-term studies are needed to assess effectiveness over time, and Jeongsuk Kim, Brittney Chesworth, Hannabeth Franchino-Olsen, and Rebecca J. Macy argue in "A Scoping Review of Vicarious Trauma Interventions for Service Providers Working with People Who Have

Experienced Traumatic Events," *Trauma, Violence, & Abuse,* March 9, 2021, https://doi.org/10.1177/1524838021991310, that interventions in vicarious trauma (VT) are self-care based and focus on general stress management, while bypassing specific effects of VT in terms of the field: nursing, counseling, veterinarian work, and here, memorial museum work. The authors therefore call for an increase in efforts "to tailor VT interventions to different service settings and participant characteristics, as well as greater attention to developing primary VT interventions at the organizational level," 1.

43 The problem of saying "never again" is that atrocities happen again and again. See note 53 on "Never Again" in chapter 4. The task is to find hope in the midst of continual human-to-human violence, starting with both self-reflection and institutional reflection, as a step toward awareness and preventative measures.

44 See Eric Fromm, *The Art of Listening* (London: Continuum, 1998).

45 The strategy points to the neurological evidence that traumatic events deactivate the logical, linguistic, and analytical left brain. Even seeing images of trauma from the past will deactivate the left brain and activate the right—the side of the brain that is intuitive, tactual, sensory, and emotional. Deactivation of the left leads to disorganization of time and interferes with the ability to make plans or learn; see van der Kolk, *The Body Keeps the Score,* 44–47.

46 Tracy, *Fragments,* 239.

47 Maya Lin writes on her website about how Vincent Scully described the World War I memorial, *Lutyen's Memorial to the Missing of the Somme* at Thiepval, as "a journey towards an awareness of loss." She realized the description fit her design for the Vietnam memorial; "Vietnam Veterans Memorial," Maya Lin Studio, accessed August 25, 2022, https://www.mayalinstudio.com/memory-works/vietnam-veterans-memorial.

48 Ricoeur brackets a conflict between interpretation conceived as the unmasking, demystification, or reduction of illusions, to interpretation conceived as the recollection or restoration of meaning; Paul Ricoeur, *Freud and Philosophy* (New Haven, CT: Yale University Press, 1965), 9. The result of the latter is faith.

49 Paul Ricoeur, *Freud and Philosophy,* 20.

BIBLIOGRAPHY

Abrams, Lynn. *Oral History Theory*. New York: Routledge, 2010.

Adler, David. "Story of Cities #19: Johannesburg's Apartheid Purge of Vibrant Sophiatown." *The Guardian*, April 11, 2016. https://www.theguardian.com/cities/2016/apr/11/story-cities-19-johannesburg-south-africa-apartheid-purge-sophiatown.

Africa Watch Committee. "The Killings in South Africa: The Role of Security Forces and the Response of the State." New York: Human Rights Watch, 1991. https://www.hrw.org/reports/1991/southafrica1/5.htm#_ftn7.

Agger, Inger. "Calming the Mind: Healing after Mass Atrocity in Cambodia." *Transcultural Psychiatry* 52, no. 4 (August 2015): 543–60.

Agger, Inger, and Søren Buus Jensen. "Testimony as Ritual and Evidence in Psychotherapy for Political Refugees." *Journal of Traumatic Stress* 3, no. 1 (1990): 115–30.

Aitchison, John. "The Pietermaritzburg Conflict: Experience and Analysis." Centre for Adult Education, University of Natal, Pietermaritzburg, 8. Quoted in Africa Watch Committee, "The Killings in South Africa: The Role of Security Forces and the Response of the State." New York: Human Rights Watch, 1991. https://www.hrw.org/reports/1991/southafrica1/5.htm#_ftn7.

Al-Ali, Mohammed N. "Communicating Messages of Solidarity, Promotion and Pride in Death Announcements Genre in Jordanian Newspapers." *Discourse & Society* 16, no. 1 (January 2005): 5–31.

Alexander, Jeffrey C. "Cultural Trauma, Morality, and Solidarity: The Social Construction of the Holocaust and Other Mass Murders." *Thesis Eleven* 132, no. 1 (2015): 3–16.

———. "Toward a Theory of Cultural Trauma." In *Cultural Trauma and Collective Identity*, edited by Jeffrey C. Alexander, Ron Eyerman, Bernard Giesen, Neil J. Smelser, and Piotr Sztompka, 1–16. Los Angeles: University of California Press, 2004.

Allen, Greg. "'Thank God You Found Me': Florida Officials Unearth a Fourth Forgotten Black Cemetery." NPR, December 20, 2021. https://www.npr.org/2021/12/20/1065178753/florida-fourth-black-cemetery-discovered.

Alvizo, Xochitl. "Being Undone by the Other: Feminisms, Blogs, and Critique." In *Feminism and Religion in the 21st Century: Utilizing*

Technology to Expand Borders, edited by Gina Messina-Dysert and Rosemary Radford Ruether, 67–81. New York: Routledge, 2015.

American Alliance of Museums. "Core Standards for Museums," 2022. https://www.aam-us.org/programs/ethics-standards-and-professional-practices/core-standards-for-museums/.

Amnesty International. "Poland: The Law on the Institute of National Remembrance Contravenes the Right to Freedom of Expression." London: Amnesty International, 2018. https://www.amnesty.org/download/Documents/EUR3778582018ENGLISH.pdf.

Anderson, Ben. "Affective Atmospheres." *Emotion, Space and Society* 2, no. 2 (2009): 77–81.

Anglican Church in Aotearoa New Zealand. *New Zealand Prayer Book: He Karakia Mihinare o Aotearoa.* San Francisco: HarperOne, 1997.

Anzaldúa, Gloria E. *Borderlands/La Frontera: The New Mestiza*, 3rd ed. San Francisco: Aunt Lute Books, 2006.

Apartheid Museum. "The Apartheid Museum's Genesis." https://www.apartheidmuseum.org/about-the-museum.

———. "The New Constitution." https://www.apartheidmuseum.org/exhibitions/the-new-constitution.

———. "Pumla Gobodo Madikazela." YouTube video, April 4, 2019, 10:41. https://www.youtube.com/watch?v=SlJS0i64EA.

Arad, Michael. "Finalists Statements." *The New York Times*, November 19, 2003. https://www.nytimes.com/2003/11/19/nyregion/finalists-statements.html.

Archbishop of Canterbury. "Archbishop of Canterbury and Chief Rabbi Visit Yad Vashem." The Archbishop of Canterbury, March 5, 2017. https://www.archbishopofcanterbury.org/speaking-and-writing/latest-news/archbishop-canterbury-and-chief-rabbi-visit-yad-vashem.

Arel, Stephanie N. *Shame, Affect Theory, and Christian Formation.* London: Palgrave, 2016.

Arendt, Hannah. *The Human Condition.* Chicago: University of Chicago Press, 1989.

Associated Press. "Cambodia Inaugurates Memorial at Khmer Rouge Genocide Museum." KSL.com, March 26, 2015. https://www.ksl.com/article/33980019/cambodia-inaugurates-memorial-at-khmer-rouge-genocide-museum.

———. "Polish Official Fired After Calling Holocaust Law 'Stupid.'" Aljazeera, January 10, 2022. https://www.aljazeera.com/news/2022/1/10/polish-official-fired-after-calling-holocaust-law-stupid.

Augustine of Hippo. *On the Trinity.* Translated by Patrick A. O'Boyle. Washington, DC: The Catholic University Press, 1963.

Auschwitz-Birkenau Memorial Museum. "Auschwitz I, Auschwitz II-Birkenau, Auschwitz III-Monowitz." http://70.auschwitz.org/index.php?option=com_content&view=article&id=87&Itemid=173&lang=en.

———. "Life in the Camp." https://www.auschwitz.org/en/history/life-in-the-camp/.

———. "Memorial Timeline." http://www.auschwitz.org/en/museum/history-of-the-memorial/memorial-timeline/.

———. "Mission Statement." http://www.auschwitz.org/en/education/iceah-general-information/mission-statement/.

———. "The Number of Victims." https://www.auschwitz.org/en/history/auschwitz-and-shoah/the-number-of-victims/.

Barash, Jeffrey Andrew. *Collective Memory and the Historical Past.* Chicago: University of Chicago Press, 2016.

Barnes, Adam. "Antisemitic Graffiti Discovered at Auschwitz-Birkenau." *The Hill,* October 5, 2021. https://thehill.com/changing-america/respect/equality/575385-antisemitic-graffiti-discovered-at-auschwitz-birkenau/.

Baxter, Tom. "South Africa: The Roller Coaster, The Casino, and Sacred Memory." SaportaReport, September 25, 2017. https://saportareport.com/south-africa-roller-coaster-casino-sacred-memory/.

Bell, Holly, Shanti Kulkarni, and Lisa Dalton. "Organizational Prevention of Vicarious Trauma." *Families in Society* 84, no. 4 (2003): 463–70.

Bell, Terry. *Unfinished Business: South Africa, Apartheid and Truth.* London: Verso, 2003.

Bennett, Caroline. "Living with the Dead in the Killing Fields of Cambodia." *Journal of Southeast Asian Studies* 49, no. 2 (June 2018): 184–203.

Besic, Vesna, Lejla Biogradlija, and Sanela Crnovrsanin. "Coffins of 19 Srebrenica Genocide Victims Carried to Potocari Cemetery." Anadolu Agency, July 11, 2021. https://www.aa.com.tr/en/europe/coffins-of-19-srebrenica-genocide-victims-carried-to-potocari-cemetery/2300728.

Beta. "Vucic: Serbia Will Not Adopt a Resolution on Srebrenica While I Am President." N1, June 6, 2021. https://rs.n1info.com/english/news/vucic-serbia-will-not-adopt-a-resolution-on-srebrenica-while-i-am-president/.

Binckes, Robin. *Vlakplaas: Apartheid Death Squads, 1979–1994.* Barnsley: Pen & Sword Books, 2018.

Black in Appalachia. "Lynching Site Soil Collection: David Hurst, Kent Junction, VA." YouTube video, November 19, 2021, 1:00. https://www.youtube.com/watch?v=fndfuNJBQ4o.

Blaser, Klaus. "No Empathy without Self Boundaries: A New Spatial Attention Concept for Understanding Empathy." *Journal of Studies in Social Science* 12, no. 2 (2005): 219–34.

Bonhoeffer, Dietrich. *Letters and Papers from Prison.* New York: Macmillan, 1972.

Bonsu, Samuel K. "The Presentation of Dead Selves in Everyday Life: Obituaries and Impression Management." *Symbolic Interaction* 30, no. 2 (2007): 199–219.

Boss, Pauline. *Ambiguous Loss: Learning to Live with Unresolved Grief.* Cambridge, MA: Harvard University Press, 1999.

———. *Loss, Trauma and Resilience: Therapeutic Work with Ambiguous Loss.* New York: W. W. Norton, 2018.

———. "Resilience as Tolerance for Ambiguity." In *Handbook of Family Resilience,* edited by Dorothy S. Becvar, 285–97. New York: Springer, 2013.

Breitenberg, E. Harold, Jr. "To Tell the Truth: Will the Real Public Theology Please Stand Up?" *Journal of the Society of Christian Ethics* 23, no. 2 (2003): 55–96.

Brotheridge, Céleste M., and Alicia A. Grandey. "Emotional Labor and Burnout: Comparing Two Perspectives of 'People Work.'" *Journal of Vocational Behavior* 60, no. 1 (2002): 17–39.

Brown, Barbra, and Timothy Longman. "Confronting Apartheid." *Facing History and Ourselves* (blog), 2018. https://www.facinghistory.org/confronting-apartheid/chapter-2/introduction.

Brown, Caitlin, and Chris Mulligan. "The Memory of the Cambodian Genocide: The Tuol Sleng Genocide Museum." *History Compass* 13, no. 2 (2015): 31–39.

Brown, Robert McAfee. *Kairos: Three Prophetic Challenges to the Church.* Grand Rapids, MI: Eerdmans, 1990.

Bullfrog Films. "Documentaries That Changed the World—Year Zero: The Silent Death of Cambodia." YouTube video, August 19, 2009, 2:58. https://www.youtube.com/watch?v=CGSuE7_HdeE. (Bullfrog Films clip.)

Bureau of Diplomatic Security. "1993 World Trade Center Bombing." https://www.state.gov/1993-world-trade-center-bombing/.

Burke, Peter. "History as a Social Memory." In *Memory: History, Culture and the Mind,* edited by Thomas Butler, 97–113. New York: Blackwell, 1989.

Butler, Judith. *Precarious Life: The Powers of Mourning and Violence.* New York: Verso, 2006.

Captari, Laura E., Joshua N. Hook, Jamie D. Aten, Edward B. Davis, and Theresa Clement Tisdale. "Embodied Spirituality Following Disaster: Exploring Intersections of Religious and Place Attachment in Resilience and Meaning-Making." In *The Psychology of Religion and Place*, edited by Victor Counted and Fraser Watts, 49–79. London: Palgrave Macmillan, 2019.

Cavanaugh, William T. *Torture and Eucharist*. Oxford: Blackwell, 1998.

Center for Substance Abuse Treatment. "Trauma-Informed Care in Behavioral Health Services: Substance Abuse and Mental Health Services Administration." No. 57. 2014.

Cheang, Sopheng. "Anti-Tank Mine Kills 3 Demining Experts in Cambodia." Associated Press, January 10, 2022. https://apnews.com/article/cambodia-land-mines-89e03ac2902e4ff1e8e628f5d1f07fa5.

Chindawongse, Suriya. "Pol Pot's Strategy of Survival." *The Fletcher Forum of World Affairs* 15, no. 1 (1991): 127–45.

Ciarrochi, Joseph, and Joseph P. Forgas. "The Pleasure of Possessions: Affective Influences and Personality in the Evaluation of Consumer Items." *European Journal of Social Psychology* 30, no. 5 (September/October 2000): 631–49.

Clark, Laurie Beth. "Ethical Space: Ethics and Propriety in Trauma Tourism." In *Death Tourism: Disaster Sites as Recreational Landscape*, edited by Brigitte Sion, 9–35. Calcutta: Seagull, 2014.

Co, Cindy. "US to Fund Project Preserving Clothes of S-21 Victims." *The Phnom Penh Post*, December 12, 2017. https://www.phnompenhpost.com/national/us-fund -project-preserving-clothes-s-21-victims.

Coates, Ta-Nehisi. "The Case for Reparations." *The Atlantic*, June 2014. https://www.theatlantic.com/magazine/archive/2014/06/the-case-for-reparations/361631/.

Cohen, Arthur A. *The Tremendum: A Theological Interpretation of the Holocaust*. New York: Continuum, 1993.

Cohen, Leonard J. *Broken Bonds: The Disintegration of Yugoslavia*. Boulder: Westview Press, 1993.

Coles, Jan, Jill Astbury, Elizabeth Dartnall, and Shazneen Limjerwala. "A Qualitative Exploration of Researcher Trauma and Researchers' Responses to Investigating Sexual Violence." *Violence Against Women* 20, no. 1 (January 2014): 95–117.

Colgan, Deirdre. "Visiting Sacred Spaces: A 'How-To' Guide with Tips & Suggestions for Groups & Individuals." Sacred Space International, 2010. https://www-tc.pbs.org/godinamerica/art/VisitingSacredSpaces.pdf.

Cone, James. *The Cross and the Lynching Tree*. Ossining: Orbis Books, 2013.

Confino, Alon. "Collective Memory and Cultural History: Problems of Method." *The American Historical Review* 102, no. 5 (1997): 1386–403.

Connolly, Kate, and Rosemary C. Reilly. "Emergent Issues When Researching Trauma: A Confessional Tale." *Qualitative Inquiry* 13, no. 4 (May 2007): 522–40.

Coopan, Vilashini. "Connective Tissue: Memory's Weave and the Entanglements of Diasporic Ethnicity." *Qui Parle* 28, no. 2 (2019): 282–306.

Copeland, M. Shawn. "Wading through Many Sorrows: Toward a Theology of Suffering in Womanist Perspective." In *A Troubling in My Soul: Womanist Perspectives on Evil and Suffering*, edited by Emilie M. Townes, 109–29. New York: Orbis Books, 1993.

Coupland, Bethan. "Remembering Blaenavon: What Can Group Interviews Tell Us About 'Collective Memory'?" *Oral History Review* 42, no. 2 (Summer/Fall 2015): 277–99.

Cowan, Brenda, Ross Laird, and Jason McKeown. "Mending the Mind and the Spirit: The Role of Objects and Exhibitions in Health and Healing." *Exhibition* 36, no. 1 (2017): 80–89.

da Silva, Ana Nunes, António Branco Vasco, and Jeanne C. Watson. "Alexithymia and Emotional Processing: A Longitudinal Mixed Methods Research." *Research in Psychotherapy: Psychopathology, Process, and Outcome* 21, no. 1 (2018): 40–54.

Daly, Mary. *Beyond God the Father: Toward a Philosophy of Women's Liberation*. Boston: Beacon Press, 1993.

Danieli, Yael. *International Handbook of Multigenerational Legacies of Trauma*. Berlin: Springer Science & Business Media, 1998.

Daughtry, J. Martin. *Listening to War: Sound, Music, Trauma, and Survival in Wartime Iraq*. Oxford: Oxford University Press, 2015.

Davie, Lucille. "Hector Pieterson Gets His Memorial." Joburg, October 24, 2001. https://web.archive.org/web/20070519061318/http://www.joburg.org.za/october/hector.stm.

Day, Katy, and Sebastian Kim. "Introduction." In *A Companion to Public Theology*, edited by Katy Day and Sebastian Kim, 1–21. Leiden: Brill, 2017.

Decety, Jean, Chia-Yan Yang, and Yawei Cheng. "Physicians Down-Regulate Their Pain Empathy Response: An Event-Related Brain Potential Study." *Neuroimage* 50, no. 4 (2010): 1676–82.

DeGruy, Joy. *Post-Traumatic Slave Syndrome: America's Legacy of Enduring Injury and Healing*. Portland: Joy DeGruy Publications, 2017.

Demick, Barbara. *Logavina Street: Life and Death in a Sarajevo Neighborhood*. New York: Random House, 2012.

Diamond, Alma. "Burying the Past and Building the Future in Post-Apartheid South Africa." *The Conversation*, February 20, 2022. https://

theconversation.com/burying-the-past-and-building-the-future-in-post-apartheid-south-africa-174010.

Dixon, Thomas. *The Clansman: An Historical Romance of the Ku Klux Klan.* New York: Grosset & Dunlap, 1905.

———. *The Leopard's Spots: A Romance of the White Man's Burden—1865–1900.* New York: Doubleday, 1903.

Documentation Center of Cambodia. "Mapping Project." http://d.dccam. org/Projects/Maps/Mapping.htm.

Doehring, Carrie. *The Practice of Pastoral Care: A Postmodern Approach.* Louisville, KY: John Knox Press, 2015.

Drummond, Andrew J., and Jacek Lubecki. "Reconstructing Galicia: Mapping the Cultural and Civic Traditions of the Former Austrian Galicia in Poland and Ukraine." *Europe-Asia Studies* 62, no. 8 (2010): 1311–38.

Duffy, Terence. "The Peace Museum Concept." *Museum International* 45, no. 1 (1993): 4–8.

Durkheim, Emile. *The Elementary Forms of Religious Life.* Translated by Karen E. Fields. New York: The Free Press, 1995.

Dzidic, Denic, and Denis Dzidic. "100,000 Bones Exhibit to Open in Srebrenica." Balkan Insight, July 7, 2015. https://balkaninsight. com/2015/07/07/one-hundred-thousand-bone s-to-open-in-srebrenica/.

Elek, Jennifer K., and Paula Hannaford-Agor. "First, Do No Harm: On Addressing the Problem of Implicit Bias in Juror Decision Making." *Court Review: The Journal of the American Judges Association* 49, no. 4 (2013): 190–98.

Equal Justice Initiative. "Slavery in America: The Montgomery Slave Trade," 2018. https://eji.org/report/slavery-in-america/montgomery-slave-trade/.

Erizanu, Paula. "Yugoslav Masterpiece and Party Hotspot: The Historical Museum of Bosnia and Herzegovina | Concrete Ideas." The Calvert Journal, November 15, 2021. https://www.calvertjournal.com/articles/ show/13280/historical-museum-of-bosnia-and-herzegovina-yugoslav-modernist-masterpiece-party-hotspot-concrete-ideas.

Etlin, Richard A. *The Architecture of Death: The Transformation of the Cemetery in Eighteenth-Century Paris.* Cambridge, MA: MIT Press, 1984.

Farber, Jessie Lie. "Symbolism on Gravestones." The Association for Gravestone Studies. https://www.gravestonestudies.org/knowledge-center/symbolism.

Farley, Edward. *Divine Empathy: A Theology of God.* Minneapolis: Fortress Press, 1996.

Fein, Helen. "Remembering for the Present: Using the Holocaust to Misunderstand Genocide and to Segregate the 'Final Solution of the

Jewish Question.'" In *Remembering the Future: The Holocaust in an Age of Genocide*, edited by John K. Roth, Elisabeth Maxwell, Margot Levy, and Wendy Whitworth, 43–54. New York: Palgrave, 2001.

Felman, Shoshana, and Dori Laub. *Testimony: Crisis of Witnessing in Literature, Psychoanalysis, and History*. New York: Routledge, 1992.

Figley, Charles R. *Compassion Fatigue: Coping with Secondary Traumatic Stress Disorder in Those Who Treat the Traumatized*. New York: Brunner/Mazel, 1995.

———. "Compassion Fatigue: Toward a New Understanding of the Costs of Caring." In *Secondary Traumatic Stress: Self-Care Issues for Clinicians, Researchers, and Educators*, edited by B. H. Stamm, 3–28. Lutherville, MD: Sidran Press, 1995.

———. *Encyclopedia of Trauma: An Interdisciplinary Guide*. Thousand Oaks, CA: Sage, 2012.

Fisher, Janina. *Healing the Fragmented Selves of Trauma Survivors: Overcoming Internal Self-Alienation*. London: Routledge, 2017.

Francis, Doris. "Cemeteries as Cultural Landscapes." *Mortality* 8, no. 2 (2003): 57–69.

Franklin, John, and Lila Petar Vrklevski. "Vicarious Trauma: The Impact on Solicitors of Exposure to Traumatic Material." *Traumatology* 14, no. 1 (2008): 1106–118.

Frazier, Patricia A., and Laura J. Schauben. "Vicarious Trauma: The Effects on Female Counselors of Working with Sexual Violence Survivors." *Psychology of Women Quarterly* 19, no. 1 (1995): 49–64.

Freedom Struggle Committee. "A Memorial to Honor Victims of Lynching in North Carolina." https://www.raleighcharterhs.org/fsc/.

Freud, Sigmund. *The Uncanny*. London: Penguin, 2003.

Fridman, Orli. "'Too Young to Remember Determined Not to Forget': Memory Activists Engaging with Returning ICTY Convicts." *International Criminal Justice Review* 28, no. 4 (December 2018): 423–37.

Friedland, Amos. "Pumla Gobodo-Madikizela, a Human Being Died That Night: A South African Story of Forgiveness." *Perspectives on Evil and Human Wickedness* 1, no. 4 (2004): 76–84.

Fromm, Eric. *The Art of Listening*. London: Continuum, 1998.

Frost, Natasha. "Horrors of Auschwitz: The Numbers Behind WWII's Deadliest Concentration Camp." History, January 21, 2020. https://www.history.com/news/auschwitz-concentration-camp-numbers.

Foucault, Michel, and J. Miskowiec. "On Other Spaces." *Diacritics* 16, no. 1 (1986): 22–27.

Fullard, Madeleine. "Some Trace Remains (An Extract)." *Kronos* 44 (2018): 163–80.

Gadzo, Mersiha. "Can Aircraft Technology Uncover Mass Graves in Bosnia?" Aljazeera, February 23, 2021. https://www.aljazeera.com/features/2021/2/23/could-lidar-help-uncover-clandestine-mass-graves-in-bosnia.

Galerija 11/07/95. "About." https://galerija110795.ba/about-gallery-110795/.

Garrison, Greg. "Slave Trade to Mass Incarceration, Museum Tells Grim Truth." Al.com, October 1, 2021. https://www.al.com/life/2021/10/slave-trade-to-mass-incarceration-museum-tells-grim-truth.html.

Gaziz-Sax, Joel. "A Brief History of Cemeteries." City of the Silent, 2011. http://www.alsirat.com/silence/history.html.

Gillett, Richard. "Workers: A Missing Link in the Theology-Economics Debate." *ATR* 92, no. 4 (October 2010): 753–60.

Gilligan, Carol. *In a Different Voice: Psychological Theory and Women's Development.* Cambridge, MA: Harvard University Press, 2016.

Gobodo-Madikizela, Pumla. "Biography." https://pumlagm.com/biography/.

———. "In Conversation with Pumla Gobodo-Madikizela." Interview by Tamar Garb, University College London, November 6, 2020. https://www.ucl.ac.uk/racism-racialisation/transcript-conversation-pumla-gobodo-madikizela.

———. "Remorse, Forgiveness, Rehumanization." *Journal of Humanistic Psychology* 42, no. 1 (Winter 2002): 7–32.

Gourevitch, Philip. "After the Genocide." *The New Yorker*, December 10, 1995. https://www.newyorker.com/magazine/1995/12/18/after-the-genocide.

Grebo, Lamija. "Bosnian Serb War Criminal Rasoslav Brdjanin Released Early." Balkan Insight, September 5, 2022. https://balkaninsight.com/2022/09/05/bosnian-serb-war-criminal-radoslav-brdjanin-released-early/.

GREENinc. "The Freedom Park Garden of Remembrance." https://www.greeninc.co.za/the-freedom-park-garden-of-remembrance.

Greenspan, Henry, Sara R. Horowitz, Éva Kovács, Berel Lang, Dori Laub, Kenneth Waltzer, and Annette Wieviorka. "Engaging Survivors: Assessing 'Testimony' and 'Trauma' as Foundational Concepts." *Dapim: Studies on the Holocaust* 28, no. 3 (2014): 190–226.

Griffith, D. W., dir. *Birth of a Nation.* 1915. Los Angeles: Triangle Film Corp. (film)

Gruspier, Katherine, and Michael S. Pollanen. "Forensic Legacy of the Khmer Rouge: The Cambodian Genocide." *Academic Forensic Pathology* 7, no. 3 (2017): 415–33.

Haglund, William D., Melissa Connor, and Douglas D. Scott. "The Archaeology of Contemporary Mass Graves." *Historical Archaeology* 35, no. 1 (2001): 57–69.

Hajdari, Una. "Bosnia's Peace Envoy Bans Genocide Denial." Politico, July 23, 2021. https://www.politico.eu/article/bosnia-peace-envoy-bans-genocide-denial/.

Halbwachs, Maurice. *On Collective Memory*. Translated by Lewis A. Coser. Chicago: University of Chicago Press, 1992.

Halifax, Joan. *Standing at the Edge: Finding Freedom Where Fear and Courage Meet*. New York: Flatiron Books, 2018.

Halili, Dafina. "Anita Mitic—Living Life as an Activist." Kosovo 2.0, September 3, 2019. https://kosovotwopointzero.com/en/a-life-of-activism/.

Halilović, Jasminko. "The Idea, Mission and Vision." War Childhood Museum, July 27, 2015. https://warchildhood.org/the-idea-mission-and-vision/.

Handschuh, David, Elana Newman, and Roger Simpson. "Trauma Exposure and Post-Traumatic Stress Disorder Among Photojournalists." *Visual Communications Quarterly* 10, no. 1 (2003): 4–13.

Harlan, Chico. "Bosnia Is Still Finding Bodies from a Genocide Some Leaders Claim Never Happened." *The Washington Post*, February 21, 2022. https://www.washingtonpost.com/world/2022/02/21/bosnia-genocide-denial-crisis/.

Hartman, Saidiya V. *Scenes of Subjection: Terror, Slavery, and Self-Making in Nineteenth-Century America*. New York: Oxford University Press, 1997.

Hašimbegović, Elma. "The History Museum of Bosnia and Herzegovina in Sarajevo." Observing Memories, December 2019. https://europeanmemories.net/magazine/the-history-museum-of-bosnia-and-herzegovina-in-sarajevo/.

Hatcher, Robert L. "Alliance Theory and Measurement." In *The Therapeutic Alliance: An Evidence-Based Guide to Practice*, edited by J. Christopher Muran and Jacques P. Barber, 7–28. New York: Gilford Press, 2010.

Hayes, Frank. "South Africa's Departure from the Commonwealth, 1960–1961." *The International History Review* 2, no. 3 (1980): 453–84.

Hennes, Tom. "Exhibitions: From a Perspective of Encounter." *Curator* 53, no. 1 (2010): 21–34.

———. "Witnessing Each Other: An Intersubjective Stance for Exhibitions Related to Substance Use and Abuse." *Substance Use & Misuse* 50, no. 8/9 (2015): 968–70.

Herman, Judith. *Trauma and Recovery*. New York: Basic Books, 1997.

Hirsch, Marianne. "Family Pictures: *Maus*, Mourning, and Post-Memory." *Discourse* 15, no. 2 (1992): 3–29.

———. "The Generation of Postmemory." *Poetics Today* 29, no. 1 (2008): 103–28.

———. "Surviving Images: Holocaust Photographs and the Work of Postmemory." *The Yale Journal of Criticism* 14, no. 1 (2001): 5–37.

Hite, Katherine. *Politics and the Art of Commemoration: Memorials to Struggle in Latin America and Spain.* New York: Routledge, 2012.

Hodalska, Magdalena. "Selfies at Horror Sites: Dark Tourism, Ghoulish Souvenirs and Digital Narcissism." *Zeszyty Prasoznawcze* 60, no. 2 (2017): 405–23.

Holocaust Memorial Day Trust. "The Srebrenica-Potočari Memorial Centre and Cemetery to the Victims of the 1995 Genocide." https://www.hmd. org.uk/wp-content/uploads/2014/04/Life-Story-Srebrenica-Genocide-Memorial.pdf.

Holocaust Museum Houston. "Virtual Lecture with Apartheid Museum Director Christopher Till." YouTube video, October 13, 2020, 57:35. https://www.youtube.com/watch?v=dsL8QtXPfSA.

hooks, bell. *Teaching Community: A Pedagogy of Hope.* New York: Routledge, 2003.

———. *Wounds of Passion.* New York: Macmillan, 1999.

Horn, Dara. *People Love Dead Jews: Reports from a Haunted Present.* New York: W. W. Norton, 2022.

Horvath, Adam O., and Lester Luborsky. "The Role of the Therapeutic Alliance in Psychotherapy." *Journal of Consulting and Clinical Psychology* 61, no. 4 (1993): 561–73.

Horwitz-Wasserman Holocaust Memorial Plaza. "Antisemitism Explained." https://www.philaholocaustmemorial.org/antisemitism-explained/.

Huener, Jonathan. *Auschwitz, Poland, and the Politics of Commemoration, 1945–1979.* Athens: Ohio University Press, 2004.

International Coalition of Sites of Conscience. https://www.sitesofconscience. org/en/home/.

In Your Pocket Essential City Guide. "KL Płaszów Concentration Camp in Kraków." March 16, 2022. https://www.inyourpocket.com/krakow/kl-plaszow-concentration-camp-in-krakow_73759f.

Isherwood, Christopher, Chester Kallman, and Wystan Hugh Auden. *The Complete Works of W. H. Auden: 1969–1973.* Princeton, NJ: Princeton University Press, 1988.

Jackson, Sharon, Kathryn Backett-Milburn, and Elinor Newall. "Researching Distressing Topics: Emotional Reflexivity and Emotional Labor in the Secondary Analysis of Children and Young People's Narratives of Abuse." *SAGE Open* (April 2013): 1–12. https://doi. org/10.1177/2158244013490705.

Jewish Virtual Library. "Jewish Holidays: Yom HaShoah-Holocaust Memorial Day." https://www.jewishvirtuallibrary.org/yom-ha-shoah-holocaust-memorial-day.

Joinson, Carla. "Coping with Compassion Fatigue." *Nursing* 22, no. 4 (1992): 116–21.

Jung, Carl. "Fundamental Questions of Psychotherapy." In *The Practice of Psychotherapy*, edited by Carl Jung, 111–25. Princeton, NJ: Princeton University Press, 1951.

———. *Memories, Dreams, Reflections*. New York: Pantheon Books, 1963.

———. *The Practice of Psychotherapy: Essays on the Psychology of the Transference and Other Subjects*. Princeton, NJ: Princeton University Press, 1951.

———. *The Psychology of Transference*. Princeton, NJ: Princeton University Press, 1946.

Justes, Emma. *Hearing Beyond the Words: How to Become a Listening Pastor*. Nashville: Abingdon Press, 2006.

Keinon, Herb, and Rebecca Anna Stoil. "Bush: Masada Will Never Fall Again." *The Jerusalem Post*, May 15, 2008. https://www.jpost.com/israel/bush-masada-will-never-fall-again.

Kent Graham, Larry. "Pastoral Theology and Catastrophic Disaster." *Journal of Pastoral Theology* 16, no. 2 (2006): 1–17.

Kenyon Emergency Services. "Mass Grave Exhumation and Identification." https://www.kenyoninternational.com/Our-Services/Disaster-Recovery-Services/mass-grave-exhumation-and-identification/.

Kershner, Isabel. "Yad Vashem Rebukes Israeli and Polish Governments over Holocaust Law." *The New York Times*, July 5, 2018. https://www.nytimes.com/2018/07/05/world/middleeast/israel-poland-holocaust.html.

Keyes, Allison. "In This Quiet Space for Contemplation, a Fountain Rains Down Calming Water." *Smithsonian Magazine*, September 21, 2017. https://www.smithsonianmag.com/smithsonian-institution/quiet-space-contemplation-fountain-rains-down-calming-waters-180964981/.

Kilgannon, Corey. "'Reopening Old Wounds': When 9/11 Remains Are Identified, 20 Years Later." *The New York Times*, September 6, 2021. https://www.nytimes.com/2021/09/06/nyregion/9-11-ground-zero-victims-remains.html.

Kim, Jeongsuk, Brittney Chesworth, Hannabeth Franchino-Olsen, and Rebecca J. Macy. "A Scoping Review of Vicarious Trauma Interventions for Service Providers Working with People Who Have Experienced Traumatic Events." *Trauma, Violence, & Abuse, epub March 9, 2021.* https://doi.org/10.1177/1524838021991310.

Kirk-Duggan, Cheryl A. "African-American Spirituals: Confronting and Exercising Evil through Song." In *A Troubling in My Soul: Womanist Perspectives on Evil and Suffering*, edited by Emile M. Townes, 150–71. New York: Orbis, 1993.

Kisicek, Gabrijela. "The Rhetoric of War: Former Yugoslavia Example." *Journal of Arts and Humanities* 2, no. 8 (2013): 75–84.

Klein, Ezra. Interview with Bessel van der Kolk. *The Ezra Klein Show*. Podcast audio, August 24, 2021. https://www.nytimes.com/2021/08/24/podcasts/transcript-ezra-klein-interviews-bessel-van-der-kolk.html.

Klein, Susan, and David Alexander. "The Impact of Trauma within Organisations." In *Managing Trauma in the Workplace: Supporting Workers and Organisations*, edited by Noreen Tehrani, 137–58. New York: Routledge, 2010.

Kleinman, Arthur. "Moral Experience and Ethical Reflection: Can Ethnography Reconcile Them? A Quandary for 'The New Bioethics.'" *Daedalus* 128, no. 4 (1999): 69–97.

Kleinman, Arthur, Paul E. Brodwin, Byron J. Good, and Mary-Jo Delvecchio Good. "Introduction." In *Pain as a Human Experience: An Anthropological Perspective*, edited by Mary-Jo Delvecchio Good, Paul E. Brodwin, Byron J. Good, and Arthur Kleinman, 1–28. Berkeley: University of California Press, 1992.

Klempner, Mark. "Navigating Life Review Interviews with Survivors of Trauma." *The Oral History Review* 27, no. 2 (2000): 67–83.

Krakow Museums. "Galicia Jewish Museum." http://www.mus eums.krakow.travel/en/muzea/id,72,trail,15,t,galicia-jewish-museum.html.

Kristeva, Julia. *Powers of Horror: An Essay on Abjection*. New York: Columbia Press, 1982.

Kritzinger, Johannes, and Martin Mande. "Theology Disrupted by the Challenge of Refugee Children." *HTS: Theological Studies* 72, no. 1 (2016): 1–10.

Krystal, Henry. *Integration and Self-Healing: Affect—Trauma and Alexithymia*. New York: Routledge, 1988.

Kucia, Marek. "The Meanings of Auschwitz in Poland, 1945 to the Present." *Holocaust Studies* 25, no. 3 (2019): 220–47.

Kwon, Heonik. *Ghosts of War in Vietnam*. Cambridge: Cambridge University Press, 2013.

Ladwig, Patrice, and Paul Williams. "Introduction." In *Buddhist Funeral Cultures of Southeast Asia and China*, edited by Patrice Ladwig and Paul Williams, 1–20. Cambridge: Cambridge University Press, 2012.

Laskowski, Cheryl, and Karen Pellicore. "The Wounded Healer Archetype: Applications to Palliative Care Practice." *American Journal of Hospice & Palliative Care* 19, no. 6 (November/December 2002): 403–7.

Lehman, K. F. "Museums and Marketing in an Electronic Age." PhD thesis, University of Tasmania, 2008.

Levine, Stephen B. "Psychological Intimacy." *Journal of Sex & Marital Therapy* 17, no. 4 (1991): 259–67.

Lewis, C. S. *The Problem of Pain*. Grand Rapids, MI: Zondervan, 2001.

Lifton, Robert J. *Boundaries*. New York: Random House, 1969.

Light, Duncan. "Progress in Dark Tourism and Thanatourism Research: An Uneasy Relationship with Heritage Tourism." *Tourism Management* 61 (2017): 275–301.

Limbs International. "Cambodia." https://www.limbsinternational.org/cambodia.html.

Linenthal, Edward. *Preserving Memory: The Struggle to Create America's Holocaust Museum*. New York: Columbia University Press, 2001.

Liphshiz, Cnaan. "In Poland, Plans to Build a Museum on Schindler Survivors' Former Camp Spark Environmental Protest." Jewish Telegraphic Agency, November 26, 2021. https://www.jta.org/2021/11/26/global/in-poland-plans-to-build-a-museum-on-schindler-survivors-former-camp-spark-environmental-protest.

López-Muñoz, Francisco, and Francisco Pérez-Fernández. "A History of the Alexithymia Concept and Its Explanatory Models: An Epistemological Perspective." *Frontiers* 10 (January 31, 2020): 1–8.

Long, Thomas G. "Habeas Corpus . . . Not." In *The Good Funeral: Death, Grief, and the Community of Care*, edited by Thomas G. Long and Thomas Lynch, 83–112. Louisville, KY: Westminster John Knox Press, 2013.

Long, Thomas, and Thomas Lynch. "Preface." In *The Good Funeral: Death, Grief, and the Community of Care*, edited by Thomas G. Long and Thomas Lynch, xxiii–xxiv. Louisville, KY: Westminster John Knox Press, 2013.

Lynch, Thomas. *The Undertaking: Life Studies from the Dismal Trade*. New York: W. W. Norton, 2010.

Machado, Daisy. "The Undocumented Woman in Aquino." In *A Reader in Latina Feminist Theology: Religion and Justice*, edited by Maria Pilar, Daisy Machado, and Jeanette Rodriguez, 161–76. New York: University of Texas Press, 2021.

Mandela, Nelson. *Long Walk to Freedom*. Boston: Back Bay Books, 1994.

Mann, Bonnie, and Jean Keller. "Why a Feminist Volume on Pluralism?" *Philosophical Topics* 41, no. 2 (2013): 1–11.

Margalit, Avishai. *Ethics of Memory*. Cambridge, MA: Harvard University Press, 2002.

Makom. "Second Conversation Chapter 4: Masada, 1942." Makom, November 8, 2013. https://makomisrael.org/second-conversation-chapter-four-masada-1942/.

Malcom, Lois. "An Interview with David Tracy." *The Christian Century*, February 13–20, 2002.

Marschall, Sabine. "Memory and Identity in South Africa: Contradictions and Ambiguities in the Process of Post-Apartheid Memorialization." *Visual Anthropology* 25, no. 3 (2012): 189–204.

Marston, John. "Khmer Rouge Songs." *Crossroads: An Interdisciplinary Journal of Southeast Asian Studies* 16, no. 1 (2002): 100–27.

Martin, Daniel D. "Identity Management of the Dead: Contests in the Construction of Murdered Children." *Symbolic Interaction* 33, no. 1 (2010): 18–40.

Maslach, Christina. "Burned-Out." *The Canadian Journal of Psychiatric Nursing* 20, no. 6 (1979): 5–9.

Maslach, Christina, and S. E. Jackson. *Maslach Burnout Inventory Manual*, 2nd ed. Palo Alto, CA: Consulting Psychologists Press, 1986.

Maslach, Christina, Tadeusz Marek, and Wilmar B. Schaufeli. *Professional Burnout: Recent Developments in Theory and Research*. Philadelphia: Taylor & Francis, 1993.

Maya Lin Studio. "Vietnam Veterans Memorial." https://www.mayalinstudio. com/memory-works/vietnam-veterans-memorial.

McCarroll, James E., Robert J. Ursano, Kathleen M. Wright, and Carol S. Fullerton. "Handling Bodies after Violent Death: Strategies for Coping." *American Journal of Orthopsychiatry* 63, no. 2 (1993): 209–14.

Menakem, Resmaa. *My Grandmother's Hands: Racialized Trauma and the Pathway to Mending Our Hearts and Bodies* (Las Vegas: Central Recovery Press, 2017).

Metz, Johann Baptist. "The Future in the Memory of Suffering." In *New Questions on God*, edited by Johannes Baptist Metz, 9–20. New York: Herder & Herder, 1972.

Meyer, Melissa. *Blood Is Thicker Than Water: The Origins of Blood as Symbol and Ritual*. New York: Routledge, 2005.

Migration Memorials Project. "Wounded Knee Memorial." https://migration memorials.trinity.duke.edu/items/wounded-knee-memorial.

Miller, John. "Greetings America, My Name Is Osama Bin Laden . . ." Frontline, February 1, 1999. https://www.pbs.org/wgbh/pages/frontline/ shows/binladen/who/miller.html.

Mills, Elizabeth Shown, and Gary B. Mills. "Missionaries Compromised: Early Evangelization of Slaves and Free People of Color in North Louisiana." In *Cross, Crozier, and Crucible*, edited by Glenn R. Conrad, 30–47. New Orleans: Archdiocese of New Orleans and the Center for Louisiana Studies, 1993.

Minow, Martha. "The Work of Re-Membering: After Genocide and Mass Atrocity." *23 Fordham International Law Journal* 23, no. 2 (1999): 429–39.

Mitford, Jessica. *The American Way of Death Revisited*. New York: Vintage Books, 2000.

Morris, Rosalind. "Giving Up Ghosts: Notes on Trauma and the Possibility of the Political from Southeast Asia." *East Asia Cultures Critique* 16, no. 1 (2008): 229–58.

Morris, Virginia. *Talking About Death*. Chapel Hill, NC: Algonquin Books of Chapel Hill, 2001.

Morrison, Kenneth. "Crossing the Rubicon: The Outbreak of War in Sarajevo." In *Sarajevo's Holiday Inn on the Frontline of Politics and War*, edited by Kenneth Morrison, 103–16. London: Palgrave Macmillan, 2016.

Muzeum KL Płaszkow. "About the Museum." https://plaszow.org/en/about-the-museum/mission-and-strategy.

Mydans, Seth. "Cambodia Profits from Killing Fields and Other Symbols." *The New York Times*, November 6, 2005. https://www.nytimes.com/2005/11/06/world/asia/cambodia-profits-from-killing-fields-and-other-symbols.html.

National Archives. "13th Amendment to the US Constitution: Abolition of Slavery (1865)." https://www.archives.gov/milestone-documents/13th-amendment#:~:text=Passed%20by%20Congress%20on%20January,slavery%20in%20the%20United%20States.

National Park Service. "Trail of Tears." https://www.nps.gov/trte/index.htm.

Ndlovu, Thabisani. "Shuttling Between the Suburbs and the Township: The New Black Middle Class(es) Negotiating Class and Post-Apartheid Blackness in South Africa." *Africa* 90, no. 3 (2020): 568–86.

Neshoma Project. "What Is The Neshoma Project?" https://neshomaproject.org/about.

Newman, Elana, Roger Simpson, and David Handschuh. "Trauma Exposure and Post-Traumatic Stress Disorder Among Photojournalists." *Visual Communications Quarterly* 10, no. 1 (2003): 4–13.

9/11 Memorial & Museum. "Collections Management Policy." 2018. https://www.911memorial.org/sites/default/files/inline-files/museum_collections_management_policy_full_1.pdf.

9/11 Memorial & Museum. "9/11 Memorial & Museum Mission." https://www.911memorial.org/about.

Nora, Pierre. "Between History and Memory: Lieu de Memoire." *Representations* 26 (1989): 7–24.

Nouwen, Henri. *Creative Ministry*. New York: Doubleday, 2013.

———. *Out of Solitude: Three Meditations on the Christian Life*. Notre Dame: Ave Maria Press, 2004.

———. *The Wounded Healer: Ministry in Contemporary Society*. New York: Doubleday, 1979.

The Observer. "'It's Getting Out of Hand': Genocide Denial Outlawed in Bosnia." *The Guardian*, July 24, 2001. https://www.theguardian.

com/world/2021/jul/24/genocide-denial-outlawed-bosnia-srebrenica-office-high-representative.

Ogden, Thomas H. "On Holding and Containing, Being and Dreaming." *International Journal of Psychoanalysis* 85 (2004): 1349–64.

Otto, Rudolf. *The Idea of the Holy*. Translated by John W. Harvey. Oxford: Oxford University Press, 1923.

Owen, Taylor. "Bombs over Cambodia." *The Walrus*, October 12, 2007. https://thewalrus.ca/2006-10-history/.

Panić, Katarina. "The White Armband Day: Activism at Its Best." Fair Planet, June 6, 2020. https://www.fairplanet.org/editors-pick/the-white-armband-day-activism-at-its-best/.

Pearlman, Laurie Anne. "Restoring Self in Community: Collective Approaches to Psychological Trauma after Genocide." *Journal of Social Issues* 69, no. 1 (2013): 111–24.

Pembroke, Neil. *The Art of Listening: Dialogue, Shame, and Pastoral Care*. Grand Rapids, MI: Wm. B. Eerdmans, 2002.

Pinn, Anthony B., and Anne H. Pinn. *Fortress Introduction to Black Church History*. Minneapolis: Fortress Press, 2002.

Ponchaud, Francois. *Cambodia: Year Zero*. New York: Henry Holt, 1978.

Pope Francis. "Speech at the 9/11 Memorial & Museum." Catholic News Agency, September 25, 2015. https://www.catholicnewsagency.com/news/32701/full-text-pope-francis-speech-at-the-911-memorial-and-museum.

Raboteau, Albert J. *Slave Religion: The "Invisible Institution" in the Antebellum South*. Oxford: Oxford University Press, 2004.

Radio Slobodna Evropa. "Bijela Traka Nije naš Izbor, Nego Njihovo Djelo." Translated by Armin Halilović. May 31, 2022. https://www.slobodnaevropa.org/a/prijedor-dan-bijelih-traka-zlocin/31877209.html?fbclid=IwAR0p7rR4hPnAM4vHlA6cQjYsrJwMT-PEMp4-aU6sniexlfQRA0vxWVbElPU.

Rafferty, Andrew. "$700 Million and Counting: 9/11 Museum Opens with Money Worries." NBC News, May 15, 2014. https://www.nbcnews.com/news/us-news/700-million-counting-9-11-museum-opens-money-worries-n106536.

Rambo, Shelly. *Resurrecting Wounds: Living in the Afterlife of Trauma*. Waco: Baylor University Press, 2017.

———. "Spirit and Trauma." *Interpretation: A Journal of Bible and Theology* 69, no. 9 (January 2015): 7–19.

———. *Spirit and Trauma: A Theology of Remaining*. Louisville, KY: Westminster John Knox Press, 2010.

Rare Historical Photos. "The Racist Signs of Apartheid Seen through Rare Photographs, 1950–1990." Rare Historical Photos, December 12,

2021. https://rarehistoricalphotos.com/signs-apartheid-south-africa-1950-1990/.

Reamer, Frederic G. "Boundary Issues in Social Work: Managing Dual Relationships." *Social Work* 48, no. 1 (2003): 121–33.

Regebr, C., and S. Cadell. "Secondary Trauma in Sexual Assault Crisis Work: Implications for Therapists and Therapy." *Canadian Social Work* 1, no. 1 (1999): 56–63.

Remembering Srebrenica. "Remembering Srebrenica Comment on the Desecration of the Srebrenica Genocide Memorial." https://srebrenica.org.uk/news/remembering-srebrenica-comment-desecration.

———. "UK National Srebrenica Memorial Day Programme and Annual Report." https://srebrenica.org.uk/wp-content/uploads/2021/07/2021-Programme-Annual-Report-WEB-01.pdf.

Resina, Joan Ramon. "The Weight of Memory and the Lightness of Oblivion: The Dead of the Spanish Civil War." In *Unearthing Franco's Legacy*, edited by Carlos Jerez-Farrán and Samuel Amago, 229–30. Notre Dame: University of Notre Dame Press, 2010.

Reznick, Charlotte. *The Power of Your Child's Imagination: How to Transform Stress and Anxiety into Joy and Success*. Westminster: TarcherPerigee, 2009.

Rice, Michael J., and Mary D. Moller. "Wellness Outcomes of Trauma Psychoeducation." *Archives of Psychiatric Nursing* 20, no. 2 (2006): 94–102.

Ricoeur, Paul. *Figuring the Sacred*. Minneapolis: Fortress Press, 1995.

———. *Freud and Philosophy*. New Haven, CT: Yale University Press, 1965.

———. *Hermeneutics and the Human Sciences*. Cambridge: Cambridge University Press, 1981.

———. *Memory, History, Forgetting*. Translated by Kathleen Blamey and David Pellauer. Chicago: University of Chicago Press, 2004.

———. *On Psychoanalysis: Writings and Lectures*. Cambridge: Polity, 2012.

Riedlmayer, András J. "Destruction of Cultural Heritage in Bosnia-Herzegovina, 1992–1996: A Post-War Survey of Selected Municipalities." Cambridge, MA: International Criminal Tribunal for the Former Yugoslavia, 2002. http://heritage.sensecentar.org/assets/sarajevo-national-library/sg-3-01-destruction-culturale-en.pdf.

Rieff, David. *Slaughterhouse: Bosnia and the Failure of the West*. New York: Simon & Schuster, 1996.

Robben Island Museum. "RIM Establishment." August 3, 2022. https://www.robben-island.org.za/organisation.

Rogers, Annie. *The Unsayable: The Hidden Language of Trauma*. New York: Ballantine Books, 2007.

Ross, Susan A. *Extravagant Affections: A Feminist Sacramental Theology.* New York: Continuum, 2001.

Rouseau, Nicky, Riedwaan Moosage, and Ciraj Rassool. "Missing and Missed: Rehumanisation, the Nation and Missing-Ness." *Kronos* 44 (2018): 10–32.

Rudic, Filip. "Hague Court Chief Criticises Serbian PM's Genocide Denial." Balkan Transitional Justice, November 20, 2018. https://balkaninsight.com/2018/11/20/hague-tribunal-chief-criticises-serbian-pm-s-genocide-denial-11-20-2018/.

Saakvitne, Karen W., and Laurie Anne Pearlman. *Transforming the Pain: A Workbook on Vicarious Traumatization.* New York: W. W. Norton, 1996.

Schauben, Laura J., and Patricia A. Frazier. "Vicarious Trauma: The Effects on Female Counselors of Working with Sexual Violence Survivors." *Psychology of Women Quarterly* 19, no. 1 (1995): 49–64.

Schwartz, Fred. "Reflecting on the Essence of Auschwitz." *The New York Times*, February 26, 2011. https://www.nytimes.com/2011/02/27/opinion/l27auschwitz.html.

Self, Will. "A Posthumous Shock: How Everything Became Trauma." *Harpers*, December 2021, https://harpers.org/archive/2021/12/a-posthumous-shock-trauma-studies-modernity-how-everything-became-trauma/.

"Serbian PM Ana Brnabic: Srebrenica 'A Terrible Crime,' Not Genocide." Deutche Welle, November 15, 2018. https://www.dw.com/en/serbian-pm-ana-brnabic-srebrenica-a-terrible-crime-not-genocide/a-46307925.

Sharma, Nitasha. "Dark Tourism and Moral Disengagement in Liminal Spaces." *Tourism Geographies* 22, no. 2 (2020): 273–97.

Shearing, Clifford, and Michael Kempa. "A Museum of Hope: A Story of Robben Island." *The Annals of the American Academy of Political and Social Science* 592, no. 1 (2004): 62–78.

Sheppard, Phillis. "Hegemonic Imagination, Historical Ethos, and Colonized Minds in the Pedagogical Space: Pastoral Ethics and Teaching as if Our Lives Depended on It." *Journal of Pastoral Theology* 27, no. 3 (2017): 181–94.

———. "Womanist-Lesbian Pastoral Ethics: A Post Election Perspective." *Journal of Pastoral Theology* 27, no. 1 (2017): 152–70.

Siad, Arnaud. "The 'Butcher of Bosnia' Radovan Karadzic Will Serve His Genocide Sentence in a UK Prison." CNN, May 12, 2021. https://www.cnn.com/2021/05/12/europe/radovan-karadzic-uk-prison-genocide-sentence-intl/index.html.

Sodaro, Amy. *Exhibiting Atrocity: Memorial Museums and the Politics of Past Violence.* New Brunswick: Rutgers University Press, 2018.

————. "Memory, History, and Nostalgia in Berlin's Jewish Museum." *International Journal of Politics, Culture, and Society* 26 (March 2013): 77–91.

Sokol, Sam. "Top Polish Institute Accused of Firing Historians over Holocaust-Era Research." *Haaretz*, November 21, 2021. https://www.haaretz.com/world-news/europe/.premium.HIGHLIGHT-top-polish-institute-accused-of-firing-historians-over-holocaust-research-1.10398136.

SouthAfrica.co.za. "Day of Reconciliation." https://southafrica.co.za/day-of-reconciliation.html.

Stein, Edith. *On Empathy*. Translated by Waltraut Stein. Washington, DC: ICS Publications, 1989.

Stern, Daniel. *The Interpersonal World of the Infant: A View from Psychoanalysis and Developmental Psychology*. New York: Basic Books, 1985.

Stroebe, Wolfgang, and Margaret S. Stroebe. "Is Grief Universal? Cultural Variations in the Emotional Reaction to Loss." In *Death and Identity*, 3rd ed., edited by R. Fulton and R. Bendickson, 117–209. Philadelphia: The Charles Press, 1994.

Sturken, Marita. *Tourists of History: Memory, Kitsch, and Consumerism from Oklahoma City to Ground Zero*. Durham: Duke University Press, 2007.

Suljagić, Emir. "Denial of Genocide and Other War Crimes Committed in Bosnia as a Form of Collective Memory." *Bosnian Studies: Journal for Research of Bosnian Thought and Culture* 6, no. 1 (2022): 4–23.

Swain, Storm. *Trauma and Transformation at Ground Zero: A Pastoral Theology*. Minneapolis: Augsburg Fortress, 2011.

Taylor, Graeme J. *Psychosomatic Medicine and Contemporary Psychoanalysis*. Madison, CT: International Universities Press, 1987.

Tehrani, Noreen. "Building Resilient Organisations in a Complex World." In *Managing Trauma in the Workplace: Supporting Workers and Organisations*, edited by Noreen Tehrani, 298–313. New York: Routledge, 2010.

————. "The Incidence of Secondary Traumatic Stress in Workers Dealing with Traumatising Materials, Victims and Perpetrators." In *Managing Trauma in the Workplace: Supporting Workers and Organisations*, edited by Noreen Tehrani, 100–14. New York: Routledge, 2010.

Terr, Lenore. *Too Scared to Cry: Psychic Trauma in Childhood*. New York: Basic Books, 1990.

Tillich, Paul. *Systematic Theology*. Chicago: University of Chicago Press, 1967.

————. *The World Situation*. Philadelphia: Fortress Press, 1965.

Thimm, Barbara. "Fragen Sind geblieben: Aber es Sind Andere." *Gedenkstätten-Rundbrief* 180 (2015): 37–43.

Thimm, Barbara, Gottfried Kößler, and Susanne Ulrich, eds. *Verunsichernde Orte: Selbstverständis und Weiterbildung in der Gedenkstättenpädagogik*. Frankfurt am Main: Brandes & Apsel Verlag, 2010.

Thimm, Barbara, and Chhay Visoth. "Displaying New Reprints at Tuol Sleng Genocide Museum Obtains New Information and Further Questions." *DK Memosis*, June 6, 2018. https://dkmemosis.wordpress.com/2018/06/26/displaying-new-reprints-at-tuol-sleng-genocide-museum-obtains-new-information-and-further-questions/.

Tise, Larry E. *Proslavery: A History of the Defense of Slavery in America, 1701–1840*. Athens: University of Georgia Press, 1987.

Tracy, David. *The Analogical Imagination: Christian Theology and the Culture of Pluralism*. New York: The Crossroad Publishing Company, 1981.

———. *Fragments: The Existential Situation of Our Time*. Chicago: University of Chicago Press, 2019.

———. *Plurality and Ambiguity: Hermeneutics, Religion, and Hope*. Chicago: University of Chicago Press, 1987.

———. "The Role of Theology in Public Life: Some Reflections." *Word & World* 4, no. 3 (1984): 230–39.

Tronto, Joan. "Joan Tronto." Interview by Ethics of Care, August 4, 2009. https://ethicsofcare.org/joan-tronto/.

———. *Moral Boundaries: A Political Argument for an Ethic of Care*. New York: Routledge, 1994.

Tuol Sleng Genocide Museum. "Home." https://tuolsleng.gov.kh/en/.

———. "Khmer New Year Blessing Ceremony." https://tuolsleng.gov.kh/en/2016/05/16/khmer-new-year-blessing-ceremony/.

———. "Support Us." https://tuolsleng.gov.kh/en/collections/archive-research/support-us/.

———. "Tuol Sleng Genocide Museum." https://tuolsleng.gov.kh/en/museum/.

Tutu, Desmond. *God Has a Dream: A Vision of Hope for Our Time*. New York: Doubleday, 2003.

212 Brdska Brigada Srebrenik. "Serbs Demolition of Mosque in Bijeljina, and Ethnic Cleansing 17.3.93." YouTube video, January 20, 2012, 6:35. https://www.youtube.com/watch?v=Vze9v9GrO5w.

Ulanov, Ann Belford. "The Space between Pastoral Care and Global Terrorism." *Scottish Journal of Healthcare Chaplaincy* 10, no. 2 (2007): 3–8.

———. *The Unshuttered Heart: Opening Aliveness/Deadness in the Self*. Nashville: Abingdon Press, 2007.

Unesco. "Tuol Sleng Genocide Museum Archives Preservation and Digitization Project." https://en.unesco.org/themes/holocaust-genocide-education/tuol-sleng-genocide-museum-archives.

United States Holocaust Museum. "Brochure for an Austrian Exhibition Titled 'Never Forget.'" https://www.ushmm.org/propaganda/archive/never-forget-brochure/.

———. "Death March from Auschwitz." https://www.ushmm.org/learn/timeline-of-events/1942-1945/death-march-from-auschwitz.

———. "International Holocaust Remembrance Day." https://encyclopedia.ushmm.org/content/en/article/international-holocaust-remembrance-day.

Unruh, David R. "Death and Personal History: Strategies of Identity Preservation." *Social Problems* 30, no. 3 (1983): 340–51.

van der Kolk, Bessel A. *The Body Keeps the Score*. New York: Penguin, 2015.

———. *Psychological Trauma*. Washington, DC: American Psychiatric Publishing, 1987.

van der Kolk, Bessel A., and Alexander C. McFarlane. "The Black Hole of Trauma." In *Traumatic Stress*, edited by Bessel A. van der Kolk, Alexander C. McFarlane, and Lars Weisaeth, 3–23. New York: The Guilford Press, 1996.

Venet, Alex Shevrin. "Role-Clarity and Boundaries for Trauma-Informed Teachers." *Educational Considerations* 44, no. 2 (2019): 1–9.

Vincent-Höper, Sylvie, Mareike Adler, Maie Stein, Claudia Vaupel, and Albert Nienhaus. "Sexually Harassing Behaviors from Patients or Clients and Care Workers' Mental Health: Development and Validation of a Measure." *International Journal of Environmental Research and Public Health* 17, no. 7 (2020): 2570.

Volcan, Vamik. *Killing in the Name of Identity: A Study of Bloody Conflicts.* Durham: Pitchstone Publishing, 2006.

von Franz, Marie-Louise. *The Problem of the Puer Aeternus*. Ontario: Inner City Books, 2000.

Vrklevski, Lila Petar, and John Franklin. "Vicarious Trauma: The Impact on Solicitors of Exposure to Traumatic Material." *Traumatology* 14, no. 1 (2008): 106–18.

Wanner, Catherine. "An Affective Atmosphere of Religiosity: Animated Places, Public Spaces, and the Politics of Attachment in the Ukraine and Beyond," *Comparative Studies* 62, no. 1 (2020): 68–105.

War Childhood Museum. "The Idea, Mission and Vision." https://warchildhood.org/the-idea-mission-and-vision/.

Ward, William A. "The Philosophy of Death in Coptic Epitaphs." *Journal of Bible and Religion* 25, no. 1 (1957): 34–40.

Warner, W. Lloyd. *The Living and the Dead: A Study in the Symbolic Representations of Americans*. New Haven, CT: Yale University Press, 1959.

Waxman, Oliva B. "The First Africans in Virginia Landed in 1619: It Was a Turning Point for Slavery in American History—But Not the Beginning." *Time Magazine*, August 20, 2019. https://time.com/5653369/august-1619-jamestown-history/.

The Week Staff. "'Butcher of Bosnia': Why War Criminal Ratko Mladic Has Hero Status Among Some in the Balkans." *The Week*, June 9, 2021. https://www.theweek.co.uk/news/world-news/europe/953073/why-ratko-mladic-butcher-of-bosnia-still-hero-balkans.

Welch, Sharon. "Dangerous Memory and Alternate Knowledges." In *On Violence*, edited by Bruce B. Lawrence and Aisha Karim, 363–76. Durham: Duke University Press, 2007.

Whalen, William J. "How Different Religions Pay Their Final Respects." In *Annual Editions: Dying, Death, and Bereavement*, edited by G. E. Dickinson and M. R. Leming, 126–28. New York: McGraw Hill, 2011.

Whitman, Walt. "Song of Myself." *In Leaves of Grass*, 1–64. Nashville: American Renaissance, 2009. Orig. pub. 1855, Brooklyn.

Whitney Plantation. "Plantation Owners." https://www.whitneyplantation.org/history/plantation-owners/#:~:text=Jean%20Jacques%20did%20more%20than,1820%2C%20Jean%20Jacques%20Haydel%20Sr.

———. "Whitney Plantation History." https://www.whitneyplantation.org/history/.

Wiesel, Elie. "40th Anniversary Symposium: Wisdom for the Next Generation." Interview by Moment Magazine. *Moment Magazine*, May–June 2015.

———. "Nobel Lecture." Speech, Oslo, Norway, December 11, 1986. https://www.nobelprize.org/prizes/peace/1986/wiesel/lecture/.

———. "Nobel Peace Prize Acceptance Speech." Oslo, Norway, December 10, 1986. https://www.nobelprize.org/prizes/peace/1986/wiesel/acceptance-speech/.

Williams, Dominic. "Punch and the Pogroms: Eastern Atrocities in John Tenniel's Political Cartoons, 1876–1896." *Canadian Art Review* 42, no. 1 (2017): 32–47.

Williams, Paul. "The Personalization of Loss in Memorial Museums." In *The Oxford Handbook of Public History*, edited by James B. Gardner and Paula Hamilton, 369–86. New York: Oxford University Press, 2017.

Wilson J. P., and R. B. Thomas. *Empathy in the Treatment of Trauma and PTSD*. East Sussex: Brunner-Routledge, 2004.

Winfrey, Oprah, and Bruce Perry. *What Happened to You? Conversations on Trauma, Resilience, and Healing*. London: Boxtree, 2021.

Wolcott, Harry F. *The Art of Fieldwork*, 2nd ed. Lanham: AltaMira Press, 2004.

Wood, Rulon, Julia Berger, and Marouf Hasain. "Public Memory, Digital Media, and Prison Narratives at Robben Island." *ESSACHESS Journal for Communication Studies* 10, no. 1 (2017): 173–97.

Writer, Jeanette Haynes. "Terrorism in Native America: Interrogating the Past, Examining the Present, and Constructing a Liberatory Future." *Anthropology & Education Quarterly* 33, no. 3 (2002): 317–30.

Yad Vashem. "Auchwitz-Birkenau Extermination Camp." https://www.yadvashem.org/holocaust/about/final-solution/auschwitz.html.

———. "Martyrs; and Heroes Remembrance (Yad Vashem) Law 5713–1953." https://www.yadvashem.org/about/yad-vashem-law.html.

———. "Mission Statement." https://www.yadvashem.org/about/mission-statement.html.

———. "Newsletter, no. 29, May 2013." https://www.yadvashem.org/yv/en/newsletters/general/newsletter_print.asp?cid=1052013.

———. "Propaganda and the Visual Arts in the Third Reich." https://www.yadvashem.org/education/educational-materials/lesson-plans/germanys-sculptor.html.

Yehuda, Rachel, and Amy Lehrner. "Intergenerational Transmission of Trauma Effects: Putative Role of Epigenetic Mechanisms." *World Psychiatry* 17, no. 3 (2018): 243–57.

Yehuda, Rachel, Stephanie Mulherin Engel, Sarah R. Brand, Jonathan Seckl, Sue M. Marcus, and Gertrud S. Berkowitz. "Transgenerational Effects of Posttraumatic Stress Disorder in Babies of Mothers Exposed to the World Trade Center Attacks during Pregnancy." *The Journal of Clinical Endocrinology & Metabolism* 90, no. 7 (2005): 4115–18.

Young, James. "The Memorial's Arc: Between Berlin's Denkmal and New York City's 9/11 Memorial." *Memory Studies* 9, no. 3 (July 2016): 325–31.

———. *The Stages of Memory: Reflections on Memorial Art, Loss and the Spaces Between.* Amherst: University of Massachusetts Press, 2017.

———. *The Texture of Memory: Holocaust Memorials and Meaning.* New Haven, CT: Yale University Press, 1993.

Zembylas, Michalinos, and Zvi Bekerman. "Education and the Dangerous Memories of Historical Trauma: Narratives of Pain, Narratives of Hope." *Curriculum Inquiry* 38, no. 2 (2008): 125–54.

Zizioulas, John D. *Being as Communion: Studies in Personhood and the Church.* Yonkers: St. Vladimir's Seminary Press, 1997.

———. *Communion and Otherness: Further Studies in Personhood and the Church.* Edinburgh: A&C Black, 2006.

INDEX

9/11, xiii, xxiv, xxvii, xxxi, 1, 5, 8, 15, 28, 30, 35, 37, 74, 75, 81, 86, 92, 116, 120, 122, 124, 175n36, 176n40, 188n50, 191n12, 195n40, 201n18

9/11 Memorial & Museum, or National September 11 Memorial & Museum, xi, xxiv, xxvii, 1, 8, 13, 16, 18, 19, 24, 28, 34–35, 37–39, 41, 43, 74, 76, 79, 84, 86, 89, 92–93, 108–11, 116–18, 121–22, 124–26, 131, 135–36, 141, 151n73, 151n74, 158n3, 166n43, 166n48, 168n57; accountant, 74, 130; Administration, Director, 54, 71, 130, 136–37, 149, 154, 217

Africa, xi, xi, 39, 43, 70, 123, 171, 179, 222

Afrikaans, xix, 26

African National Congress (ANC), xix

Affective, affectivity, xxxv, xxxvii, 4, 14–15, 17, 72, 87, 92, 139, 168n61, 169n62, 182n18, 191n17

Agger, Inger, 183n21, 184n24

Aitchison, John, 26–27, 175n30

al Qaeda, xxiv

Alabama, United States, xxiv, 28

Ali, 69–70, 70n44, 73, 101, 110–11, 141

Alliance, xxxiii, 41, 83–84, 86, 89, 91, 113, 191n13, 199n1

Ambiguity, xxxvii, 4, 7–8, 10–12, 17, 27, 29, 30, 34, 140, 141, 159n7, 159n8, 168n61

Ambiguous Loss, xl, 29, 30, 31–34, 176n40, 176n42, 176n43

Amnesty International, xvi, 147n25

Ancestors, 13, 39, 58, 69–71, 73, 101, 111, 166n48, 187n44

Antisemitism, 7, 171n1

Apartheid, x, xiii, xviii, xix–xxi, xxxi, 18, 21–22, 26–27, 30, 43, 59–61, 63, 109, 112, 141, 171n3

Apartheid Museum, xix, 13, 16, 37–38, 59–61, 63, 66, 79, 83, 97, 105, 108, 111, 131, 149n47, 166n43, 175n31, 184n29

Arad, Michael, 1, 157n1

Arbeit Macht Frei, 51, 79

Archetypes, xli, 157n30

Architecture, 4, 8, 15

Archivist, 45, 55–56, 58, 109, 127

Arlington, Virginia, United States, xxiv

Augustine, of Hippo, Saint, 190n8

Auschwitz-Birkenau State Museum, Auschwitz I and Auschwitz II,

xiii–xiv, xv–xvi, 4, 7, 13, 16, 24,
37, 38, 45, 50–52, 79, 121, 134,
141, 145n10, 145n11, 145n12,
145n13, 145n14, 146n24,
147n28, 167n51, 167n52,
173n18, 173n19, 174n20,
195n38, 201n17

Balkan States, xxi
Baptist Metz, Johann, 157n27,
161n14
Barmen Declaration, 6
Barth, Karl, 6–7
Belford Ulanov, Ann, 153n3,
195n40, 196n41
Belzec, 49
bin Laden, Osama, 21
Black History Month, 19
Blood, 6, 17, 40–44, 56–58, 64,
120, 179n64, 186n43
Bloomberg, Michael, xxv
Boundaries, 123–27, 129, 133,
137, 141, 161n12, 201n19,
201n20, 201n21, 202n22,
202n23
Bosnia, x–xi, xxi–xxiii, xxviii, 5,
18, 21, 27, 35, 42, 66–68, 93,
100, 105, 107, 110, 122, 133,
138, 149n58, 172n6, 175n32,
185n34, 186n36, 186n37
Bosnian War, xiii, xxi–xxiii,
Boss, Pauline, 159n8, 176n40,
177n48
Breitenberg, E. Harold, 161n16,
162n18
Brnabic, Ana, xxiii
British Commonwealth, xix
Buchenwald, 53, 129, 137

Buddhism, 7, 22, 26, 39–40, 58,
179n62
Burnout, 49, 181n8, 181n9,
189n1
Bush, George W., 198n52

Cambodia, x–xi, xvi–xviii, 13, 18,
22, 25–26, 30, 40–41, 45,
53–58, 79, 94, 96, 100, 109,
116–17, 123, 128, 135, 141,
147n30, 148n40, 148n44,
177n50, 193n29
Cambodian Genocide, xxxi, 57
Cape Town, South Africa, xx
Caregiving/givers, xl, 80, 82, 180n8,
190n11, 191n18, 192n26,
199n5, 202n21, 202n23
Caribbean, xxv
Cemetery, xxiii, 11, 16, 22–24, 26,
31–33, 74, 83, 167n51, 170n69,
174n26, 175n34, 177n51
Chaplains, chaplaincy, 37, 81–82,
131–32, 191n12, 196n40,
201n18
Children, x, xxiv, xxvii, xxxiii, xl, 10,
25–26, 30, 41, 45, 58, 65, 90,
103–4, 110, 115, 141, 164n29,
177n56, 187n45, 194n34
Choeung Ek, xvii, 5, 24–26, 39–40,
174n26
Christianity, Christian, 6, 14,
22, 160n9, 162n16, 166n44,
171n3, 196n44
Christian Church, 6
Civil War, xxv
Clinton, Bill, 6
Clinton, Hilary, 6
Closure, Myth of, 89, 116

Index 233

Coaches, 128–30, 133
Collector, 8, 83, 86, 89, 91
Collected Memories, xxxiv,
155n8
Colonialism, xxv, 22
Communication, 28, 79–80, 96,
114, 130, 133, 135, 137–38,
176n39, 192n20, 205n41
Community, x, xxiii, xv, xvii–xviii,
xxii, xxxv, xl, 7, 9, 12, 28,
30–32, 38, 42, 64, 71, 80,
82–83, 87, 90, 92, 99, 102, 103,
107, 109–10, 113–14, 133–35,
139–40, 142, 162n16, 170n69,
182n14, 194n34, 195n38,
196n43, 197n46
Compassion Fatigue, 13, 49,
166n42, 180n8, 181n8,
191n10, 201n18
Cone, James, 164n27, 172n5
Conflict Resolution, 140
Connective Tissue, x, 41, 44,
143n5
Constitution Square, 43
Contemplation, xxxiv, 16, 114
Cremation, 5, 40
Crimes Against Humanity and
Genocide Museum, xxiii, 37,
115, 141
Culture, ix, xxxi, xxxiv, 4, 21, 23,
41–43, 58, 100, 103
Cummings, John, xxv, xxvi
Curator, 5, 8, 14–15, 80, 84–91,
125, 141

Dangerous Memories, xl, 3, 161n14
Day of Reconciliation, 18
Day of the Vow, 18

Dayton Peace Agreement, xxi
Deutsche Christen, 6
Death, xiii, xvii, xix, xxvi, xxxix,
xl–xli, 1, 7n21, 13, 18–20,
23–34, 36–42, 44–45, 47–48,
51–52, 57–58, 67, 74–77, 79,
82, 86, 90, 102, 121, 126,
141–42, 143n1, 144n6,
156n23, 163n21, 165n38,
170n69, 179n64, 183n22
Death Camp, 3, 48, 167n51
Democratic Kampuchea, 25
Department of Environmental
Affairs and Tourism, xix–xx
Development, xvii–xviii, 180n5,
190n11, 195n38
Disney World, 74
Dixon, Thomas, 172n5
DNA testing, 28
Documentation Center of
Cambodia, 25, 174n23
Dodik, Milorad, 67
Doehring, Carrie, 157n29, 165n37,
191n15
Donor, xiii, 80, 83–84, 86–87,
90–91, 116, 140
Du Bois, W.E.B., 164n27
Durkheim, Emile, 167n50, 168n58,
170n68, 177n51

Economics, x, xiii, xix, xxi, xxv,
xxxi, xxxiv, xli, 2, 4, 10, 22,
39, 134, 155n17, 158n4,
193n29
Education, xxii–xxiii, xxvi, xxxii,
xxiv, 11, 15, 18, 21–22, 39–40,
46, 53–56, 59, 79, 80, 87, 97,
103–5, 107, 109, 125, 127–29,

133, 137, 154n5, 183n19,
196n45, 197n46, 205n40

Educators, 26, 103, 128, 130,
182n18, 196n46

Earth-Making, 81–84, 87–88

Empathy, 49–50, 80, 92, 94,
97, 114, 122, 158n6, 165n40,
191n18, 192n28, 199n9,
200n10, 201n18, 201n20,
201n21, 202n21, 205n39

Equal Justice Initiative, xxvi,
152n77

Ethics, xii, xl, 12, 37, 94, 158n4,
162n16, 193n32

Ethics of Care, 81, 84, 89, 107,
191n20, 192n20

Ethical Fatigue, 49

Evil, xxxi, xxxviiin22, xxxix, 4, 8,
43, 48, 156n22, 159n7,
185n44

Exhibitions, xiv, xv, xxiii, xxiv, xl,
31, 35, 37, 67, 80, 86–87,
96–97, 99–100, 103, 121, 129,
192n21, 192n22, 197n51,
200n12

Faith, xxix, xxxvii, 1, 7, 15, 31, 103,
142, 156n17, 159n8, 162n16,
165n29, 170n69, 176n47,
196n44

Father Mychal Judge, 37, 81

Figley, Charles, 180n8, 181n8

Fire and Safety, 116

Flashbacks, 67–68

Florida, United States, xxvii, 28

Fragments, xxvi, xxxi, xxxiv,
xxxvi–xxxviii, xl, 22, 28, 38–40,
42, 82, 153n2, 178n59

France, xi

Freedom Park, xx, 16, 42, 149n55,
166n48, 179n67

Forgiveness, 105–6, 197n49

Foucault, Michael, 174n26

Freud, Sigmund, 160n12, 166n45

Fromm, Eric, 166n41, 206n43

Galicia Jewish Museum, xiv, xv,
41, 46, 49, 99, 103, 146n18,
146n19, 146n20

Gallery 11/07/95, xxii, 35, 65, 100,
110

Genocide, xvi, xviii, xxii–xxiii,
2, 13, 18, 25, 27, 37, 54–58,
65, 67–68, 134, 144n6, 153n1,
172n6, 185n34, 196n43,
198n53

Germany, xi, xiii, 6–7, 53, 128

German Federal Ministry of
Economic Cooperation
and Development, xvii

Goodness, xxxvi, xxxviii, xxxix,
xli, 19, 101, 196n40

Ghost, 47, 58, 169n64, 183n22

Gift, xxxv, 3–4, 18, 82, 84, 89–90,
105, 118, 190n8

Gillett, Richard, 155n17, 156n17,
157n26

Graffiti, 40, 57, 120

Great African Steps, 43

God, xxxvii–xxxviii, xxxix, 4, 13,
27, 98, 141–42, 156n18, 171n3,
190n7, 190n8, 196n41

God in America, 15

Gobodo-Madikizela, Pumla, 64,
106, 175n31, 184n29, 185n30,
197n50

Ground Zero, xxiv, 1, 28, 37, 43, 81, 116, 191n12

Growth, xxxviii, xl, 105, 113–14

Guardians of Memory, 13–14, 83, 166n43

Halbwachs, Maurice, 143n4

Halifax, Joan, 166n42, 199n8, 201n18

Halilović, Jasminko, xxii

Hall of Execution, 59

Hall of Names, 34

Haunting, xxxix, 58, 63, 68

Healing, xxxiii, xli, 18, 30, 42–43, 109, 113, 139, 145n8, 154n3, 156n22, 159n6, 188n48, 192n21

Hector Pieterson Museum, 26, 149n51

Hennes, Tom, 191n16, 192n22

Herman, Judith, 154n4, 155n13, 155n14, 155n15, 155n16, 159n8, 178n61, 180n1, 182n14, 184n28, 185n33, 186n41, 188n49, 189n2, 193n31, 193n32, 194n33, 196n42, 197n49, 205n40

Hitler, Adolf, 6

Hirsch, Marianne, 177n52, 177n53

Historical Museum of Bosnia and Herzegovina, xxi, 150n61

History, xii, xiv, xviii, xx, xxii, xxvi, xxxii–xxxiv, xxxviii, xl, 7–8, 13, 23, 25–26, 32, 34, 39–41, 45, 47–48, 51, 55, 58–59, 61–66, 69, 72–73, 76, 79, 83, 85, 88, 92–94, 96–97, 99, 103, 106–10, 125, 129, 133, 154n5, 178n59, 179n67, 182n15

History Museum of Bosnia and Herzegovina, xxii, 79, 103, 150n62, 150n63

Historical Exhibit, 37, 75, 121

Holding space, 82–83, 91, 190n11

Holocaust, x, xiii, xv, xvi, xxxi, 7, 13, 18, 23, 30, 32, 34, 39, 47–49, 51–52, 56, 65, 88, 90–91, 99, 103, 121, 147n26, 147n27, 147n29, 168n59, 177n49, 177n52, 177n53, 178n60, 193n30, 197n51, 201n18

Holocaust Martyrs' and Heroes' Remembrance Day, x

hooks, bell, xli, 157n31, 196n46, 197n46, 197n47

Hope, xxix, xxxii, xxxv, xxxviii, 3–5, 10, 15, 19, 43–44, 52, 54, 82, 101–13, 141–42, 161n14, 165n34, 180n2, 196n40, 196n43, 205n42

Horror, x, xxv, xxxii, xxxiv, xxxv, xxxvi, xxxvii, xxxix, 4, 12, 26, 29, 36, 38, 44, 46, 51–52, 54, 57, 61, 63, 66, 68, 77, 91, 107, 121, 135, 141, 194n33

Hungry Ghost, Preta, 18, 26

Hurst, David, 42, 179n65

Hyperarousal, 46, 137, 182n18

Imagination, xiv, 5, 23, 73, 82, 117

Imperial War Museum, xxiii

Indifference, xxii, 9, 60, 142, 167n50

Indigenous Knowledge Systems, 43

Insomnia, 68

Institute of National Remembrance, xv

Integration, Integrating Trauma, 13, 62, 65, 83, 114, 182n14

International Freedom Center, xxiv

Interpretive Guide, 48, 136

Intimacy, 56, 86, 89, 124, 202n23

Intrude, Intrusion, 63, 67–68, 126

Isivivane, 16, 179n67

Islam, 7, 30–32

Israel, Jerusalem, xi, xiii, xv–xvi, 84, 121, 146n24, 198n52

Japan, xii, xvii

J.C. Royal Company, xvii, 174n25

Jewish life, xv, 21–24, 50, 103; history/heritage, 18, 39, 41–42, 46, 79, 197n52; people, x, xiii–xvi, 32, 88, 99, 146n24, 197n51

Jim Crow, 73

Johannesburg, South Africa, xix, xx, 43, 172n9

Juneteenth, 19

Jung, Carl, 157n30, 199n1, 199n2, 199n4, 199n5

Kairos, 10, 162n17

Karadžić, Radovan, 21, 150n59, 172n6

Khmer, 7, 116–117, 162n20

Khmer Rouge, xiii, xvii, 18, 21, 25, 30, 34, 36, 40, 45, 54, 57–58, 96, 109, 147n30, 172n4, 174n24, 193n29

Killing Fields, xvii, 25, 41

Kleinman, Arthur, 144n7, 170n70

Klimowicz, Teresa, 32, 42, 141

Kovno Ghetto, 90

Koßler, Gottfried, 128, 203n29

Knesset, xv, 198n52

Kraków Museum, xiv

Kraków-Płaszów, xiv, 22–23, 47–48, 50, 145n16

Kristallnacht, 22

Korea International Cooperation Agency, xvii

Kosovo, 107

Ku Klux Klan, 21, 172n5

Legacy Museum, xxvi, 28

Lewis, C.S., 166n46, 168n62

Life-Giving, 81–82, 103–7, 110

Lifton, Robert J., 201n19

Linenthal, Edward, 163n26, 167n51, 168n59, 168n60, 173n15, 179n63

Listening, xxxvi, 8–9, 11–12, 20, 48, 82, 94, 105, 166n41, 193n30, 199n1, 205n39, 206n43

Long, Thomas G., 176n38, 177n47

Louisiana, United States, xi, xxv, xxxiii, 13, 69, 175n33

Love, xxviii, xxix, xxxviii, xli, 28, 65, 82, 109, 112, 190n8

Lublin, Poland, 32, 51

Lynch, Thomas, 173n17, 176n38, 177n47

Lynching, xxvi, 21, 28, 42, 172n4, 172n5, 179n65

Machado, Daisy, 10, 164n33, 165n36

Malinck, Shlomo, 88

Mandela, Nelson, xix–xx, 18, 64, 149n53

Margalit, Avishai, 155n11, 155n12

Marketing/communications, 74, 79, 80, 96, 154n5

Maslach, Christina, 181n8, 181n9, 189n1

Mass Atrocity, xxix, xxxiii, 2, 33–34, 82, 102, 141, 183n21, 198n53

Mass Incarceration, xxvi, 73, 175n35

Mass Trauma, ix, xi–xii, xvi, xxxi– xxxii, 11, 29, 31, 36, 40, 45, 53, 81, 84–85, 102, 106, 114, 120, 123, 127–28, 131, 134, 140, 144n6, 145n8, 153n1, 190n7, 193n29, 194n36, 195n38

McCarroll, James E., 202n24, 202n25, 202n26, 202n27, 203n28

Memorial, xvii, xx, xxiii, xxvi, xxxiii, 2, 16, 35, 44, 53, 72, 120–21, 126, 128, 130, 154n5, 170n69, 203n32

Memorialization, xi–xiii, xviii, xxiii, xxxii, xxxvi, xli, 5, 7, 10, 13, 15, 27–28, 33, 39–40, 45–46, 51–53, 56, 65, 67, 80, 90, 103, 107, 123, 133–35, 137, 156n22, 156n23, 158n5, 163n21

Memorial Museum, xi–xii, xvi–xvii, xxii–xxiii, xxv–xxvi, xxxii–xli, 2, 4–5, 7–13, 18, 28, 33, 36–39, 42, 44, 53–54, 63, 69, 70, 72, 74–77, 80, 82–84, 86–89, 91–92, 96–97, 100, 102, 105, 107, 115–16, 121, 124, 130, 136, 139, 141, 144n6, 155n17, 158n4, 160n12, 161n14, 161n15, 168n59, 169n62,

169n64, 170n69, 178n60, 179n62, 182n14, 187n47, 194n34, 195n38, 196n40, 196n41, 205n40

Memorial Stupa, xvii, 141

Memory, x– xii, xiv, xxiii, xxvi, xxxii–xxxiv, xxxviii, xxxix, xl, 2, 4, 8, 10, 13–14, 16–17, 25, 28, 30, 33–34, 38–41, 44, 46–48, 50–52, 59–60, 66, 68, 72, 75, 77, 80, 82–86, 88, 91, 99, 102, 107–8, 111, 115, 122, 154n5, 154n8, 155n8, 161n14, 163n27, 166n43, 167n50, 169n64, 178n59, 180n2, 180n5, 182n14, 185n34, 191n14, 195n38

Memory Studies, xii, xli

Metanoia, 11

Ministry of Tourism, xviii, 100

Ministering, xlii, 81, 199n2

Mission, xiv, xv, xx, xli, 84, 88, 96, 108–10, 115, 120

Mission Statement, 145n14, 146n22, 146n23

Mitic, Anita, 107, 108, 198n56

Moghul, Haroon, 79

Morality, 191n20

Morawiecki, Mateusz, xvi

Morgan, Suzanne, 15

Mosque, 11, 22, 30, 32, 42, 68, 173n13

Mount Herzl (Mount of Remembrance), xv

Mourning, xi, xxxii–xxxiii, xxxix, 1, 7, 9, 11, 13–14, 18, 19, 23, 28, 30, 33–34, 44, 72, 76, 82, 118

Museum of Jewish Heritage,

Musić, Sudba Bubi, 27, 42, 151n70

Muslim, xxi, 21, 22, 79

Ministry of Culture and Fine Arts of Cambodia, xvii

National Day of Hatred, 18

National Day of Remembrance, 18

National Gallery, xxii

National Heritage Resources Act, xx

National Library of Bosnia and Herzegovina, xxii

National Memorial for Peace and Justice, xxvi

National Museum of Bosnia and Herzegovina, xxii

National Museum of African American History and Culture, xxvi

National September 11 Memorial & Museum, *see* 9/11 Memorial & Museum

National Party, xviii, 171n3

Native American, xii, xxv, 151n75, 152n76

NATO, xxi

Nazi, xiii, xv–xvi, 6, 18, 21–24, 30, 47, 90, 121, 146n24

Nelson Mandela National Museum, xx

New Yorkers, 1

New York City, New York, United States, xi, xxiv, 1, 22, 37, 43, 74, 84

New York City Fire Department, 37

New York Historical Society, 5

New York University, xxvii, 79

Netanyahu, Benjamin, xvi

Never Again, xxxii, 103, 107, 110–12, 144n6, 197n52, 198n53, 205n42

Never Forget, xxxii, 103, 107, 111, 197n51

NGO, 31, 148n40

Nightmares, 25, 54, 68, 77, 182n18

Nonbeing, 12

Nora, Pierre, 145n10

North Carolina, United States, xxvi

North Tower, 1

Nouwen, Henri, 14, 158n6, 166n44, 196n44, 199n2, 199n3, 200n11

Numinous, the, 5, 17, 161n13, 166n46, 168n59, 169n64

Number Four Prison, 43

Nožić, Suada, xxiii

Obama, Barack, 16

Okinawa Museum, xvii

Oral History, xl, 52, 54, 56, 76, 87, 93–94, 116, 123, 125, 195n38

Oral Historian, 43, 79–80, 92–95, 123, 135, 141, 192–3n28

Oświęcim, Poland, xiv, 51, 79

Pain, xxxi–xxxii, xxxv, xxxvii, xl, 1–3, 6, 9, 11, 13–15, 19, 29, 46, 51–52, 56, 61, 71, 76, 79, 80–82, 91–97, 99–102, 105, 107, 109, 112–14, 117–18, 123–25, 139–41

Pain-Bearing, 81–82, 96–97, 100, 107

Parapets, xxix, 1, 19, 35

Pastoral, as a framework or process xl, 3, 187n47; as care, 82,

157n29, 165n37, 169n63, 190n6, 195–6n40, 196n41, 199n1, 205n39

Pataki, George, xxiv

Peace, xxi, xxix, 2, 7, 16, 34, 40, 54, 58, 65, 179n67, 180n2–3

Pedagogy, 55, 128, 196–7n46

Pentagon, xxiv, 22

People Work, 49–50, 52, 77, 80

Pieterson, Hector, xix, 149n51, 212

Phnom Penh, xvii

Pluralism, xxxvii, 158n4, 160n10

Prijedor, Bosnia, xxiii, 27, 30–31, 42, 122

Pol Pot, xviii, 21–22, 40, 54–55, 79, 147n130–31

Poland, xi, xiii–xvi, 25, 32, 47–48, 51, 55–56, 58, 79, 99–100, 128, 145n10 and 15, 146n18, 147n25–27

Politics, xiii, xxiii, xxvi, 2, 10, 63–64, 100, 136

Pope Francis, 1, 19, 157n2, 171n71–72

Post-Conflict Research Center, 67

Post Traumatic Stress Disorder, 143n3, 180n8, 200n14

Pretoria, South Africa, xx, 16, 42

Propaganda, 21

Public Health, 102

Public Memory, xxii, xxxvii–xxxviii, xl,

Public Service, xli – xlii

Psychiatrist, 97, 192–93n28

Psychoeducation, 137, 140, 205n41

Psychology, xii, 69

Racism, xix, 109, 111–12, 159n8

Rambo, Shelly, 143n1, 155n11, 156n22, 165n38, 187n46

Reconciliation, xix–xxi, 18, 67, 70, 109

Reconstruction, xix, xxxi, xxxvi, 23, 32, 38–39, 41, 73, 83–84, 102, 111, 182n14

Recovery, ix, xxi, xxiv, xxxi, xxxiii, xxxviii, 2, 23, 33, 38–39, 43, 66, 102, 106, 116, 155n17, 176n40, 184n26, 185n33, 186n43, 197n51, 205n40; recovery workers, xxiv, 6, 81, 116

Red Cross, 131–32

Religion, as a discipline xxvi, 2, 16, 19, 23, 155n17, 156–7n23, 160n11, 167n49; as practice, xvii, xxxvii, xxxix, 15–16, 21–23, 34, 163–64n27, 172n5; symbols of, xli, 16, 19, 22, 34

Religious, xxvi, xxxvi, 5, 161–2n16, 165n37, 168–9n62, 170n70, 171n3

Remembrance Day, x, 121

Repair, xxii, 41, 63–65, 81, 106

Resilience, xxxv, xl, 17, 39, 71, 79, 105, 138, 153n85, 159n8, 181–82n13

Revisionism, 101

Rhetoric, 6, 12, 21, 107, 172n5 and 7

Ricoeur, Paul, 157n24, 161n13, 163n21, 166n45, 168n59 and 61, 169n64, 170n65, 178n59, 191n14, 206n47–48

Rituals, 7, 18–19, 33, 35, 43, 58, 170n69; as commemorative

anniversaries, xxiv, xxix, 121–22, 140, 146n24, 180n3

Robben Island, South Africa, xx, 61; Museum, xx, 149n54, 184n25, 195n38

Rogers, Ashley, 71, 136–37, 141, 154n6, 205n39

Roma, xiii, 24

Sacred, xxv, xxxix, 1, 4, 14, 15–19, 28, 33–34, 80, 90, 93, 157n24, 161n13, 163n21, 165n37, 168n59–61, 168–69n62, 170n65 and 69, 177n51

Sacred Spaces, 1, 15–18, 167n49–50

Sacred Space International, 15, 166n47

Safe Area, xxi

Safety, xxxv, 25, 27, 56, 61, 77, 89, 94–95,116, 124, 126, 137, 140, 193n31; as stages of recovery, 185n33, 205n40

Samarah, Tarik, xxii

Sarajevo, in Bosnia and Herzgovinia, xxi, xxiii, 37, 65, 67, 69, 103, 115, 141, 149–50n58

Šarić, Velma, 67–68, 133–34, 137, 141

Seck, Dr. Ibrahima, xxv, 10, 16, 71, 73, 141

Secondary Traumatic Stress, xl, 49, 137, 180n5, 180–81n8, 183n19, 200n16

Security Prison 21 (S-21), xvii, 25, 45, 54, 57, 148n38

Segregation, 60, 73

Self-care, 55, 126, 140, 180–81n8

Sendyka, Roma, xiv, 173n14

Sensory Overload, 56, 188n51

Serbia, xi, 65, 151n68 and 69; Military, xxi, 150n59; people of, xxiii, 30, 68, 100

Serbian Republic of Bosnia and Herzegovina, *Republika Srpska*, 27

Security Guard, 75, 122

Self-understanding, 127, 137

Sen, Hun, xviii

Service, as in helping or in service of, ix, xxxii, xxxv, xli, 2, 19–20, 31, 48, 90, 116, 124, 132, 188–89n1, 200n11; as assistance, 128; as care or love, 19–20, 114; Diplomatic Security, xxiv; prayer, 1; visitor services, 121

Shanksville, Pennsylvania, United States, xxiv

Sheppard, Phillis, 12, 187n47

Shoah, the, xv, 173n18

Sinti, xiii, 24

Situation, the, xiii, xxvi, xxxvii, xxxix, xli, 2–4, 7–8, 11–12, 15, 20, 51, 68, 81, 94, 98, 101, 105, 121, 130, 133, 141–42, 153n84, 156n19, 158n4, 165n34

Slaughter, in Bosnia xxi, 5, 54, 149n58, 150n59; of Native Americans, 152n76

Slavery, xii–xiii, xxv–xxvi, xxxi, 11, 16, 28, 39, 70–73, 152n76–79, 159n8, 172n5, 186–7n44, 187n45

Social groups, 2, 44

Social Media, xviii, 74, 80

Social Work, 50

Srebrenica, xxi–xxiii, 31, 107, 122, 134, 151n68

Srebrenica Massacre, xxiii, 67, 110

Srebrenica Memorial Center or Srebrenica–Potočari Memorial and Cemetery, xxiii, 13, 16, 24, 27, 107, 150n67, 166n43, 168n56

Srebrenica–Potočari Memorial and Cemetery, xxiii

Stein, Edith, 199n9, 200n10 and 13

Stevenson, Bryan, xxvi

Stewards of History, 13

Solidarity, xxi, 12, 64–65, 77, 106, 134, 163–64n27, 178n60, 197–98n52

Sophiatown, Johannesburg, South Africa, 22, 172n9

South Africa, xi, xx, 16, 18, 21, 26–27, 42–43, 59–61, 97–98, 106, 112, 138, 149n50 and 56, 166n43, 167n55, 170n66, 174n28, 179n67, 192n22; apartheid government, x, xviii, xix, 61–63, 148n45–46, 171n2 and 3, 175n29 and 30; people of, xxi, 22, 45, 63–65, 195n38

South African Institute of Race Relations, 26

South African Wars, 42

South Tower, 1

Soweto, South Africa, xix–xx, 18, 26, 45, 109

Soweto Heritage Trust, xx

Soweto Uprising, xix, 18, 26, 195n38

Stalin, Joseph, xiii

Stakeholders, xxxv, 86, 132

Stupa, xvii, 5, 18, 39, 40, 141

Suffering faith, xxxvii, 7

Survivor Tree, 43

Swain, Storm, 81–83, 88, 106, 189n5, 190n6–7 and 9–11, 191n12–13 and 17, 192n23–27, 194n35, 195n37

Symbols, xvi, xxxi, xxxiv, xxxvii, xli, 8, 11, 14, 17, 22–23, 39–41, 43–44, 154–55n3

Synagogue, 11, 22, 120

Tehrani, Noreen, 200n16, 204n37

Temple, 11, 22

Terrorism, xxiv, 152n76, 195n40

Terrorist Attack, xxv, 1, 5, 8, 21–22

Testimony, traumatic xxxiii–xxxv, xxxix, 13, 20, 24, 40–41, 47, 56, 69, 79, 81, 85, 87, 92, 96, 132, 156n18, 173n16; personal 17, 33, 38, 47, 81, 191n12; workers', ix–xiii, 48, 56, 59, 68, 85, 94, 144n6, 160n10; pages of testimony (Yad Vashem), 34

The Uncanny, 3–4, 5, 15, 17, 19–20, 156n19, 169n64; C.S. Lewis and 166n46, 168n62; Freud and 160n12

Theodicy, 156n22

Theology, xii, xxxvii–xxxviii, 3–8, 19–20, 143n1, 155n11 and 17, 158n4, 159n8, 165n38; pastoral, 169n63, 189n5, 194n35; public, xxvii, 8, 156n20, 161–62n16, 163n24; theology of suffering,186–87n44

Therapy, 53, 128–29; testimony method, 184n24; Donald Winnicott, 190n6

Thimm, Barbra, 53, 128–131, 137, 141, 182n15, 16, and 18, 203n29–32

Thirteenth Amendment, xxv

Tillich, Paul, 153n84, 156n19, 158n4, 161n15

Tombstones, 24, 28

Tour Guides, xx, 13, 25, 49, 61–62, 69, 79–80, 97–101, 103, 105, 109–10, 137

Traces of Memory, xv, 41, 99

Tracy, David, 3, 8, 153n84, 156n19–21, 159n7, 160n9, 161n14, 163n23–24

Tradition, 4–5, 7, 40, 100

Training, of memorial museum occupations, xl, 77, 80–81, 205n41; psychological or pastoral, 3, 97, 114, 123, 140, 182–3n18, 188–89n1, 203n23–24; lack of 94; Barbara Thimm's method, 128–37, 203n31–32

Trauma, historical, ix, xli, 64

Trauma, Logic or Dialectic, xxxii, xli, 46, 51, 67, 70, 103, 154n4, 180n1

Trauma of Human Design, xii, xxxvii–xxxviii, 8

Traumatic Memory, xii, xxxiii, xxxvi–xxxvii, 38, 51, 77, 82–83, 91, 99

Traumatic Stress, xvi, xxiv, xl, 45–56, 128–138, 143n3, 180–81n8, 184n26, 188n50, 188–89n1, 200n14 and 16, 203n31

Traumatic Triggers, triggered, xli, 53, 56, 62–64, 94, 116, 125, 138–39, 153, 188n51

Tremendum, 18, 102, 161n13, 169n64

Tronto, Joan, 189n4, 198n55

Truth and Reconciliation Commission, xx, 64

Tuol Sleng Genocide Museum, xvii, 7, 18, 25, 37, 39, 53–55, 57, 110, 128, 148n36–39, 162n20, 167n54, 182n16

Tutu, Desmond, 10, 164n31

Twin Towers, xxiv, 1, 24

Ulrich, Susanne, 128, 182n15, 203n29

UNESCO, xvii

Unexplainable, the, 4, 7, 142; in Freud, 160n12

United Nations, xxi, 67, 146n24

United States, xv–xvii, xxiv–xxv, 5, 72, 134; definitions of museums, 154n5; history of slavery in, xxv, 72, 172n5

United Airlines Flight 93, 37

Unsayable, 8–9

van Der Kolk, Bessel, 157n25, 181n11, 184n26, 186n40, 188n51, 194n34, 206n44

Verunsichernde Orte: Slbstverständnis und Weiterbildung in der Gedenkstättenpädagogik (Disconcerting Sites: Self-Understanding and Capacity Building on Education Memorial Sites), 127, 131–32, 182n15, 203n29

Vhuwaelo, 43, 179n67

Vicarious Trauma, 49, 132, 143n3, 180n8, 181n9, 183n19, 205n41

Vietnam War, xvi

Virgil, 28

Vocation, xii, xli, 12, 113

Voiceless, xii, xxxiv, xlii, 3, 5, 13, 51, 102

Vučić, Aleksander, xxiii

Walker, Peter, 1

Washington D.C., United States, xxiv, 22

War Childhood Museum, xxii, 41, 115, 131, 150n65

Warsaw Ghetto Uprising, 88, 146n24

Wat, 22

Welby, Justin, 7

Well of Memory, 32

Wiesel, Elie, 41, 47, 163n26, 179n63, 180n2–4,

Whitney Plantation xxv, 152n80–81; museum, xxxiii, 10, 16, 19, 39, 69–71, 79, 110, 136, 141

White Armbands, xxiii–xxiv

White Armband Day, 18

Whitman, Walt, 199

Winfrey, Oprah, 181

Winnicott, Donald 190n6, 192n24

Witness, act of ix–xv, xxv, xxxvii–xlii, 27, 29, 36–52, 164n33; types of, xxxvi, 48, 66, 115, 155n11, 173n16, 191n16

Womanism/womanist, 12, 159n8, 186n44, 186–87n44

World Heritage Site, xx, 195n38

World Trade Center, xxiv, 1, 8, 15, 21–22, 24, 28, 37, 39, 41, 45, 75, 79, 81, 86, 151n72, 200n14

World War I, 42

World War II, xiii, xv, xxi, 42–43, 171n1

Wounded Healer, xli, 113–14, 140, 157n30, 166n44, 199n2–6, 200n11

Wounding, xii, xviii, xxxix, xl–xli, 3, 49, 113–14, 116, 120, 122–23, 127, 131, 137, 139, 140–41, 196n41

Xhosa, 60

Yad Vashem, x, xv–xvi, 7, 16, 18, 34, 45, 49–50, 79, 84–85, 87, 90, 121, 141, 146n21–23, 147n26, 162n19, 171n1, 174n20

Yehuda, Rachel, 200n14

Yom HaShoah, 18

Yousef, Ramzi, xxiv

Youth Day, 18, 146n24

Youth Initiative for Human Rights, 107–8

Young, James, 154n8, 177n49

Yugoslavia, xxi, 149n57, 172n7, 173n13

Zbylitowska Góra, 25

Zizioulas, John D., 159, 199

Zulu, 60–61